Going Home Again

Roy Williams, the North Carolina Tar Heels, and a Season to Remember

ADAM LUCAS

THE LYONS PRESS
Guilford, Connecticut
An imprint of The Globe Pequot Press

The Library of Congress has previously cataloged an earlier (hardcover) edition as follows:

Lucas, Adam, 1977-
 Going home again : Roy Williams, the North Carolina Tar Heels, and a season to remember / Adam Lucas.
      p. cm.
   Includes index.
   ISBN: 1-59228-551-1 (trade cloth)
Williams, Roy, 1950- 2. Basketball coaches—United States—Biography. 3. North Carolina Tar Heels (Basketball team) I. Title.
GV884.W58L83 2004
796.323'092—dc22

                                                                2004057729

Dedication

For Stephanie and McKay, whose smiles are
the best part of going to a game—
and coming home from one.

Acknowledgments

One of Dean Smith's best known innovations was requiring a player who scored a basket to point to the player who had thrown him the pass that led to the hoop. "Thanking the passer" became a trademark of Carolina basketball, pleasing Smith, who often commented that while everyone was celebrating the player who scored, the player who threw the pass went virtually unnoticed. Under Smith, the Heels also tracked assists differently: any good feed to the post resulted in a coach's assist, even if the shot was missed.

That's how I feel about this book. Without assists from numerous people, it never would have been written. Quite obviously, the 2003–04 University of North Carolina basketball players were essential, and they were continually even more cooperative than I had hoped. They answer thousands of questions from the media each season, but none of them—Justin Bohlander, Raymond Felton, Damion Grant, Rashad McCants, Phillip McLamb, Jackie Manuel, Sean May, Jonathan Miller, Wes Miller, David Noel, Damien Price, Byron Sanders, Melvin Scott, Reyshawn Terry, and Jawad Williams—ever complained about fielding their eighth "How did that make you feel?" query of the day. Most of them have been through the most trying era in Carolina basketball history and have emerged in a way that should make even the most cynical Tar Heel fan proud. Eric Hoots belongs in the players' category as well, because he put in at least as many hours as everyone on scholarship and was the unquestioned guru of the Dr. Dish machine.

For the Carolina coaches, and especially Roy Williams, it must have been jarring to accept a high-profile job and discover a few months later that a book was being written about their exploits. As Joe Holladay said at one point, "You're writing a book? I didn't know you knew that many words." He was right, I don't, but Williams, Holladay, Steve Robinson, Jerod Haase, and C. B. McGrath were patient with someone they'd never met before April 14, 2003, and helped me understand their program, both on and off the court. They are one of the best examples I've ever seen of a group of individuals working together as a cohesive unit. Two decades after being a member of what may have been the best staff in college hoops history—with Dean Smith, Bill Guthridge, and Eddie Fogler—Williams now employs a staff that rivals that one.

Of course, they wouldn't be quite as efficient without the basketball office staff. Emily Cozart, Armin Dastur, Jennifer Holbrook, and Kay Thomas keep one of the top college programs in the nation running smoothly and were never too busy to give a quick smile. It has been suggested that they deserve to be honored at halftime of a basketball game—but all are too modest to ever consider the idea.

What few fans realize is that sportswriters don't actually do much work. Sports information staffs across the country do it all for them, providing stats and the sort of facts and figures that make a good article a great one. After following the Tar Heels across the country over the past several years, I am quite convinced that Steve Kirschner and Matt Bowers in UNC's basketball sports information department are the best in the business.

Everyone at *Tar Heel Monthly* made the past twelve months a fairly painless publishing year. That publication would be a mere shell without the hard work of Jeffrey Camarati, Bill Cole, Jennifer Engel, Grant Halverson, John Kilgo, Matt Morgan, Mick Mixon, and Lee Pace. Jones Angell also is an invaluable contributor to the magazine—and a fast-rising star in the broadcast business—but was even more essential as someone to bounce ideas off of throughout the writing process.

I would be remiss not to thank the following folks: Neil Amato, Woody Durham, Larry Gallo, Bill Guthridge, Clint Gwaltney, Jeff Jeske, Cody Plott, Dean Smith, Sandra Umstead, and Jill Whitaker. All helped in some fashion, although they may not have even realized it. Tom McCarthy at The Lyons Press was excited about the idea from the first day he heard about it and had considerable patience with a writer who is not a veteran.

The highlight of Carolina's end-of-season basketball banquet are the senior speeches. Most of the graduating players make it through dry-eyed until they reach the part where they have to thank their families. Now, I see why. My dad, Jim, still claims he thought of the idea for this book. I'm not sure about that, but I am sure my parents are the ones who first started taking me to basketball games when I was too little to know the difference between a block and a charge. My wife Stephanie is one of the few women in the world willing to consider a sports event a "date night." She also has an underappreciated knowledge of college basketball, right down to Larry Miller's jersey number. My daughter McKay had the misfortune to be born at the same time her father signed a book contract. Watching games with her cast everything in a new light and gave me a greater appreciation for some of the sacrifices coaches have to make. I will never hear the song "Jump Around" in quite the same way.

There is one other important group of people to thank—Carolina basketball fans. The thousands who read *Tar Heel Monthly* and pack the Smith Center make projects like this possible, and enabled someone who never quite grew tall enough to play power forward to still make a living going to basketball games.

All of the people mentioned above contributed immeasurably to this book. Mark them down for, at minimum, a coach's assist.

Prologue

The first loss of the Roy Williams era at the University of North Carolina takes place in front of a few hundred kids. It is not reported in any newspapers. It does not hurt the Tar Heels' NCAA Tournament chances. Very few Carolina fans will ever know the game was played.

But the loss makes Williams extremely concerned.

Every summer, the University of North Carolina holds its annual summer basketball camp at the storied Dean E. Smith Center. It is the most popular camp in the state, and for many years potential campers had to be referred by a member of the Rams Club, the school's athletic fund-raisers. In the summer of 2003, the camp offered three sessions, each filled to maximum capacity of some five hundred school-age children eager to learn from current players and the new coach of the Tar Heels, who had been on the job just over two months.

For most of the campers, the highlight is the counselors' game, which matches the current Carolina players against alumni, who frequently return to Chapel Hill in the summer to work out and play pickup. Rosters vary, but it's not unusual to see at least a handful of NBA players walking the halls of the Smith Center before the game. Each side wants to win, but not in the desperate way that they might want to beat Duke, or win an Atlantic Coast Conference Tournament or an NBA playoff game. It is, at best, an exhibition game, and the Smith Center looks the part. The lower-level seats are pushed back on one side, the cushy courtside chairs are stashed away, and the usual high-tech scorer's table has been replaced by a folding table, where team manager Eric Hoots operates the scoreboard. There is no band, no piped-in arena music. There are no uniforms, so players on both sides wear a mishmash of T-shirts and shorts. It's a laid-back atmosphere. The most energy seems to belong to the younger campers (the teenaged campers try to maintain bored smiles), who scream passionately for the player who had coached their group earlier in the day. Some players, like sophomore David Noel, even take the time to cultivate their own cheering sections, cupping hand to ear to prompt more volume.

It is not particularly surprising when the current players sleepwalk through the counselors' game during the second session of camp, losing to the alumni in a rout. Rising Carolina sophomore Rashad McCants sits out the game with an injury, remaining on the sideline and occasionally answering his bleating cell phone. The winners exchange high fives, and everyone immediately forgets the final score.

Except Roy Williams.

NCAA rules prohibit him from watching the game, but rumors travel the Smith Center faster than a high school cafeteria, and it's only a matter of minutes before the outcome reaches him.

That night, the members of Williams's first Carolina team are spread out across the various gyms used for camp, finishing up their day as counselors, when they receive a surprise visitor—their new head coach.

"How'd the game go today?" he asks each of them. He already knows the answer, and they know he knows. They respond sheepishly.

"What was the problem?" he asks.

The answers focus on lackadaisical defense and bad shot selection. Their coach's response is simple: "Well, if I was you, I'd try to change that."

"I let them know individually that to me, it's not OK to lose," Williams says. "If you think it's OK to lose, that's how you lose thirty-six games in two years. Winning is important. It's not OK to just go through the motions, whether it's a pickup game, pool, or marbles. You should compete to the best of your ability and invest something in every competition we have."

The next counselors' game is scheduled for June 24. The setting is the same, but there is a new electricity crackling through the current Tar Heels. McCants is playing this game, and he works up a sweat almost immediately. Early in the game he makes a jaw-dropping drop-step and spin on the baseline against NBA veteran Shammond Williams that results in a highlight-reel two-hand dunk, sending the hundreds of campers watching into a high-fiving frenzy. In the previous game, both teams usually freelanced, relying on individual moves to create scoring opportunities rather than functioning as a team. This week, point guard

Raymond Felton occasionally calls out set plays, screens are set, and bodies go sprawling as both sides try to draw charges. Last week, individuals sometimes played to the campers. This week they appear to have completely forgotten the audience, immersed instead in what is no longer a meaningless game. Neither team can muster a lead of more than 5 points.

"I've never played in a pickup game that intense," Baltimore native and junior Melvin Scott says. "Baltimore pickup games are tough. They are physically tougher. But there's not as much talent."

It is a challenge for the officials to keep the game civil. Alumnus Shammond Williams, one of the toughest competitors in Carolina history, ups his intensity even higher when he realizes how hard the current Tar Heels are playing. Fouls are contested. No easy layups are given. There is none of the good-natured bantering between players that marked the previous game; instead, the only sounds are the squeaking of shoes on the Smith Center hardwood and the occasional quibble with an official. With the score tied at 78 in a game being played to 80, Williams has the ball and a chance to win. He thinks he has drawn a foul on McCants, but the referee doesn't call it. The current Tar Heels recover the ball and set up a play, and Jawad Williams drains a game-winning three-pointer from the right side to end the game. As Williams accepts hugs and high fives, the celebration among the current players resembles a conference game. Shammond Williams is so incensed with the no-call that he spends a half hour trying to track down the game referees to argue his case. "You saw it," he says to a bystander. "Tell them it was a foul."

That night, Roy Williams again stops by each camp station to find out the outcome of the day's contest. The players tell him about the game with broad smiles.

The season-opening game against Old Dominion is five months away. But Roy Williams may have already earned his first victory as Carolina head coach.

This time, it looked like Bill Guthridge was serious.

The longtime assistant to Dean Smith, the winningest coach in the history of college basketball, had stepped in after Smith's sudden retirement in the fall of 1997, taking the job virtually no one could have handled: Smith's successor. After guiding the Heels to a miraculous upset dash to the Final Four in 2000, his second such appearance in three seasons, Guthridge began seriously mentioning retirement. He formally announced his retirement on June 30, 2000. Some reporters at the press conference, which was also attended by Smith, believed that an agreement was already in place for Roy Williams to become Carolina's next head coach. The logic seemed simple: although he'd been coaching at Kansas for thirteen seasons, Williams still possessed that North Carolina twang. He had served as an assistant coach to Dean Smith from 1978–1988. His son Scott had played at North Carolina, and his daughter Kimberly performed with the dance team. Numerous members of both his family and his wife's family lived in North Carolina. He owned a beach house in South Carolina.

Besides, there was no way Guthridge would retire so close to the start of college basketball's July recruiting season without lining up a replacement—coaches would begin scouting prospects in less than a week. The media and fans who assumed the line of succession was clear had good company. Smith felt confident Roy Williams would return to Carolina, as did Guthridge, former UNC assistant coach Eddie Fogler, and Bill Miller, a close confidant of Smith and Guthridge.

UNC Athletic Director Dick Baddour was not as certain. "We're going to treat this like he is our top recruit and he doesn't know us at all," he told Smith. Baddour contacted Kansas for permission to speak to Williams, and Williams arrived in Chapel Hill on the first weekend in July, where he was promptly greeted by . . . nothing. It was a holiday weekend, the Fourth of July, and Baddour and Williams found a deserted Carolina campus. The area was such a wasteland that when Associate Athletic Directors Steve Kirschner and Larry Gallo went to hunt down some authentic North Carolina barbecue for what they hoped would be a taste of home for the future Tar Heel coach, they had to make a ninety-minute drive to Wilber's Barbecue in Goldsboro.

At the time, the lack of frenzy on campus seemed like a blessing. Williams could get on and off campus without being harassed by fans or the media. He was able to discuss the job in detail with Baddour, asking pointed questions about the amount of authority he'd be given and getting answers that pleased him. Hours stretched into days, and it became obvious he was the lone candidate. Later Baddour drew criticism for failing to line up alternate candidates in case Williams said no. But at the time, aware of Williams's emotional state and the delicate nature of the situation, Carolina's athletic director felt that interviewing other candidates might be perceived by Williams as a sign that he wasn't needed in Chapel Hill. That was not the case. He was, as Baddour told Smith, Carolina's top recruit, and the Tar Heels wanted to treat him that way.

After his trip to Chapel Hill, Williams retreated to his beach house in Isle of Palms, South Carolina, a Fourth of July tradition that included close friend and business partner Lee King.

"We'd go out to play golf early in the morning, and Carolina and Kansas was the basic conversation all the way around the golf course," King says. "He was very torn about making the right decision. It was tough to leave Kansas because he had it made there. He'd established his own program."

Williams returned to Kansas on July 5. Still clearly undecided, he shook hands with King before departing.

"Whichever job you take, it's fine with me," his friend told him. "You have to do what is right for you and your family."

With Williams on his way back to the University of Kansas, King returned to his family's condominium, where wife Sarah was waiting.

"Until right at that moment, I never thought that he wouldn't take it," King says. "But when I got back I told her, 'Roy's not going to take the Carolina job.' "

The rest of the world was not as certain. Although Baddour was getting nervous, the rest of the Carolina insiders, including Smith and Guthridge, remained resolute. Roy was coming. The Tar Heels knew Williams was a meticulous planner. Perhaps, they thought, his very public struggling was his way of preparing the KU faithful for his departure.

Williams is a man of emotion, a trait he can usually mask with a well-conceived plan. But without an established procedure for making this decision, emotion was important. And in stark contrast with the deserted surroundings he'd found in Chapel Hill, when Williams returned to Lawrence he found the KU campus awash in a Roy Williams lovefest. Emails imploring him to stay piled up by the hundreds. Signs and flowers adorned the path to his office at Phog Allen Fieldhouse.

One day later, on July 6, Roy Williams had made a decision. There was going to be a press conference.

In Lawrence.

"He could never answer the question, 'What am I going to tell my players?' " says his close friend Cody Plott.

Baddour already knew what the substance of the press conference would be. After waiting nervously around his Smith Center office for most of the day, he finally decided to make the short drive home and wait for Williams's decision there. He was sitting in his den when the phone rang.

"I just can't do it," Williams told him.

"Is there anything I can do?" Baddour asked. "Do you need more time?"

"No, more time won't help," Williams said.

Baddour's cell phone rang. It was Dean Smith. Carolina's athletic director was now holding one phone to each ear. He was literally right between Williams and Smith, one who was going to stay in Kansas and one who was going to be very disappointed.

"Tell him I'll call him later tonight," Williams said.

Crestfallen, Baddour returned to the Smith Center, where a handful of media had been on stakeout during most of the job search. During their phone conversation, Williams had assured the Carolina athletic director that he had been very satisfied with how UNC had handled the interview process. He would, in fact, make a point of praising Baddour and the search. But the meeting with the local media was not likely to be pleasant. Steve Kirschner, who is responsible for the athletic department's media relations, told the athletic director he'd have to make some kind of statement to the press.

"Do you want anyone up there with you?" Kirschner asked, aware that Smith had been a part of Guthridge's retirement press conference.

"No, I've got to do this one alone," Baddour said.

The Kansas press conference was played live on the video board at KU's football stadium in front of a crowd symbolically estimated at 16,300—the capacity of Allen Fieldhouse. It turned into a Royapalooza, and Carolina fans everywhere gnashed their teeth over the way they perceived Williams had shoved his decision in their collective face live on ESPN. In truth, it was one of the few times that the coach had little control over his program. Emotionally spent from the past week, he simply went along with what people told him to do, a decision he would later regret.

Baddour was left with a handful of choices to lead Carolina's program, none of them without flaws. Roy Williams had been the slam dunk. NBA wanderer Larry Brown, the most logical next option, had strong support from key members of the Tar Heel basketball family, but he was miffed that he had not been the first choice to replace Guthridge; after his jump to the NBA in 1988, Kansas was placed on probation for violations during Brown's tenure, an unappealing detail to UNC.

There was, it seemed, one potential compromise candidate who could solve most of Carolina's problems. And so, when Baddour concluded his press conference after Williams's "I'm stayin'" announcement, he made just one phone call: to Matt Doherty.

Doherty, a member of Carolina's 1982 championship team, had worked as an assistant to Roy Williams at Kansas for seven years before becoming Notre Dame's head coach. Notre Dame had fallen off the basketball map since the departure of Digger Phelps, but in his one season in South Bend, Doherty's youth-oriented approach gave the Irish buzz again.

But Doherty was not a unanimous choice for Carolina. He had points in his favor: major college coaching experience and youth. If things worked out, he could very well be at Carolina for the next thirty years. It might be an opportunity to hire the next Dean Smith. But he also had drawbacks: he had just one year of major college coaching experience, and not everyone was sold on his qualifications to lead one of the best programs in America. His one year in South Bend had been marked with heart-pounding upset victories and some deflating upset losses.

Baddour, however, felt he was the best compromise candidate and, just as everyone expected, Doherty did not say no. His hiring once again created one big, happy Carolina family.

For about five minutes.

It was about that long into his press conference when he announced he was bringing his staff of assistant coaches with him from Notre Dame, displacing Guthridge assistants Phil Ford, Pat Sullivan, and Dave

Hanners. Doherty believed that by importing his own staff he was displaying the type of loyalty Dean Smith had always tried to instill in his protégés—rewarding the assistants who had helped him reach this point in his career. But the displaced assistants had all played at Carolina and had been recruiting for the Tar Heels during the coaching transition. Despite Doherty's intentions, the shift in the coaching staff was perceived as a very un-Smith-like move, and it created an immediate rift at Chapel Hill.

He compounded the problem a few days later. Under Smith and Guthridge, the Carolina basketball office had never been palatial, but it didn't matter because their status trumped the subpar office space. As a second-year head coach without the unimpeachable reputation of his predecessors at Carolina, Doherty believed he needed surroundings that would impress recruits. He assigned assistant coach Doug Wojcik the job of sprucing up the office, including the outer lobby area. Wojcik spent the better part of a week doing basic housekeeping chores. The transformation seemed inconsequential, but it angered at least one longtime member of the office staff who felt that the new coach was invading her space.

In less than a month, Doherty had brought in four new assistant coaches and dramatically altered the physical appearance of the basketball office. The message seemed clear: this isn't Dean Smith's program anymore. The message was not entirely unintended. Doherty wanted to put his own stamp on the program, to prove that he was in charge. He was too busy—or too naive—to realize that what he thought was effective leadership was being perceived quite differently within the program.

His first team went 26–7 and was ranked number one in the country for two weeks in February. After that, they imploded. They suffered an embarrassing 26-point loss to Duke in the Atlantic Coast Conference (ACC) Tournament final after an ill-timed Doherty blowup in a team meeting the day before. One week later, a team that was falling apart at the seams—including serious friction between two of the leading scorers, Joseph Forte and Jason Capel—was sent home from the NCAA Tournament by a less talented Penn State team.

Because of a lack of depth, the next season was one Doherty had feared since taking the job. The Tar Heels limped to an almost inconceivable 8–20 finish, missing the postseason entirely. Off the court, things weren't much better. Complaints were growing about Doherty's management style. The freshmen—Jawad Williams, Melvin Scott, and Jackie Manuel—who were supposed to be the sign of hope for the future, were stunned to find that the suave, smiling coach who had recruited them often blistered them on the practice court. This confusion about Doherty's true personality caused an erosion of trust between the players and the coaching staff, which combined with growing complaints about his management style proved fatal.

Doherty's third season turned into a soap opera. With a highly touted recruiting class in place that included Sean May, Raymond Felton, and Rashad McCants, the Tar Heels raced out to a 5–0 start, including a Preseason National Invitation Tournament championship that featured a win over Roy Williams and Kansas. From there, the season fell apart. Carolina lost back-to-back games to Illinois and Kentucky by 27 and 15 points, respectively. Doherty's style was grating on his players, his staff, and other members of the athletic department. One of his assistant coaches was unwittingly fueling the rumor mills by holding casual conversations with fans about the problems within the team. Doherty was never physically abusive—he never had one big blowup that would have served as justification for his dismissal. Instead, it was a series of smaller events that, taken as a whole, wore on those around him. In Doherty's very first game as Carolina's head coach, a game against Winthrop in the Smith Center, Forte threw an ill-advised behind-the-back pass that was intercepted. At the next timeout, Doherty berated Forte—an established star who in his freshman year had been named ACC Rookie of the Year and the MVP of the NCAA's South Regional as he led the Heels to the Final Four—calling him a "motherfucking prima donna." Coming off a year under the more tranquil Bill Guthridge, the players were shocked by the harshness of Doherty's tone. This would be a theme throughout his stay in Chapel Hill. The trust between the players and their head coach continued to deteriorate, helped along by one incident in which Doherty during a team huddle brought up a personal issue of one of the players, which he had only learned about in confidence. Doherty later acknowledged the move was a mistake.

That lack of trust crushed Doherty as his tenure wound down, because his players never felt comfortable telling him the truth about their concerns, instead telling him whatever they thought he wanted to hear. Despite a serious foot injury to Sean May, the Heels advanced to the 2003 NIT, where they looked listless in a third-round home loss to Georgetown. The same night that the Hoyas ended Carolina's season, many of the players met in their nearby dorm. They were aware they would probably be called to meet with Baddour, and they resolved to do one thing: tell the truth.

Baddour was faced with a tricky decision. Based on what he had heard from within the athletic department and from the players, it seemed a change would be healthy. But he also realized that most of the public would never understand the reasoning behind his decision, because he wouldn't be able to talk about it in public. To reveal the details would be severely damaging to Doherty's future job prospects. Doherty was not thrilled with the idea of resigning, and in the hours before the press conference, two statements were prepared, one in the event that UNC was announcing a firing, one in the event of a resignation. Baddour persuaded skeptical members of the Carolina family that the coach should be allowed to resign, since a resignation would be better for Doherty's finances and his long-term job prospects. That bit of generosity went unknown by the public, however, and miffed Carolina fans directed most of their anger at Baddour, not the deposed coach.

Meanwhile, in Lawrence, Kansas, Roy Williams got the news of Doherty's ouster while sitting in the coaches' locker room. He immediately left friends with the impression that he might be leaving to take a new job.

"I was with him when he found out," says Randy Towner, the golf pro at Alvamar Country Club, where Williams lived. "He kind of shrugged, and he got this look on his face like, 'I've kind of got to go.' "

The circumstances were not entirely favorable. There were some unmended fences in Chapel Hill, where Smith had taken his pupil's rejection well three years earlier, but others had not. Guthridge, who had set the whole process in motion with his retirement, was especially upset, and he and Williams did not speak during the period after Williams said no and before the courtship was renewed. Those types of hurdles were significant to Williams, for whom loyalty is a prized virtue.

But his life in Lawrence was not as perfect as it had been in 2000. Kansas supporters had forced out Athletic Director Bob Frederick, a close Williams friend, because of perceived weaknesses in fund-raising and in the football program. Frederick had been replaced by Al Bohl, who immediately proved to be a better fund-raiser but, more importantly, who also had a special talent for getting on people's nerves.

There were other reasons to return to Chapel Hill. Williams had two ailing family members living in the area, a significant detail for a man who prizes family. Nick Collison and Kirk Hinrich, two Jayhawks with whom Williams had developed a father-son relationship, were graduating.

After Kansas finished their season by losing to Syracuse in the national championship game, Williams attended an awards ceremony in Los Angeles. He stayed with Dana Anderson, a Kansas booster and a close friend. Cody Plott, a North Carolina graduate who had been invited by Williams, stayed at the Downtown Athletic Club and played golf with Williams's group at the Los Angeles Country Club on Saturday and Bel Air on Sunday. Plott left Los Angeles with a nagging feeling that this time, his friend's decision might be different. "That's your heart talking and not your brain," said his wife, Becky, well aware that her husband would love to see Williams return the Tar Heel program to prominence.

But Dick Baddour was getting the same feeling. This time, it seemed, the circumstances were different. The strong emotional pull Williams had felt to so many things in Lawrence in 2000—to Frederick, to Collison and Hinrich—was weakening. He'd also had the chance to see what his decision to turn down Carolina had done to the Heels, as they'd missed the NCAA Tournament for two straight years and fallen behind Duke in the hierarchy of the ACC. That was important to a man who valued his Tar Heel heritage.

This time, though, Carolina was not locked in on Roy Williams. He was the primary candidate, of course, but the coaching world had changed in the three years since his last decision. In 2000, most coaches handled their own business affairs. Three years later, virtually every major college coach had an agent, creating a new avenue through which interest in a job could be gauged, interest could be expressed, and contact could be made indirectly. Through these back channels Dick Baddour knew that even if Williams turned down the Tar Heels, the program would still end up in the hands of one of any number of top coaches who had used an intermediary to express interest. Last time, Williams was the lone big hitter. This time, Carolina seemed to have several sluggers on deck.

The only public relations home run, however, was to hire Roy Williams. Baddour was well aware that he was the only person in the entire situation taking a risk. No one was going to blame Dean Smith if Williams again spurned the Heels. Williams would only more firmly entrench himself at Kansas if he said no a second time. Baddour, however, stood to take a major hit. He had already overseen two botched attempted hirings—the first try with Williams and a similar situation with the football program when a nationally respected football coach indicated he would accept the Carolina job, only to renege at the last moment, leaving Baddour without a high-profile coach.

This time, he got the sense that he was going to land his man. Williams was in Los Angeles, agonizing yet again over whether to accept the head coaching job at his alma mater. After several rounds of golf and the awards ceremony, he flew back to Lawrence on a KU plane with Randy Towner, changing his mind several times on the flight.

"I wasn't sure what he was going to do that night," Towner says. "But when you're buddies with a guy for fifteen years, you can get a pretty good feeling based on the way someone is acting. And I had a feeling he was going."

He was. Baddour had enlisted a private plane co-owned by two Carolina supporters, Paul Lawing and Bill Jordan. An elaborate ruse had been set up to thwart any cell phone eavesdroppers or overeager members of the media. If Baddour called Lawing and said the word "Houston," where Lawing frequently traveled for business, that was the signal to send the plane to Lawrence to pick up Williams. Monday morning, the code was given. The coach was coming home.

Williams wore a red tie at the press conference announcing his hiring, angering some Carolina fans who were expecting him to be decked out in full Tar Heel blue. Carolina's previously scheduled basketball banquet was the next evening, and he chose not to attend. Over the next few days, he would hand out Krispy Kreme doughnuts at the Old Well to fawning students, get acquainted with his office in the Smith Center, do a whirlwind of interviews, and fly back to Lawrence to attend the Kansas banquet—where a fan shouted "Traitor!" at him before being shouted down by, among others, Nick Collison's father.

One of his assistant coaches, Ben Miller, was retained by new Kansas coach Bill Self, so Williams brought Joe Holladay, Steve Robinson, Jerod Haase, and C. B. McGrath with him to Chapel Hill. That left no room for Phil Ford, a situation that had caused an outcry when Doherty left the popular former point guard off his staff. This time, there was silence. That was the same sound coming out of the basketball office, where the leaks and gossip that had plagued Doherty were immediately stanched.

"There is only one source for Carolina basketball," Williams said about two weeks after his hiring, "and that is me. That was one of the problems that made it so difficult here before. There were so many sources. It came out that Matt was doing this or Matt was doing that, and somebody forgot to ask Matt."

No one would forget to ask Roy. He would make sure of it.

At noon on Friday, October 17, Neill Wessell should be at work. An employee of the computer shop on UNC's Chapel Hill campus, Wessell, a senior business major from Wilmington, is scheduled to be on duty for most of Friday afternoon. But instead of spending the unseasonably warm afternoon amid hard drives and monitors, Wessell spends his day enjoying the sunshine.

Wessell's decision to spend the day outside isn't unusual among Carolina students—Wilmington, a popular beach destination, is less than three hours away by car. But he isn't going to the beach. Instead, he sets up his lawn chair, drink cooler, and laptop computer outside the Dean E. Smith Center. North Carolina's first basketball practice of the year begins at midnight, and Wessell wants to be first in line.

He makes it, but just barely. Although it was announced that the doors wouldn't open until 6:30 P.M., a crowd of about one hundred has formed outside the Smith Center main entrance by early afternoon. "I kind of skipped out on work," Wessell says. "But it's just a job. I told my boss I had to do it."

Wessell might have been the first to arrive, but he didn't have the longest trip. A mother-and-son team, Lorraine and Barry Greer of Fork Union, Virginia, left their home before noon in order to stand in line for three hours before the doors opened. The Greers have attended every midnight practice in Tar Heel history, making the four-hour drive each year since 1992.

And a four-hour drive is nothing to the Singleterry family. Paul and Judy Singleterry live in Mulvane, Kansas, a small community just outside of Wichita. They are attending the midnight practice at Chapel Hill for the third straight year, a feat made even more impressive by the fact that they drive from Kansas to North Carolina for the event. Their itinerary for 2003: Monday night in Kansas City; Tuesday night in Benton, Illinois; Wednesday night in Newport, Tennessee; and a Thursday afternoon arrival in Chapel Hill, the culmination of a 1,400-mile trip.

The response from fans eager to see Roy Williams's first team was exactly what the Carolina sports marketing team had hoped for when planning the event. The idea of holding the year's first practice at midnight on the first day has been around college basketball even longer than the three-point line. The pioneer is generally agreed to be Lefty Driesell, the former coach at Maryland who was frustrated several times during the mid-1980s by Dean Smith's patented Carolina comebacks.

Driesell's first team in College Park finished a disappointing 13–13 during the 1968–69 season. To motivate the team, he decided to start practice the next year at the earliest possible moment. Unwittingly—and his detractors would tell you that Lefty did most everything unwittingly—Driesell had given birth to Midnight Madness.

Across the college basketball world, the event grew in popularity throughout the 1980s, evolving into a college basketball holiday that was covered by ESPN, which dispatched Dick Vitale to report on the happenings at certain schools. At Carolina, however, head coach Dean Smith resisted the trend, saying he didn't want to keep his players and the students out past midnight on a school night.

In 1992, however, the NCAA moved the start of practice back to November 1. October 31 fell on a Friday, and Smith relented. The first-ever "Tar Heel Tip-Off" drew a sizable crowd to the Smith Center. The highlight came when senior guard Henrik Rödl, a German who spoke with a slight accent, picked up on the Halloween mood and stepped forward during team introductions to pronounce over the microphone, "We're going to be so good this year, it's scaaaary." Rödl's announcement was a source of much hilarity but he turned out to be a prophet, and after the Tar Heels captured the 1992–93 national championship, he repeated his fearsome declaration at the welcome-home party at the Smith Center celebrating the title.

Midnight Madness was an off-and-on happening throughout the 1990s, shuttling between the Smith Center and Carmichael Auditorium. It hit a high point in 2000 during the first year of the Matt Doherty era, as the Tar Heels held "Midnight with Matt and the Tar Heels" at Carmichael Auditorium. Carmichael Auditorium was filled to the rafters, and over 1,200 fans had to be turned away.

It took exactly one day for the sniping to begin. Bitter insiders complained that the name of the event, "Midnight with Matt and the Tar Heels," put too much emphasis on the head coach and not enough on the Carolina ideal of all participants being equals. The inference was that Doherty's ego was dominating the program, an assertion that gained steam when he made the much talked-about decision to mount a 6-by-8-foot photo of Michael Jordan's game-winning shot in the 1982 national championship game against Georgetown in the lobby of the Carolina basketball office. Some people didn't see Jordan. They only saw a certain Tar Heel sophomore named Matt Doherty standing in the background of the photo, looking on as Jordan took the shot. Only a few people knew that hanging the photo hadn't even been Doherty's idea; it was the brainchild of assistant coach Doug Wojcik and sports information director Steve Kirschner. But almost before it had been hung, word was being spread by a disgruntled basketball staffer that Doherty had removed photos of former players and was putting up pictures of himself, and the word traveled quickly among former Tar Heels. The myth was soon accepted as fact. The photo was such a lightning rod that it was removed before the 2001–02 season. Later Doherty would marvel that anyone would care so much about a wall decoration.

"We chose the one with me in the background for recruiting purposes," he said. "We wanted a recruit to walk in and say, 'Oh, he did play with Jordan. He was on the same court with [Georgetown's] Patrick Ewing.' But people take things the wrong way, and so it wasn't worth it."

The removal of the photo wasn't the only alteration before the second season of Doherty's tenure. When the midnight practice was held again the next year, the name had (not coincidentally) been changed to "Midnight with the Tar Heels."

After Williams arrived, the name of Midnight Madness suddenly became less important. When it was announced that the 2003 version would be known as "Late Night with Roy Williams," just as it had been in Kansas, no one batted an eye.

And so on October 17 there is plenty of excitement among Wessell and his fellow early-arriving fans, and there is even a hint of anticipation inside the 21,750-seat basketball palace as the operations crew begins getting the floor ready for the night's events. The script for the evening is tightly choreographed: doors open at 6:30 P.M., a Carolina-Duke volleyball match begins at 7:30, and basketball team introductions at 10:30. A handful of companies are presenting giveaway items to the night's earliest arrivals; observers guess that the hottest item will be the 2003–04 team poster.

An annual tradition, the team poster used to simply be a way to introduce fans to the players and list the year's schedule. In the marketing-intense twenty-first century, however, it has become an essential promotional tool. Posters from the previous two years had featured only certain players, but with the beginning of a new era in Carolina basketball, the UNC marketing gurus made the decision to include the entire team—and a certain much-loved head coach.

After scouting out Chapel Hill for appropriate locations for the photo shoot, photographer Bob Donnan and Norwood Teague, the associate athletic director for marketing, decided on the DuBose House, a vintage home located in a leafy subdivision of Chapel Hill. The house, all ornate trim and shiny fixtures, fit the bill. The decision had already been made to feature the players and Williams wearing suits and ties, at least partially in response to some criticism the program had taken several months earlier.

The whirlwind of events preceding Matt Doherty's resignation had ended quickly. After a week of speculation following Carolina's season-ending loss to Georgetown in the NIT, eager reporters staked out the Smith Center parking lot. The intrigue finally concluded on April Fool's Day, a Tuesday, as it became apparent that Doherty would be removed. A press conference was scheduled for 8 P.M., but it wasn't clear until moments before the event began whether it would be announced that Doherty had resigned or that he had been fired.

In the end, lawyers hammered out a deal that included Doherty's resignation. But while attorneys and athletic department officials had been meeting constantly over a period of several days, the Tar Heel players had been kept out of the loop. On the Tuesday of the press conference, none had been told that he might have to make an appearance later that night. Team leader Jawad Williams was waiting while getting his truck washed when he saw teammates Melvin Scott and David Noel on television doing a live interview from the Smith Center parking lot. Williams carries two cell phones, but neither one rang; it was a television anchorman who informed the viewers—and Carolina's star sophomore, watching from his freshly cleaned truck—that Doherty was leaving the Tar Heel program.

At about 6 P.M. Tuesday evening, the players who could be located were called and told to attend a team meeting at 7 P.M. in the Carolina locker room. They were not told the subject of the meeting, just that they should be in attendance. Many arrived straight from the weight room or study hall. The meeting, which lasted almost thirty minutes, was run by Dick Baddour. He informed the players of Doherty's departure and, without mentioning Roy Williams by name, told them, "I'm going to go out and get you the best coach in the country." When the players were asked if they had any questions, Raymond Felton asked the first two: first, about the scholarship status of his close friend David Noel, who had paid his own way as a freshman under a promise by Doherty that he would go on scholarship as a sophomore, and second, about the status of strength coach Thomas McKinney, a confidant to many of the players. (Williams wisely decided to retain McKinney.)

The meeting broke up less than forty-five minutes before the scheduled start of the 8 P.M. press conference. The players were told they had the option of attending the press conference. Some, including Noel and Felton, chose to leave. Others stayed, but in the hectic atmosphere that night none of the UNC administrators, including some who stood directly behind the players at the press conference, ever thought to suggest that the players should change clothes before facing the cameras. Many wore baseball hats and sweatshirts; most had their shirts untucked.

It was an image of Carolina basketball that many fans were unaccustomed to seeing. For thirty-seven years, Dean Smith had rigid rules regarding the appearance of his players in public and on television. Since the earliest days of the Smith era, suits and ties had been required on road trips. During the 1960s, freshmen were ineligible for varsity competition. Teams fielded freshman squads that were essentially glorified junior varsity teams, and Smith coached the Carolina freshman squad during his tenure as an assistant coach to Frank McGuire. The year before Smith assumed the head coaching position for the 1961–62 season, he left an indelible impression on one member of his freshman squad.

"The last Dixie Classic was my freshman year," remembers Mike Cooke, who earned three letters as a Tar Heel point guard. "It was a big event, and I had gotten a brand-new sweater for Christmas, and that was a big deal. The freshman team had tickets to sit in the stands for the Dixie Classic, and I was all decked out in my new sweater. When we came back to school, Coach Smith passed me at the gym and said, 'I saw you at the Dixie Classic. You didn't have a coat and tie on. Don't let me ever see you without a coat and tie on.'"

That rule remained in place as the importance of television grew during the 1980s. At many schools, players would do their postgame interviews moments after stepping out of the shower, usually still wrapped in a towel. At Carolina, players were required to get dressed before appearing on television. Skeptics of the Tar Heel basketball program often referred to them as the "IBM of college basketball." The joke was intended as a slight at the buttoned-down image of the Tar Heels, but it also illustrated just how refined the public concept of Carolina basketball had become.

So when UNC's players appeared looking like teenagers rather than corporate executives, a firestorm ensued. Several things about the press conference created controversy, from the way Chancellor James Moeser alluded to the questionable leadership of the Doherty regime to the way some players went public with their criticism of the coaching staff. But most infuriating to some observers was the way the Carolina players were dressed—although few critics understood the circumstances. Leading the charge was CBS college basketball analyst Billy Packer, a former Wake Forest University player who is the antithesis of better-known college hoops analyst Dick Vitale. Vitale is all sunshine and roses, a huge booster of college basketball who prefers to accentuate the positive; Packer, by contrast, has no problem with pointing out negatives and often seems to enjoy being surly. Just two years earlier, he had been required to issue an apology to a stadium usher at Duke after responding belligerently to her request to see his press credential, and in 1996 he called Georgetown's Allen Iverson a "tough little monkey" on the air.

Packer's response to what the Tar Heel players wore to the press conference came on the FOX network: "One of the things that really troubled me was a photo of those players who attended the press conference with baseball caps turned to the side," he said. "They looked like a rap group, as opposed to collegiate athletes . . . If those were the guys Athletic Director Dick Baddour listened to, I would really worry about that."

Almost everything about Packer's response was wrong, from the notion that the players had somehow gotten the coach fired to the idea that anyone with a baseball cap turned to the side was in a rap group. (Several weeks later many Kansas players would wear similar attire to a Jayhawk press conference, but no national frenzy ensued.) But he seemed to capture the feelings of many disgruntled fans who longed for the days of Dean Smith, when Tar Heel players were seen wearing one of two things—a basketball uniform or a suit. When it was announced on April 14 that Roy Williams would be Carolina's new head coach, Kirschner made certain the players wore suits.

So it was decided that the 2003–04 team poster would feature the Tar Heel players in a dressy setting. Donnan snapped the photo of the squad and their new coach standing on the DuBose House steps, and the poster—with the double-edged tagline "Class is in Session"—was ready for distribution just a few weeks later.

The day of "Late Night with Roy," sports marketing employees set up a table bearing hundreds of posters in the Smith Center concourse. When ushers finally throw open the arena doors, some fans grab handfuls of posters at a time, desperate to have multiple copies of the first tangible evidence that Roy Williams is indeed the head coach of this year's Tar Heels. Within minutes the table is barren.

The rest of the evening is part celebration, part state fair, part improvisational comedy show, and part (a very little part) basketball. When Roy Williams arrived in Kansas in 1988, "Late Night" was already a three-year tradition. The new coach made his own contributions to the program, and by the time he left, it had become an annual event featuring more humor than hoops.

That recipe is somewhat foreign to Chapel Hill. As plans were being made for the inaugural "Late Night with Roy" during the summer of 2003, staffers for the Carolina Athletics Association—a student support group for athletics responsible for distributing tickets and other tasks—were told to create skits highlighting the players. Accustomed to thinking of the players as exactly that—basketball players—the staffers came up with initial skit ideas centered around the hardwood. Told that the theme should be different, Norwood Teague, the assistant athletic director for sports marketing, met with Kris McGrath, the wife of basketball administrative assistant C. B. McGrath, in early August. Kris, a former KU tennis player, had worked in sports marketing at Kansas and had been involved extensively with the "Late Night" production in Lawrence.

For the Tar Heels, McGrath produces a handful of sketches that will thoroughly entertain the crowd of over 21,000, a gathering that forces the Smith Center operations staff to close the doors at 11:30 P.M., a half hour before the year's first official practice. The skits and dances are new to the fans, but they were just as unexpected for the players a few days earlier when the team met on Sunday evening for their first rehearsal.

For five straight days, McGrath and the Carolina Athletics Association staffers rehearse with the team for two hours each night. Early rehearsals are difficult, as the team gets used to the idea of being dancers and actors rather than basketball players. But the players eventually warm to the idea. When McGrath passes out vintage Tar Heel uniforms that will be used in one skit, the Tar Heels are so taken by the old-school jerseys that they dash into the tunnel while still wearing the classic togs and then run out onto the court in perfect formation. After "Late Night" is over, the players are so appreciative of McGrath's efforts that they pool their money to buy her four baskets of flowers.

David Noel proves to be the most natural thespian on the roster, easily fitting into each sketch. When the show finally hits the big stage in front of over 21,000 fans, one skit requires the team to perform a chore-ographed dance to Gatorade's popular 1991 jingle, "Be Like Mike," a reference to former Tar Heel Michael Jordan. As the number finishes and the rest of his teammates walk off the darkened court, Noel pauses, causing McGrath, sitting in the stands, to wonder if he has forgotten what to do. But then, after capturing the attention of the crowd, Noel walks off the floor in a dead-perfect imitation of Jordan's loose-limbed gait.

In a later skit, Noel—who goes by the name "Divine" in the skit—dresses as a woman and tries to sort through suitable candidates in a parody of the 1970s game show *The Dating Game.* In fact, the skit was originally written to feature Jawad Williams in the female role. Williams practiced the role at the previous Sunday's rehearsal, reading through the script with a skeptical eye. But the day before "Late Night" was to debut, McGrath pulled out a hot pink wig in a dress rehearsal and Williams, who had expressed some reservations, declined the role. Noel steps in and fills the role smoothly.

That Williams declines to take on such a potentially embarrassing task is no surprise. The quiet junior has an unusual personality for a player at his level. Most Division I basketball players are naturally out-going, having performed on the public stage since elementary school. In high school they get used to being flown around the country to compete in a variety of high-profile basketball tournaments. They are used to being fawned over by college coaches who tell them what superstars they will become; they are used to having adults twice their age try to latch on to them in the hopes of riding their coattails as they rise to NBA stardom and claim the riches that come with it.

Today's college basketball player arrives in school already used to talking to the media, having fielded nightly calls from the "journalists" who breathlessly cover college recruiting for Internet sites. High school seniors are virtually antiques; it's now common for recruiting junkies to be well acquainted with the best high school freshmen players in the country. As soon as a player shows a flash of talent, he is immediately asked which schools he favors, so interacting with strangers becomes second nature.

Although he was an extremely coveted recruit who earned the high school basketball golden seal of approval—selection to the McDonald's All-American team—Jawad Williams never developed that easiness with strangers. The son of a Cleveland Golden Gloves champion boxer and the brother of Nasheema Williams, who played women's basketball professionally in the short-lived American Basketball League, Jawad was a bit of an enigma during his freshman season at Carolina. On his right shoulder he sports a "Loved by few, hated by many" tattoo, which he chose after first seeing it on Mike Tyson. But despite once playing a game of pickup basketball at Tyson's home, where the boxer kept a caged tiger just steps from his outdoor court, Williams never showed any Tyson-like characteristics. His father tried to steer him toward boxing before giving up when his son kept bouncing a basketball while wearing his gloves. If anything, Williams was too passive as a Carolina freshman, too unwilling to bang under the basket, too hesitant to take over a game with his formidable talents. He rarely strung together more than a couple of sentences at a time in public. After he went public with criticism of Doherty after the 2001–02 season, some concluded that Jawad Williams was a sullen malcontent.

It was almost inconceivable, then, when several of his teammates began to cite his leadership as a key to the 2002–03 team. After games, at press conferences, word was beginning to trickle out: Williams was the glue that was holding this team together. His quiet leadership became a constant during the turbulent 2002–03 season, and by the time the year ended Williams was publicly being compared to George Lynch, the revered senior leader of the national champion 1993 Tar Heels. It was a role that had partly been forced on him. Doherty wanted to foster his growth as a leader and often used him as a go-between for the coaches and players. At first, the responsibility pleased Williams. But as more issues arose between the two groups, and as Doherty continued to go to him over issues that might have been better addressed with the players involved, it turned into a stressful situation. Williams is an extremely coachable player—during his freshman year, Doherty and the staff worked with him to add a head fake to his post repertoire and then watched with surprise when he used it flawlessly in a game just days later. Yet Williams is one of the few players in major college basketball who isn't entirely self-confident. Most players at the Atlantic Coast Conference level go beyond self-confident to cocky, but Williams sometimes needs reassurance, both on and off the court. He has an elaborate set of superstitions which he follows before every game and which he refuses to discuss with anyone out of fear that someone will try to interfere with them. One example, which he let slip on an unguarded occasion, is that if he steps on a line with his right foot on a game day, he must step on another line immediately with his left foot. Any line, any time of game day. And the clean-shaven Tar Heel firmly believes that his superstitions contribute to his success on the basketball court. As members of the program learned how to relate to him, and came to understand that he was more shy than arrogant, the 6-foot-9 player became a much-loved Tar Heel.

"I can get the label of being arrogant," Williams admits. "But I'm from Cleveland, and where I'm from you don't walk around speaking to people you don't know. I'm not arrogant at all, I just don't know who to speak to."

He wasn't exaggerating about his background. Afraid of the sketchy characters who sometimes infiltrated their neighborhood, Williams's parents chose to send their son to St. Edward's High School, a parochial school in west Cleveland, an hour's bus ride away. His father, Joe Williams, who managed a recreation center located just a block from the family's home on East 143rd Street, had an easy response to any potential bad influences on his son.

"I don't know karate," the Golden Gloves champion would tell gang members looking to indoctrinate young Jawad, "but I do know ka-razy."

That comment, along with a well-placed gleam in his eye, was enough to keep his son free of undesirable influences.

After a sophomore year that included an All-ACC honorable mention, the only nagging complaint about his floor game was the occasional suggestion that he might be a little soft—too willing to settle for a perimeter jump shot when he could have scored in the paint. He attempted 136 three-pointers during the 2002–03 season, more than any other Tar Heel apart from the guards. Most tellingly, he attempted more three-pointers than any player on Roy Williams's 2002–03 Kansas squad except one, the sharpshooting Kirk Hinrich. Roy Williams favors throwing the ball inside and then swinging the ball back to the perimeter after the defense has collapsed, rather than the kind of perimeter-oriented attack that Carolina often used in the two seasons before his arrival. Occasionally, the Tar Heels got bogged down with too much dribbling last season, so Williams emphasizes the need to move the ball with passes rather than dribbles in several early-season practices. The goal is simple: use better ball movement to create better shots for several players, including Jawad Williams.

Over the summer, Williams adds a staggering nineteen pounds to his formerly wiry frame, and he enters his junior season listed at 223 pounds, up from 204 as a sophomore. Summer pickup games show off a more physical Williams; during one memorable game, he throws down a vicious one-handed dunk over the significantly beefier Sean May, prompting teammate Damion Grant to say, "Oh, Sean, I'm really sorry about that Sean." Williams now seems as comfortable taking the ball straight at the basket as he does settling for a jump shot.

The "Late Night" festivities count as an NCAA-regulated practice, but the Tar Heels don't begin the season in earnest until the next day, when they gather for their first "official" practice at 6 P.M. The workout caps an odd six months for the Carolina coaching staff. After being hired on April 14, Roy Williams spends most of the summer on the road recruiting with his assistants. During one late-April stretch, the new head coach hits eleven states in six days.

The cross-country journeys are good for recruiting (one of the stops is Washington, D.C., the home of shooting guard Marcus Ginyard, a highly regarded class of 2005 guard prospect who will commit to the Tar Heels a month later) but not great for getting to know the players already on the roster. NCAA rules tightly limit the amount of contact coaches can have with their players over the summer, so while most of the current team spend their afternoons playing pickup games at the Smith Center, the coaches are barred from the gym.

After crisscrossing the country in the early spring, the coaches spend most of May and June completing their moves from Kansas to North Carolina. There are homes to sell, new homes to buy, families to uproot, and boxes to pack and unpack. Steve Robinson, an assistant coach who spent five years as the head coach at Florida State, has the most difficult move. For the second time in two years, he has to move three school-age children—eleven-year-old daughter Kiaya, twelve-year-old son Denzel, and fifteen-year-old son Tarron. Robinson, fired as the head coach at FSU in the spring of 2002, signed on as an assistant to Williams at Kansas, where he had previously spent seven years as an assistant from 1988 through 1995. Now, after just one season in Lawrence, he has to move his family back across the country to Chapel Hill.

"The toughest thing about the move is the impact on my family," he says. "We've still got boxes we haven't unpacked from the last move. It's hard for the kids. They get mad at you for a little bit."

Much of the moving burden falls on the coaches' families because the men spend so much of the summer recruiting. July is an active recruiting period during which the staff travels to numerous AAU basketball tournaments—multiple-day basketball fests attended by the very best high school players in the country. In August, Williams spends twenty-six straight days with the United States national team, where he serves as an assistant coach for fellow Tar Heel Larry Brown. Williams returns to Chapel Hill in September and the recruiting resumes; he conducts all the in-home visits with Tar Heel prospects.

So while most Carolina fans are intimately familiar with the playing styles of the returning Tar Heels, the coaching staff has seen very little of them. In late August, a friend mentions to assistant coach Joe Holladay that he has seen Tar Heel freshman Reyshawn Terry play during the on-campus pickup games.

"Oh, really?" Holladay says. "I've never seen him play basketball before."

Such is the logic of the NCAA. Roughly forty-five days before he and the coaching staff will be expected to mold Terry and his teammates into a top-25 team, Holladay has never seen the rookie pick up a basketball. The NCAA does allow four-man workouts to begin in the early fall prior to the start of practice, but because of the recruiting calendar, most of the workouts are conducted by Jerod Haase, a twenty-nine-year-old assistant coach who has impressed many in Chapel Hill as a rising star but who is nevertheless the third man on the assistant coaching totem pole. Word from the annual summer pickup games is that rising sophomore forward David Noel appears ready to explode after a solid freshman campaign. Reports range from glowing to gushing about the Durham native, who would be an important piece of the puzzle for a team lacking frontcourt depth.

Williams doesn't have to see his team in action to realize that his top seven Tar Heels are talent-heavy but unproven—none of the players, he notes, has ever won anything on the college level—and after them the team lacks depth. Carolina's best four players—Rashad McCants, Raymond Felton, Sean May, and Jawad Williams—are among the most physically talented starters in the country. But beyond junior reserves Jackie Manuel and Melvin Scott and sophomore David Noel, the bench provides woefully little support.

The 2003–04 Tar Heels feature zero scholarship seniors, a product of Doherty's tenure in Chapel Hill. Guards Adam Boone and Brian Morrison were recruited by Bill Guthridge but never played for him, entering the program before the 2000–01 season and transferring after their sophomore seasons due to personality differences with the new head coach.

There had been another transfer during Doherty's three-year tenure, a 7-foot-6 post player named Neil Fingleton. A native of England, Fingleton was selected as a McDonald's All-American for reasons no one could quite understand. Possessing slow feet and poor hands, he was not among the twenty best high school players in the class of 2000, but his formidable height and recruiting attention from a powerful program like North Carolina's earned him the McDonald's distinction. After redshirting his first year at Carolina, he transferred to Holy Cross in December of the next season, making very little impact with the Crusaders.

Fingleton's transfer was the least controversial of the trio. He had solid reasons to leave—a desire for more playing time and to be closer to his American host family—and most Carolina fans realized that he was not going to be a major player for the Tar Heels. But for the 2003–04 squad, his absence meant that, apart from Sean May, the depth in the paint was almost nonexistent. Because of a combination of factors, Carolina had failed to recruit a highly regarded big man other than May over the past two seasons.

First among them was the fact that, in the twenty-first century, several talented big men were choosing to go straight to the NBA. Three high school players who stood 6-foot-9 or more went in the first round of the 2003 NBA Draft, depleting the recruiting class of its best post prospects. This depletion of the available interior players led to further recruiting misses. Several centers, including DeSagana Diop and Kendrick Perkins, who were recruited by Doherty, went straight to the professional ranks.

But there were also misses on players who attended college. David Harrison, a 7-footer from Nashville, had compelling reasons to attend other schools on his final list when he made his college choice in the fall of 1999: his father was an assistant football coach at Vanderbilt, and his brother, D. J., played at Colorado. Still, very few people in the basketball world believed that a player with NBA aspirations would choose a mid-level program like Vandy or CU over a national powerhouse like Carolina. The Tar Heels seemed to have the inside track on Harrison until his official visit to Chapel Hill. During the game against Duke, which he watched from behind the Tar Heel bench, his eyes went wide after he heard Doherty tell assistant coach Doug Wojcik to "Shut up" during a team huddle. After the weekend visit, he suddenly seemed to look for reasons to go elsewhere. Official visits are usually wine-and-dine experiences set up to showcase the very best of a school. This time, however, Harrison had heard things from the current Carolina players that led him to look more seriously at other schools; Harrison eventually chose Colorado, where he became exactly what the Heels needed—a 7-footer able to score and rebound in the paint and a 2003–04 Wooden Award candidate.

One year later, one of the top high school centers was Torin Francis. Carolina was the acknowledged leader for Francis throughout much of his recruitment, but the situation soured during his recruiting visit, as his mother peppered the UNC staff with tough questions that the Tar Heel coaches believed had been planted by the staff of another team. Francis later picked Notre Dame.

That same year, the Heels missed on Jason Fraser, another player who appeared to be a good fit but who eventually selected Villanova, saying his recruitment by Carolina had been "too intense." Fraser was overwhelmed by the almost daily communications from the Carolina coaches. UNC suffered another setback when Brad Buckman spurned the Heels. The Carolina staff devoted considerable energy to Buckman, a Texas native who had grown up in the same Austin neighborhood with Longhorn athletic director DeLoss Dodds and was on a first-name basis with several members of the UT athletic department. Not surprisingly, Buckman picked Texas.

David Padgett's decision came two years later and was equally hurtful. Padgett seemed to prefer playing in Chapel Hill, but he wanted to play for Roy Williams. When he made his college choice, the coach won out—Padgett announced for Kansas, actually citing Roy Williams as one of the primary factors in his decision.

Carolina filled its post needs with a pair of lesser-known players, Byron Sanders and Damion Grant. Sanders, a native of Gulfport, Mississippi, better known as "Big Breadmenz" to his teammates, was the state player of the year in Mississippi but was not offered a scholarship by most of his in-state schools. He jumped at the chance to attend Carolina when it became clear the Tar Heels had to add a big body to their incoming class of 2002. Although Sanders's willingness to do the little things—set screens, rebound, and pass the ball—endears him to his teammates and the coaching staff, his limited offensive game restricts his role in the Carolina offense.

Grant is more of an enigma. A native of Jamaica, he looks impressive in his uniform, standing 6-foot-11 and weighing 262 pounds. His easygoing personality charms his teammates, who know him strictly as "Deebo," a nickname he earned for his startling resemblance to a character of the same name in the 1995 film *Friday*.

But Grant has been hampered by a number of debilitating injuries. He undoubtedly went through a painful freshman year during the 2002–03 season, as he battled tendinitis in his knees and a torn meniscus that was not repaired until he underwent surgery after the season. His injuries, which also included a torn ligament in his thumb, forced him into a vicious cycle. He was rarely able to practice on back-to-back days, which made the coaching staff hesitant to put him into games.

"I'd get up and hope and pray that by the next practice my knees would have calmed down so I could run," Grant said. "I couldn't walk up steps or down steps. I had a class on the third floor and it was like getting on the Stairmaster. It got really annoying."

Grant's medical condition was a concern. Instead of remaining in Chapel Hill for summer school like the rest of the Tar Heels, he went back to New Jersey for the entire break to live with his uncle and have two surgical procedures, one on his knee and one on his thumb. Those procedures left him unable to practice. Given his absence over the summer and injury-plagued freshman season, his return for a second season never seemed certain. Asked upon his return whether he knew when he left that he would come back to Carolina rather than transfer, Grant just laughed and shook his head.

The easygoing nature that makes him popular with his teammates is sometimes frustrating to his coaches. A new tattoo that appeared on his back after his freshman season seemed to illustrate his confusing personality. The top half of the image was a globe with the caption, "Rise above all odds." Below was a basketball with the phrase, "To thine own self be true."

Grant loves basketball enough to tattoo one on his back. But does he love it enough to dedicate himself to overcoming his painful injuries? In early November, as he sits out practice after practice, it looks doubtful.

His absence leaves Carolina in an unfamiliar quandary. Although Sean May possesses surprising dexterity for a man his size and solid post fundamentals, he is not the prototypical North Carolina center. Dean Smith won hundreds of games with centers who rarely ventured more than 6 feet from the basket and were much more likely to shoot a hook shot than a jump shot.

There is no one who fits that description on the 2003–04 roster. The hole in the post behind May is the primary concern, but Roy Williams also has no viable backup to Raymond Felton at the point guard position and an overall lack of talented depth. Although the NCAA allows Division I teams to include thirteen scholarship players, this year's Tar Heels feature just ten. As the head coach evaluates his roster in the early days of practice, what he sees is both promising and worrisome.

"I like the personnel that we've got very much, except I'd like to have more of them in certain spots," Williams says as he reflects on early practices. "It's a fact that Raymond Felton is the only true point guard in our program. There's nobody else. And it's a fact that Sean May is the only big guy that has proven he can play at this level . . . I've never coached a team that had just one point guard. Every other team I've coached has had three."

The lack of depth shows as the squad is split up for the annual Blue-White game, an intra-squad scrimmage played two weeks into practice. Quite simply, there are not enough scholarship players to go around. The White team starts walk-on senior Damien Price and freshman Reyshawn Terry, who has barely been in Chapel Hill long enough to know the keypad password that must be used to access the Tar Heel locker room. The Blue squad starts walk-on senior Jonathan Miller. Of the four players who come off the bench as substitutes, none is on scholarship.

It seems to many in the crowd of over 8,000, who pay $10 apiece for the privilege of watching the scrimmage, that the teams are stacked in favor of the Blue. The Tar Heels have two players who no one else on the team can guard: Raymond Felton and Sean May. Both suit up for the Blue squad, making even assistant coach Joe Holladay wonder if the

sides are skewed when the teams are formed a few days in advance. The
Blues do indeed notch a 77–70 victory, but what Holladay knows, and
few others in the Smith Center realize, is that the day before, the White
team puts a hurting on the Blues in a not-for-the-public scrimmage—
testament to Jawad Williams's rapid improvement and Jackie Manuel's
growing sense of his place in the offense.

"We don't have enough post players to field two teams, especially if
you have to have a substitute," Roy Williams admits after the game.

Two days later, the situation gets worse. Sophomore David Noel, a
versatile player who stands just 6-foot-6 but was Carolina's best post
defender at the conclusion of the 2002–03 season, is going through a
regular Tuesday afternoon practice session when he bumps into
Reyshawn Terry and hyperextends his thumb. Ligaments in his right
thumb tear, an injury that Tar Heel team doctors estimate will take up to
eight weeks to heal. The recovery process will be further complicated by
the fact that Noel has a cut on his hand in the same area as the injury,
making it unwise to operate until the cut heals due to the risk of infec-
tion. Even if he recovers rapidly, doctors project Noel will miss the
Atlantic Coast Conference opener against Wake Forest and a nationally
televised trip to Kentucky on January 3.

The injury complicates matters for an already thin team and slows
Noel's adjustment to Williams's system, which was already progressing
haltingly. The sophomore from Durham isn't yet an instinctive basketball
player. Unlike most of his teammates, Noel was a multisport athlete
throughout high school. Instead of spending his summers traveling the
United States with AAU basketball teams, he spent considerable time on
football, a sport at which he was so proficient that he received several
major Division I scholarship offers on the gridiron. He does not have
the same amount of game experience on the hardwood as his teammates. In early practices he seems a step behind his teammates and he
struggles to live up to the glowing reviews he had received from fans
and Tar Heel insiders prior to mid-October.

The day after Noel's injury, the Heels have the day off. When they
reassemble two days later, Noel shows the work ethic that made him a
fan favorite as a freshman. The rest of the squad goes through a typically
rigorous Roy Williams practice, but Noel's heavily bandaged right hand

prevents him from taking part in any of the drills. Instead, Noel works on his left-hand dribble and practices his shooting form left-handed. Without being asked, Noel selects one player to "shadow," and mirrors that player's running throughout drills. When the group he would usually be working with makes a defensive mistake, and Williams tells them to line up on the baseline for a series of sprints as punishment, Noel drops the basketball he is using and lines up beside his teammates, running sprints for an error he did not commit.

The Tar Heels look impressive four days later in an exhibition against an overmatched squad from a nearby Division II school, North Carolina Central, notching a 97–60 victory. Raymond Felton turns in a 12-assist, 11-point performance, but Noel can only watch from the sidelines as Central—which features just one regular player over 6-foot-8 and has nowhere near the inside talent of any team in the ACC—out-rebounds the Tar Heels 42–36 and grabs a disturbing 22 offensive rebounds. Carolina will start the season with walk-on Justin Bohlander and sophomore Byron Sanders behind 6-foot-9 Sean May in the post.

The national media are not impressed by the apparent lack of depth and by Williams's constant reminders that the Tar Heels lost thirty-six games over the past two seasons. When the preseason Associated Press top-25 poll is released the following day, Carolina is picked ninth in the country despite finishing the previous season completely out of the rankings and returning with essentially the exact same roster. After North Carolina State posts an exhibition victory over a team of traveling all-stars in early November, junior star Julius Hodge expresses some doubts about his team's archrival.

"Who has Carolina got new coming into their team?" Hodge asks reporters. "Basically, we've both got the same teams [as last year]. And they're ranked in the top ten? And what are we, twenty-four?"

A writer informs Hodge that the Heels have a new coach. The confident New York native has just one response: "Can he play?"

Despite the skepticism in Raleigh, the expectations of the Tar Heel fans mirror those of the poll voters. When extra tickets to the regular season opener against Old Dominion are put on sale three weeks before the game, they sell out in less than a day. All 21,750 tickets were snapped up nearly a month before tip-off.

Both for the media and for the fans, there is one key difference from last year: Roy Williams is back in Chapel Hill. And as the first blast of cold weather pushes the temperatures at Chapel Hill into the 50s, he is starting to feel at home.

Again.

The first essential fact about Roy Williams is this: he's not kidding about the putter.

When the North Carolina head basketball coach speaks in public, he's fond of noting that one of the only things that's been with him longer than his wife, Wanda, is his golf putter. It sounds like a neat throwaway line, the kind a coach comes up with at dinner and then uses at booster club meetings for the rest of his career. It's not expected to be true, not in the year 2003, when any number of companies would love to fill Williams's golf bag with the newest, shiniest, most technologically advanced equipment. All complimentary, of course.

But Williams, who is an obscenely good putter, especially for someone who doesn't play golf during the basketball season, uses a putter that he estimates is fifty years old—a heavy, offset-blade model made by a company that doesn't exist anymore. He's been using it for thirty-four years. The average golfer misses one putt and starts shopping for new equipment. When Roy Williams misses a putt, he puts his putter back in the bag, confident that it will come through the next time.

"That putter is ugly as homemade sin," says Cody Plott, one of his close friends and a frequent golfing companion. "It's not just old. It's rusty, it's got that old blade. But he can flat putt the ball."

He hasn't changed wives, unlike many of his friends in the coaching business. He hasn't changed putters. Ask people around Chapel Hill, and they'll say he hasn't changed much, period, since he left town fifteen years ago to accept the head coaching job at Kansas.

Sometimes it seems that even casual basketball fans know the Coca-Cola story. By the fall of 2003, it's become a part of Roy Williams's essential biography, an easy capstone to any profile written about him. It belongs right up there with other essential Tar Heel folklore, like Michael Jordan being cut from his high school basketball team, or Dean Smith being hanged in effigy.

Roy Williams's family had little money when he was born in Marion, North Carolina, on August 1, 1950 (an occasion mistakenly listed in the index of the McDowell County Register of Deeds as the birth of "Roby Williams"). Sports were a major part of his childhood, and like most kids of his era, he and his buddies rotated from football to basketball to baseball depending on the season. Since home was North Carolina, though, basketball was king. Everett Case was building a powerhouse program at North Carolina State University; Frank McGuire, who had arrived at UNC in 1952, was challenging Case both on and off the court for supremacy over the Atlantic Coast Conference, which was formed prior to the 1953–54 season. When McGuire took the Tar Heels to the 1957 national championship, the final game against Wilt Chamberlain's Kansas team was televised in North Carolina and drew a breathless audience, many of whom flocked to Raleigh-Durham Airport to meet the Heels upon their triumphant return.

In the same way that football ruled Texas, Florida, and western Pennsylvania, basketball was ingraining itself in the fabric of North

Carolina. When Roy was a child, the Williams family lived less than a mile from Biltmore Elementary School. If snow fell, as it was prone to do in the mountains, he and best friend Walt Stroup would walk to the outdoor courts at Biltmore and shovel the snow off the asphalt court. Their palace cleared and their breath visible in the frosty morning, they'd start out playing in jackets, sweaters, long-sleeve shirts, and hats. Slowly, as the game grew more intense and the score increased, layers of clothes would begin to come off, until anyone observing who was unaware of the climate might have thought it was a spring day.

When the weather was better and enough players gathered for a full five-a-side battle, the postgame routine was simple: a stop at a local service station to indulge in a Coca-Cola. There were days when Roy Williams did not have the dime to spare on a soft drink, and this was the genesis of the Coca-Cola story. Later, after he had become the head basketball coach at the University of Kansas, he kept a refrigerator in his garage. His most important visitors, like his mother Lallage and his high school basketball coach Buddy Baldwin, were shown the contents of the appliance: endless rows of Coca-Cola's, stacked from front to back on each shelf.

The way the story is sometimes told by well-meaning individuals, it makes it sound as though Roy Williams led a deprived childhood—it conjures images of a youthful Roy wearing shoes made of cardboard, sitting on his front porch, staring wistfully into the mountains, thinking that if only he could drink a Coca-Cola, he might be a happy boy. It sounds like the opening scene to a movie, *The Roy Williams Story*.

Except that it didn't happen that way. Within his circle of friends in Asheville, where his family moved when he was eight, no one exactly had Coca-Cola on tap.

"There were times that all of us went over to that service station and drank water," says Stroup. "The first time I read that Coca-Cola story in an article and the writer made it sound so bad, I thought, 'What the hell are they talking about?'"

"After paying the electricity bill and rent and water and food, there was not a lot left over," Williams says. "But as far as I was concerned it was a great place to live, and I appreciated what we did have."

Williams adored his mother, who quit school after tenth grade to work in a cotton mill and then spent more than twenty years working in the Vanderbilt Shirt Factory. She was, by book learning standards, uneducated, the kind of woman often looked down upon and underestimated by people in other parts of the country. But Southern women of that generation and background understood that a diploma had very little to do with intelligence. It wasn't unusual for her to clock a sixty-hour workweek to make sure her family had enough money to pay for rent and food. It was just enough, usually, to pay for the essentials. There was no family car; there were no vacations. Extras were something to be worked for. When Roy wanted to attend a basketball camp at Western Carolina University that cost $25 for a week's instruction, families in the neighborhood chipped in to pay for it, and he spent the summer doing odd jobs and working the concession stand at Little League games to pay them back. When Roy was a teenager, his mother would come home from work at the shirt factory and begin her second job ironing clothes—ten cents for a shirt, twenty cents for a pair of pants.

"My mom was my hero," Williams says. "I idolized her and how much she cared about her family. I don't think she knew it was the Golden Rule, but she always talked about treating people the way you'd want to be treated. She just thought it was the right thing to do."

Missing from most accounts of his childhood is Williams's father, Babe Williams. He was, at best, an absent father, and he is the one topic about which Roy Williams—normally bluntly honest on every subject—grows reticent. The effect of that absence can be seen in the way Williams conducts himself today, especially toward his own children. Family dinners, which were rare when Roy was a child, were required in the Williams household. The life of a modern Division I basketball coach is frenzied, even during the offseason, but Williams's son Scott remembers a father who made a pointed effort to keep his family together.

"A lot of people ask me, 'What was it like never getting to see your dad?' " says Scott. "But he went out of his way to see us. He was actually a bigger pain in the tail than a normal dad, because whenever he was in town we had to have dinner together at a specific time. My mom fixed dinner, and we sat down at the table. That was our family time. And every summer we'd take off to the beach. The quantity may not have been there, but he really stressed the quality of our time."

During the 1984–85 season, when Williams was an assistant coach at UNC, the Tar Heels were in Japan for a pair of games dubbed the Suntory Bowl. Carolina waxed Wichita State in the opener, 80–69, and then defeated Arizona State in Tokyo two days later. The team was scheduled to travel as a group from Japan to Hawaii, where they would participate in the Hawaii Pacific Invitational beginning on December 29. But instead of missing Christmas with his two young children, Williams spoke individually to the players and told them how important the holidays were to his family. The assistant coach asked if it would be acceptable if he flew home and then met the team in Hawaii. Given the seal of approval from his players and fellow coaches, Williams jetted halfway across the globe—flying from Tokyo to Seattle, Seattle to Chicago, Chicago to Charlotte, and Charlotte to Asheville—to open presents with his family. After spending Christmas Eve and Christmas Day with his wife and children, he flew back across the country and arrived in Hawaii in time for practice on December 26.

While at Kansas, he was perhaps the only head coach in the country who doubled as a short-order chef. When Scott and Kimberly were in high school, every day that Roy Williams was home, he rose early enough to fix them breakfast. Sometimes it was as simple as toast and cereal, but he made the effort. He and Wanda raised a family that is almost absurdly tight-knit—the kind people don't think exists anymore. On Easter 2004, the most highly paid member of Carolina's athletic department could be found scurrying around his house hiding Easter eggs, the centerpiece of Easter Sunday activities that included dinner with Wanda, Scott, Kimberly, and some of his children's close friends, followed by an Easter egg hunt for the nine 23- to 28-year-olds in attendance.

"First of all, Wanda did a great job with our kids," the head coach says. "I always knew the quantity of my time with them might not be there, so I tried to make our time together of a higher quality. To this day, my son and daughter have never seen me come home from work and lay on the couch and fall asleep. When I came home, if they were up, I was up. It made no difference how tired I was."

He carries that family-first philosophy over into his dealings with his assistant coaches. Over the 2003 Christmas break, the Tar Heels have three days off from practice before Christmas Day. The staff wants to watch Marvin Williams, a talent every recruiting analyst ranks in the top five in the class of 2004 who has already signed with the Heels, and another prospect play during the break. The initial schedule calls for assistant coach Joe Holladay to be on the road before Christmas— NCAA rules limit teams to two coaches on the road at any given time. But Holladay's son Mathew is deployed in Iraq and his daughter Heather is visiting Chapel Hill for the last time before leaving for London for two years. When Williams learns of Heather's visit, he rearranges the recruiting schedule. "If you go recruiting, you're fired," he tells Holladay, and then takes one of the recruiting assignments himself, going to see Marvin Williams play in a holiday tournament in Florida.

Roy Williams does not drink alcohol, a choice almost certainly related to the damaging effects it had on his childhood home. Babe Williams was an alcoholic and his condition had miserable ramifications for his wife and children. Money had a way of disappearing into drink, and there were times when the father's condition drove his son out of the house. Some neighbors marveled at the dedication Roy Williams had—at his willingness to shovel snow off a basketball court just to shoot a few hoops. But the alternatives were not always pleasant, and the choice to get out of the house for a few hours was deliberate.

"Things at home were fairly tough at times," Williams says. It's as close as he will come to admitting the difficulties of his childhood. "The playground or the basketball court was one place I could go and lose myself."

His relationship with his father remained strained and full of contradictions. Babe mounted a Kansas Jayhawks license tag on his pickup truck during his son's tenure in Lawrence, but never made the trip to Allen Fieldhouse to see him coach. Roy occasionally asked his father if he wanted a ticket to see the Jayhawks play, but the offer was consistently declined. Later, Babe Williams would say that the lack of visits had nothing to do with his son, but rather with airplanes. Many years before he took a turbulent flight from New York City to Asheville, and upon touching down he declared that he would never fly again. And when a stubborn mountain man makes a declaration like that, it's likely to hold up, even if it means missing his son fulfill his lifelong dream. Once his son was hired by Carolina, Babe Williams walked out to his truck and changed the license tag from Kansas to North Carolina—which was not easy to do, given his back problems. Six months after moving back to Chapel Hill, though, Williams has not yet made the five-hour drive to Asheville to see his father. "He's been so busy," his father says just before Roy's first season at Carolina begins. "He's been gone about all the time whenever I call. I've probably talked to his wife more than I've talked to him."

When his father dies on May 16, 2004, the Carolina head coach keeps it quiet, not wanting to make a complex situation even more awkward. The Associated Press doesn't pick up on the story until nearly a week later.

His father missed much of the childhood that propelled Roy toward a future in coaching. He played the cerebral positions in all sports, lining up at point guard in basketball and playing the middle infield and occasionally pitching on his baseball team. He quickly realized that his future was not on the diamond. When his Babe Ruth team called Walter Stroup into service as a catcher, he informed the coaches that the only player he would catch was Roy Williams. Not because he was the team's best pitcher, but because Stroup was bat-shy and the only player who threw soft enough to allow him to see the ball was his buddy, Williams. On the basketball court, he had more success. He was never a superstar, but he was the kind of heady player coaches love. He spent two years with the junior varsity at T. C. Roberson High, playing a major role on the team despite standing just 5-foot-6 as a freshman. He was just as likely to dive on the floor for a loose ball as he was to sink a long jumper, never one to make a behind-the-back pass when a simple bounce pass would work just as well.

Opposing guards got the same treatment Stroup had received in the duo's endless games on the Biltmore School asphalt courts. "Roy was a good player, very tenacious," he says. "Whatever it took to win, within the rules, was what he tried to do. I'm about four inches taller than he is, and he'd do anything and everything to try and stop me. I'd come away with my arms just as red as could be."

Williams's role was as a passer and a leader. He could score when necessary—he racked up thirty-five points against Owen High as a senior, a school record that stood for seventeen years—but he preferred to get his teammates involved. He was already developing the mind for the game that would later serve him well as a coach and the self-deprecating sense of humor that would remind everyone that he wasn't impressed with his status. During a Roberson game against a crosstown rival, Williams took a handful of shots in the first half that uncharacteristically all fell short. As he warmed up for the second half, his jumpers were again clanging the front of the rim. Stroup, a teammate on that squad, saw an opportunity to needle his friend as only a buddy can.

"You're a little short tonight, aren't you?" he asked.

Never missing a beat, Williams responded, "Yep. About five-foot-eight."

His height would eventually end his playing career. Williams chose to attend North Carolina, surprising some of his high school teachers who expected him to go to Georgia Tech. Roy was a bright student who was a nominee for the Morehead Scholarship, the most prestigious academic award given by UNC. Many Roberson teachers expected him to put his mind to use as an engineer, doctor, or lawyer.

NCAA regulations prohibited freshmen from playing in varsity competition during the 1968–69 season. The Tar Heels were wrapping up a streak of three consecutive Final Four appearances, a level of success that had bolstered their recruiting under head coach Dean Smith, who had taken over the program from McGuire in 1961 as an unknown assistant. The new recruits had to spend their first year on the freshman team, where they dominated most of the playing time. The rest of the roster was filled out with players like Williams, athletes not quite good enough to play on the major college level but willing to spend endless hours practicing just for the chance to sit on the bench. That season marked the end of Williams's playing career.

He did not move up to varsity the next season but stayed involved with the program, occasionally charting statistics. Smith kept myriad complicated stats that went well beyond points, rebounds, and assists; when friends from Asheville came to visit Roy, they would marvel at how he would have the complete statistics in Smith's hands five minutes after the end of practice.

When Williams arrived in Chapel Hill thirty-five years later to be introduced as Carolina's new head basketball coach, he was flown in by private plane and met at the airport by a fleet of well-wishers. But as a college freshman he hadn't owned a car, and when he wanted to visit his mother, he hitchhiked from Chapel Hill to Asheville and then back to Chapel Hill again, a journey he made five times during his first year in school. As a sophomore, he lived in the basement of a church and cleaned the sanctuary for part of his rent. The fridge was not yet stocked with Coca-Colas.

He finished his college degree in four years and went on to earn a master's degree in 1973. As a graduate student, he was a regular in the Carmichael Auditorium rafters, where he frequently shared space with a Tar Heel football graduate assistant named Al Groh, who would go on to coach in the NFL and at the University of Virginia. Both men were fascinated with the structure of a Carolina basketball practice, with the tight organization and attention to detail. No action, not even a missed layup, went unnoticed by the coaching staff, and everything had consequences.

Watching a few practices, however, didn't amount to a terrific coaching background, so when Williams was hired as Owen High School's new basketball coach in 1973, it was greeted with significant skepticism. He had never won a game on any level, and some Owen boosters believed that Principal Charles Lytle had made a gross error in bypassing more qualified candidates in favor of a neophyte who, to make matters worse, had played at a rival school. But Williams quickly won over his players by introducing a fast-paced, full-court style of play, and eventually their enthusiasm for the new coach spread to the fans.

The Owen program was run just like a college team—and more specifically, like North Carolina's team. Practices were planned to the minute and frequently included drills that forced the players to practice taking charges. Turnovers were a plague punished by one suicide—a dreaded full-court sprint—at the next day's practice for each turnover committed. Centers had thirty seconds to complete the suicide; everyone else had twenty-eight. If one player fell short, everyone had to run again.

A frequent Williams ploy—something he still does today—was to allow a player to shoot a free throw to determine whether the conditioning drills were finished. If the free throw was made, the running stopped. If it was missed, the running continued. Occasionally, he would offer to shoot the free throw, but with the situation reversed: if he made it, the running continued. After suffering through a couple of early-season swishes, the Owen squad quickly learned to decline his offer to shoot.

The players found their coach to be intense but caring. Halftime talks could have an edge to them, but never with a malicious tone. Snow is common in the mountains of North Carolina, and the team sometimes practiced when the roads were covered in powdery fluff. Skip Anderson, an end-of-the-bench reserve, usually had trouble making those practices; his father had passed away years earlier and his mother was legally blind. Without fail, Williams would call him and show up in his blue Ford Mustang to drive Anderson and any other players who needed a ride to practice. As head coach, Williams inherited a team with a problem he was very familiar with: the players did not have enough money to attend basketball camp in the summer. Their coach promptly organized a bottle and can collection drive that spanned the county on Saturday mornings to locate bottles the team could turn in for camp funds. When they finally collected enough money to pay the camp fee at Gardner-Webb University, Roy Williams of Owen High School was named "Outstanding Coach of Camp."

During the summers, Williams worked at the University of North Carolina basketball camp, a crucial networking opportunity for coaches hoping to climb the ladder of their profession. In the coaching profession, countless job openings have been filled this way. A coach becomes impressed with another coach's work ethic or mind for the game, and when that first coach eventually becomes a head coach, he remembers that scrappy coach he met at camp several summers ago.

The more senior coaches at Carolina's camp—coaches who came back year after year and were deemed reliable—were usually put in charge of a gym. Because of the enormous attendance, the Tar Heel hoops camp stretched out over several gyms, meaning that each coach in charge of a gym was like a mini-camp director. Within a year, the

Carolina coaching staff had taken notice of Roy Williams and assigned him a gym. "He was fantastic at our camp," longtime Tar Heel Bill Guthridge says. "Usually coaches would work several years before they got a gym, but we put him in charge right away and he was so reliable. Parents were thrilled and the players were thrilled."

And in the way coaching usually works, when the NCAA allowed Division I programs to add a third assistant coach before the 1978–79 season, Guthridge and Smith's first thoughts were of that former freshman team player who was so effective at their summer camp. Williams joined the staff that fall, becoming the fourth member of a coaching staff that eventually would be acknowledged as one of the best of all time. Smith, of course, became college basketball's all-time winningest coach. Guthridge won the National Coach of the Year award after taking over from Smith in 1997 and guiding the Tar Heels to the Final Four, and second assistant Eddie Fogler also earned national coaching recognition after taking the head coaching job at Wichita State in 1986 and guiding the unheralded Shockers into the top twenty in the country.

Although taking the job was a no-brainer in the basketball world, there was at least a slight hesitation in the Williams household. His wife Wanda had a good job teaching English at the local high school, and the couple had an infant son, Scott. NCAA rules limited the third assistant's salary to the equivalent of a full scholarship, which meant he'd be making less than $3,000 a year. Accepting the job at Carolina meant taking a pay cut and doing less than glamorous work. Since the program had worked just fine for several years with two assistants, a large part of the job of the third assistant coach would be administrative.

And, as Williams soon found out, it also meant putting endless miles on his car. Carolina had statewide appeal, and Dean Smith taped the standard coach's television show—a smattering of game highlights and player features—each week that aired on a network of stations each Sunday. This was 1978, well before satellite transmission, before even ESPN, or reliable overnight delivery. To make extra money, Williams volunteered to drive the tapes of Smith's show across the state and hand-deliver them to the stations that aired the show. Every Sunday, he'd rise before the sun, make the hour-plus drive to WFMY in Greensboro, continue nearly three more hours to Asheville, drop off another tape, have lunch with his mother, and make it back to Chapel Hill in time to run the junior varsity practice in the evening. For making the deliveries, a round-trip of approximately 500 miles and eight hours, he was paid an extra $113 per week.

Another income supplement was through the sale of team calendars. Being associated with the Tar Heels was good for business, so companies across the state often liked to have on hand a supply of the squad's annual team calendars, which featured a photo of each player on the team and a listing of that year's basketball schedule. Televised games weren't a regular occurrence in 1980, and in some parts of the state, the team calendar was where some fans first saw the new players. Williams started selling the calendars in lots of 125 for $100. In his first year, he sold 10,500 of them, driving 9,000 miles in nine weeks to make his sales, from which his portion of the proceeds was $2,400. As with coaching a basketball team, however, he quickly realized that he could streamline the operation. His winning personality and his ability to connect with the calendar buyers soon translated into increased sales. Eight years later, when the price of the calendars had increased to $160 per 100 units, he sold 55,000 of them in just four weeks, driving "only" 4,000 miles. Williams had developed a reliable network of buyers; on one especially memorable day, he left Chapel Hill at 5 A.M., drove to Rutherfordton, about 200 miles away, to meet a customer, made the hour drive to Morganton for another meeting, kept a tee time in Hickory with three customers, stopped in Gastonia, and arrived back in Chapel Hill at 11 P.M. having sold 9,000 calendars in one day.

On the basketball court, Williams was forming an equally formidable philosophy. Carolina was one of the few squads still fielding a junior varsity team, a quaint throwback to the days when freshmen weren't eligible, which Dean Smith believed kept the basketball program close to the student body. Open tryouts for the team were held across the university. After toiling for two years on the squad—which some students didn't even realize existed—players would occasionally get a chance to move up to the varsity as walk-ons, athletes who were not on scholarship but fully participated in all activities of the basketball team. Coaching the junior varsity usually fell to the most junior assistant, and Williams accepted the role with enthusiasm. He prepared the team relentlessly, frequently playing tight games against prep school teams with rosters of players who would go on to earn Division I scholarships. The junior varsity also often took part in varsity practices, where they would serve as defenders while the Tar Heels installed a new offense or worked on breaking a unique defense. Even in practice, Williams's work with the JVs caught the eye of Dean Smith. "The first time I thought, 'Wow, this guy is special,' was with his work with the JV team," Smith said. "We'd have the junior varsity come and play defense against us, and each time they were so well taught."

When Roy Williams set out to prepare the Tar Heel varsity team to meet Old Dominion in 2003, he did almost exactly the same things that he did preparing the Carolina junior varsity to beat Fork Union Military Academy in 1984.

In the days approaching the season opener on November 22, the Monarchs are receiving roughly the same amount of attention as the Washington Generals, the squad that serves as the Harlem Globetrotters' regular punching bag. When Williams meets the media—wearing shorts, becoming the first Tar Heel head coach in anyone's memory to attend a scheduled press conference with exposed knees—two days before the game, twenty-nine of thirty minutes have passed without a single question about the opponent, a team that was within 7 points of the Tar Heels with 2 minutes to play in last season's game, although no one seems to remember this. All the attention is on Williams: on how he will feel when he walks out of the Smith Center tunnel for the first time, on what it will be like to assume the seat that once belonged to Dean Smith. Finally, the last questioner of the day asks Williams what he knows about Old Dominion.

"It's not the kind of game you go into trying to decide where to go eat after the game," Williams says. "We realize we have to go out there and play. When somebody has four of their top six guys back and played us very well last year, we have to understand that we have to respect everyone and fear no one."

The comment echoes a persistent preseason theme from the head coach. His team is immensely talented. Point guard Raymond Felton and shooting guard Rashad McCants were preseason candidates for the

Wooden Award, given to the best college player in the country. Post player Sean May was outstanding in limited action during the 2002–03 season, averaging 11.4 points and 8.1 rebounds over ten games before suffering a broken foot in December that kept him out of all but one of Carolina's remaining games. After a sophomore season during which he improved his scoring and rebounding markedly, junior Jawad Williams has added almost twenty pounds to his frame and looks to be capable of providing the Tar Heels with some added bulk in the paint, where they are desperate for someone to supplement May. Fellow juniors Melvin Scott and Jackie Manuel have responded well to the new coach and appear to fit into their roles—Scott as a starter counted on to supply outside shooting and ballhandling, Manuel as a sixth man usually responsible for guarding the other team's best backcourt player. The lack of depth, especially without Noel, is troubling, but the team is undeniably talented.

Sometimes, Roy Williams thinks, they can be too impressed with their physical talents. After all, the Tar Heels won just twenty-seven games over the past two seasons while losing thirty-six. It is not a point lost on the new head coach, who went 30–8 last year at Kansas and who finds the idea of losing thirty-six games in two years deplorable. Over the past four seasons, he lost just twenty-nine.

Finally, during practice two days before the ODU game, his players push him too far. During a simple drill late in the session, Williams instructs the team managers to give the Blue team, the substitutes, an 86–80 lead over the White team, the starters, on the Smith Center scoreboard. Three minutes are placed on the clock, and the teams play a live game situation. The challenge is simple: the starters have to take the lead before the clock goes to zero. "Take your time," the head coach tells them. "Get it back."

But with the White team on defense, there is a miscommunication as the Blues work the ball around the defense. McCants and Felton disagree on who is responsible for guarding the ball handler, with each believing the other has the duty.

Williams blows his whistle.

"I don't like the arguing," he says, intensity slowly rising. "Just say, 'I've got the ball.' Gosh dang it, we have to play in forty-eight hours!"

It is then that McCants makes a critical mistake—he cuts his eyes away from his head coach and looks at the floor.

"Look at me when I'm talking to you!" Williams booms. "If we're gonna win, we're gonna do it together. We've got a game in forty-eight hours. I'm sick of you arguin' like frickin' third-graders. Your way got your ass kicked. Every single time. Thirty-six frickin' losses. Do it my way. If you don't like it, get your ass out because I'm gonna frickin' win, with you or without you."

Although the public perceives Roy Williams as a golden-mouthed country boy who never curses, he knows how to place a few well-timed expletives. And though he is much more likely to use "frickin'" than the other f-word favored by most coaches, he is, as he admits in a less intense moment earlier in the preseason, "better at cursing than most people think."

He makes his point, as the White team does recover the lead in less than 3 minutes. More important, however, are the reactions of his players to the instruction. As a freshman, Rashad McCants almost certainly would have sulked for the remainder of practice. Instead, as the team runs sprints at the end of practice, when Williams looks for a volunteer to run the length of the court and back two times in thirty-three seconds, McCants volunteers. He easily accomplishes the task, winning his teammates a reprieve from any more running that day.

That McCants would be temperamental is not entirely surprising. Probably the most physically talented player on Carolina's roster, the Asheville native endured a roller-coaster freshman season both on and off the court. He began his freshman campaign as an outwardly emotional superstar. In the season opener against Penn State, he scored a game-high 28 points, made 11 of 14 field goals, and grabbed 7 rebounds. In that game, he waved his arms to the crowd to get them more involved, flashed a megawatt smile after making baskets, and crossed his arms in the "X" gesture, which he told his teammates stood for "total domination." He scored 18 points against Rutgers in Carolina's next outing, all while wearing a harness on his left shoulder, as he would through the first twelve games, to compensate for an injury he had suffered in an October practice. With 10 seconds remaining against the Scarlet Knights and the Heels nursing a 2-point lead, McCants had a chance to seal the game with a pair of free throws. The rookie came through, swishing both of them.

"There was no doubt I was going to sink them," McCants said after the game. "That's all I used to practice growing up. It wasn't a last-second shot, it was clutch free throws. I always wanted to come through with clutch free throws at the end of the game."

It was to be one of the last times during his freshman year that his confidence was unshaken. Slowly, seemingly insignificant little things began to chip away at his confident veneer. Late in Carolina's next outing, a win at Old Dominion, head coach Matt Doherty noticed that McCants was making a phantom kiss gesture before each of his attempted free throws. Doherty turned to assistant coach Doug Wojcik on the Tar Heel bench and instructed him to write down that the coaches should order McCants to stop performing the ritual. It was the first clash between player and coach in what turned out to be a season full of them. McCants considered himself a player who thrived on emotion, a swashbuckling dueler who loved to feed off the crowd. When the Tar Heels journeyed to Cameron Indoor Stadium two months later to face Duke and their vaunted Cameron Crazies crowd, McCants went through his pregame stretching routine waving his arms and encouraging the full-throated fans to get louder. Doherty, meanwhile, wanted his team to eliminate the gestures, the interplay between themselves and the crowd. "When somebody tries to change the way you've been playing all your life, it's a hard adjustment," McCants said.

The coach himself sometimes had trouble meeting that standard. Upon entering the court for his first visit to Cameron as Carolina's head coach, Doherty was heckled by a courtside fan who informed the rookie coach that he had been the Heels' third choice. Doherty stopped, turned around, and flashed four fingers, signifying that he was actually the fourth choice, not the third.

McCants earned MVP honors during the Preseason NIT, as he spearheaded Carolina's upsets of Kansas and Stanford; for his performance he was named National Player of the Week by ESPN and *The Sporting News*. He continued to score in double figures for most of the next two months, becoming the first Tar Heel player ever to score at least 10 points in his first twenty games, but trouble was bubbling beneath the surface. Accounts differ, but at least some say the breaking point came in a practice in which Doherty called the freshman a "pussy," a word that seems no worse than a handful of others regularly used by coaches to motivate players but which crossed an unspoken line of respect. The insult infuriated McCants and caused the already introverted player to retreat even further inside himself. He went through a miserable 5-of-18 shooting performance and even worse, a lackluster defensive showing at Georgia Tech on January 29. After Doherty rode him even harder at the next day's practice, the freshman cried during practice, out of eyesight of the head coach. He was removed from the starting lineup for the team's next game against Wake Forest. Humiliated, McCants played just 20 minutes and proceeded to make just five of his twenty-eight shots over the next three games, coming off the bench in all of them and nursing a painful injury that was caused at least in part by his benching. Relegated to the Blue team in practice, McCants was in the process of showing everyone why he deserved to be a starter the day before the game at Duke.

"I was playing as hard as I've ever played in my life," he said. "On the last play of practice, I went up for a reverse layup, made it, and when I came down my back went out."

Over the remainder of the season, McCants's defense—or lack thereof—and effort—or lack thereof—were regular topics of conversation among Carolina fans and, sometimes, the coaching staff. Doherty noted in press conferences that McCants needed to make some defensive improvements, an accurate observation but one that chafed the player. Their relationship got worse at midseason when a member of the coaching staff invited the player to meet with "a friend of the program." When McCants arrived at the meeting, he learned that the "friend" was actually a sports psychologist. It is not uncommon for college athletes, including Tar Heels, to consult with sports psychologists, and many players have benefited. But coaches usually present it as an option, and any meeting is arranged only with mutual consent. McCants took umbrage at the way the meeting was sprung on him. Although Doherty made efforts to repair their relationship later in the season, once even inviting McCants to his house for dinner, the two men never fully understood each other and their discord hurt team chemistry. The feud sapped McCants's trademark confidence to the point that friends watching him on television commented that he looked unhappy. Of course, it didn't take a psychic to read his displeasure—he occasionally sat on the bench with a towel draped over his head, and sometimes declined to offer the customary high fives when removed from a game.

It turned into a vicious cycle: the player failed to meet expectations, the coach punished him; the player responded with outward displeasure and subpar play, the coach punished him. Neither party grasped the intent of the other, and both suffered.

"A common mistake people make with Rashad is they think they understand him by his facial expressions or body language," says his former prep roommate and current UNC teammate Wes Miller. "But a lot of times what you think when you look at him from a distance is not even close to what's going on in his mind."

"I coached him for three years," says Cliff Knight, the Charlotte Royals head coach during McCants's tenure with the team. "I can see how he can be misinterpreted. The biggest thing you have to understand about his personality is that he wants to please everybody. He wants someone to be happy with everything he does. When he thinks he's not pleasing people, he's like most teenagers—he sulks. That's what teenagers do. I've had a whole team of them."

McCants's sulking was magnified by his instant distrust of virtually everyone he met. All UNC basketball players realize somewhere in their subconscious that every new person they meet could be trying to take advantage of them. They might want tickets, or an autograph to sell on eBay, or just to be able to say they know a famous basketball player. For most of the Tar Heels, their first inclination is to give strangers the benefit of the doubt. McCants is the opposite: he assumes he's being used and then makes others prove him wrong. He has close friendships, but most of them were formed long before he arrived in Chapel Hill. Buddies declare there is an engaging, outgoing personality underneath his tough veneer, but to outsiders McCants can seem gruff. It is a reputation he does not entirely dislike. He rarely makes eye contact with media members and sometimes sneers at questions he considers silly, leading them to write articles describing him as "moody" or "temperamental." He has been known to answer his cell phone while sitting in class, a brassy move most students would never attempt. His moodiness intensified during the 2002–03 season when the Tar Heels were only winning sporadically and, for the first time in his life, McCants was not always the best player on the floor.

It was a painful freshman season for McCants, who was accustomed to being the superstar of every team he had ever played on. When he was removed from the starting lineup, it was the first time since his freshman year of high school that he hadn't started. That he would be a basketball prodigy seemed almost predetermined. Just weeks after he was born on September 25, 1984, his father James wrote in his son's baby book, "The next Michael Jordan." It was a gesture with several layers of meaning. To some, James McCants was simply a proud parent, a physically imposing man who had passed on much of his genetic blessing to his son and was eager to watch him fulfill his potential. To others, however, it seemed that James occasionally pushed his son too hard, making Rashad feel that without the game of basketball his life had little importance. Some people saw pressure in the father's pride.

Father and son had an occasionally touchy relationship that centered on basketball. James would frequently take Rashad to the gym when he went to work out, and as he neared puberty, Rashad would pass the time by playing basketball at one end of the court with kids his age while James played on the other end with the men. By the time Rashad was twelve, James informed him that he was too good to play with kids, and from that point forward he would play in the men's game. The seminal moment came after McCants was left off the eighth-grade team at Asheville Middle School. The family had Rashad transferred to the Erwin Middle School district so that he could play basketball, but he missed the tryout date by one day. So as not to languish without any competition for a season, Rashad played rec league basketball, the equivalent of Barry Bonds moonlighting in a church softball league.

"I've still got film footage of that," his dad says with a smile. "He was flying over everybody. He took over the place. I told him right then, 'No more playing with kids for you.'"

And so before he could vote, buy a beer, or drive a car, Rashad McCants was no longer a kid. That designation was fitting, because he had never looked like a kid. Today he stands 6-foot-4, a chiseled 207 pounds, and he has had that frame for most of his adolescent life. While other players were going through a gawky phase, McCants was simply smooth. As a freshman at Erwin High School, he played all five positions. When head coach Van Allen designed the Erwin full-court press, he designated his star freshman as the last man back, a position usually occupied by the center. On paper, it looked a little silly. During games, it looked like genius.

"We'd let him roam the back of the press back there," Allen says. "The other team would think they had a layup, and he would send it back and then we'd be on the fast break. That was just incredible, because I'd never seen anyone who could do that. He had great timing."

His freshman season, McCants blocked a staggering 62 shots. He blocked over 100 during his two-year Erwin career. Still, he was struggling in an environment that didn't value basketball as much as he did. He was all basketball, all the time, and Erwin was all basketball for about two months out of the year. Offseason on-court workouts were discouraged, which for McCants was like oxygen deprivation. He was, first and foremost, a basketball player. A bright student who could occasionally remove the detached facade and become surprisingly engaging, he needed an environment that would recognize his growing hoops potential.

McCants played AAU basketball during the summer with the Charlotte Royals, a formidable traveling team that also produced former UNC standout Antawn Jamison. One of McCants's teammates on that squad was Wes Miller, who had just finished his first year at New Hampton Prep, a prep school little known outside basketball circles. Inside the basketball world, however, New Hampton was part of one of the best prep school basketball leagues in the country, a conference in which each team regularly included a handful of top Division I prospects. It was, Miller thought, the perfect atmosphere for McCants, and after taking a visit, McCants agreed. He enrolled before his junior year and quickly became the team's best player.

Now that he was the acknowledged superstar on a top-level prep team, the college recruiting process for McCants was wide open. He received interest from every top program in the country, and also generated attention from several Ivy League schools who thought he mixed athleticism and academics in the way they required. But all the phone calls, all the letters from suitors, were meaningless. McCants, who was ranked among the best ten players in the nation in his high school class, had made up his mind: he wanted to go to North Carolina.

"He never even took a visit," Knight said. "Not one visit. I've been through the system with a lot of kids and you just don't hear about kids doing that. How many kids, when they are given the chance to go on free trips and be recruited, are going to turn that down? But that's what he did, and he signed with Carolina before he ever took an official visit to Chapel Hill."

Doherty spent seven years as an assistant to Williams at Kansas, so McCants and the other players realize that the old coach and the new coach will have some things in common. But Williams's ability to critique a player while maintaining his respect is key, as is his résumé, which includes 418 victories at Kansas. So when Williams sets his sights on McCants in practice, the capricious sophomore does not react as if he's being singled out. He takes it as an opportunity to improve, and just a few minutes later, he is volunteering for extra sprints. It is a rededicated Rashad McCants who prepares for his team's season opener two days away against Old Dominion.

Roy Williams remains concerned about his new team's overconfidence. The Thought for the Day—a Dean Smith innovation in which some nugget of wisdom, basketball-related or not, is dispensed to the team before each practice—in the last practice before the Heels meet the Monarchs is, "Respect is not inherited. It must be earned every day." But if Williams wants to infuse some reality into his inexperienced team, his task only gets tougher after the game against Old Dominion. Almost everything goes as scripted for the Tar Heels in their debut under their new head coach. The head coach goes home after the team's pregame walk-through and takes his customary pregame nap, and then returns to the Smith Center, where Dean Smith and Bill Guthridge are among the sellout crowd of 21,750. Williams gets a standing ovation when he walks onto the Smith Center court twenty minutes before tip-off. Later he recalls thinking, "I never saw myself walking out of this tunnel as the head coach at North Carolina." His team goes through pregame drills, which are capped with a defensive drill that includes two choreographed dives onto the floor.

The drill gets a standing ovation.

Williams gets another standing ovation when he emerges onto the court just before tip-off, perfectly playing to the students by firing three T-shirts into the student section to the right of the Tar Heel bench. The shirts bear the slogan, CAROLINA BASKETBALL AND CHAPEL HILL: WORTH COMING HOME FOR. Once the game begins—almost an afterthought to the ceremonial appearance of the returning head coach—Williams's preseason emphasis on shot selection instantly pays off. The Tar Heels attempt just four first-half three-pointers and seven for the game, instead choosing to work the ball inside to Sean May for high-percentage shots. The Heels make almost 60 percent of their field goals and cruise into the locker room with a 40–23 advantage. The second half is more of the same, as even Rashad McCants flashes a new facet of his game. Sometimes criticized for hunting for his own shot rather than working the ball to his teammates, McCants hands out a career-high 8 assists. He also earns cheers from the crowd when he has the ball stolen on the offensive end but then races 70 feet to chase down the offending Old Dominion player and swat away his layup attempt.

Every player seems to understand his role. Raymond Felton choreographs Williams's up-tempo attack, May fills the paint, and walk-on Justin Bohlander provides 14 minutes off the bench for the depth-shy Tar Heels. Five Carolina players finish in double figures as the Heels overwhelm ODU in a 90–64 thrashing. The most noticeable improvement is by junior Jackie Manuel, who last season was a free-shooting offensive liability. Against the Monarchs, however, he takes just seven shots and makes six of them, contributing 12 points and a major energy boost off the bench. Manuel was Williams's major offseason reclamation project. A 27-percent shooter from three-point range as a sophomore, Manuel was given two choices by his coach: start making the shots or stop taking them. After a day of wondering whether he wanted to play at a place where he couldn't shoot, he chose the latter and immediately seemed to understand his place in Carolina's new system.

"I can't say enough about Jackie Manuel," Williams says. "I talked to him early on to see if he was happy here. I told him he couldn't shoot the ball very much. Not a lot of guys would have accepted that. But I told him yesterday that if he was better looking, I'd have kissed him."

As the final seconds tick off the clock, the students in the riser section behind the Carolina basket begin a muffled chant. The fans who earn riser tickets are frequently the heartiest Tar Heel basketball fans and are certainly the most visible, as they stand throughout the game, usually decked out entirely in Carolina blue. They would have been among the first students to line up for ticket distribution for the Old Dominion game one week earlier, when the crowd was greeted at 6 A.M. by Williams and his coaching staff motoring around the line in a golf cart handing out doughnuts. Late in the game, they begin a chant that causes the head coach to think he hears his name. He turns his head to the risers, trying to decipher the chant. Then it becomes clear:

"We love Roy," clap, clap, clap–clap–clap.

The Tar Heel head coach smiles and turns his head back to the game. Then, almost imperceptibly, he turns back to the students and gives them a quick smile and wave. For at least one night, Roy Williams is perfect as the Carolina head coach.

His perfection continues two days later when the Tar Heels travel to Charlotte to meet the Davidson Wildcats. Davidson, a tiny private school located just outside Charlotte, was formidable under Lefty Driesell in the 1960s, but has long since chosen to emphasize academics over athletics. In terms of raw physical talent, they do not belong on the same court as the Tar Heels—which made it all the more surprising when they came into the Smith Center two years ago and emerged with a stunning 58–54 victory. That win sparked unabashed giddiness on the Davidson campus, and some students arrive at the Coliseum two years later sporting T-shirts that memorialize their earlier victory. As part of the contractual agreement between the schools, the game is not being played in the Wildcats' potentially raucous on-campus Belk Arena, but a large portion of the student body still makes the short trip to Charlotte for the game, along with a large contingent of Carolina fans. The arena is packed with 16,356 fans—a record-breaking attendance for a Davidson home game.

One of those fans is Babe Williams, who is watching his son coach for only the second time in his life. "We haven't been as close as I would like and probably as he would like," the head coach says of his father. Babe's other game was the 2002 Final Four in Atlanta, when he watched the Jayhawks lose to Maryland. This time, he will see his son get a win.

Williams, as is becoming a ritual, gets a standing ovation when he comes onto the court. His team again jumps out to a halftime lead, this time boasting a 43–25 advantage at the break. The Tar Heels get 38 points off 27 Davidson turnovers and a career-high 28 points from Jawad Williams on their way to a 91–68 victory. But the game is not without incident. Davidson coach Bob McKillop's son, Matt, plays for the Wildcats, and like many coaches' sons, he plays with a mixture of limited athletic ability and hard-nosed desire. That intensity rankles Carolina's Sean May early in the game, when McKillop swats May during a dead ball. Late in the second half, the pair tangle again. McKillop commits a hard foul on Rashad McCants and quickly discovers all 6-foot-9 and 260 pounds of May in his face.

"I was just protecting one of my players," May said. "That was about the third hard foul they'd had. Those guys are my brothers out there and anybody who goes after my brother, I've got their back."

It is not an insignificant gesture, since May was one of the Tar Heel players most frustrated by McCants's moodiness last season. "Halfway through last season, I was done with him," May said of his fellow freshman. "On the court we could play, but after that I wanted to go my way and him to go his way." But the duo spent several weeks together during the summer of 2003, and after a long talk on a plane flight to California, where they were serving as counselors at Michael Jordan's basketball camp, May began to better understand McCants's perspective. So it is with renewed vigor that May comes to his defense in Charlotte, eager to stand up for his teammate after McKillop's perceived cheap shot.

Except May is able to stand up for McCants for only a fraction of a second before Roy Williams bounds off the Carolina bench and heads straight for May. At first glance, it appears that the head coach is also frustrated by the physical play. But then it becomes clear that the target of his advance is May, not McKillop.

"I was upset with our guys," Williams says after the game. "The ref called a hard foul and I didn't like the way our guys reacted. I perceived they were talking too much."

Chastened, Carolina's burly post star digs himself in further when he refers to Davidson as "dirty" in his postgame remarks to the media. Eager reporters naturally seize on the comment, which appears in the next day's game story in at least two newspapers. It does not look flattering in print—for the 260-pound May to call 170-pound McKillop "dirty" sounds like Goliath complaining about David. May regrets the comment almost as soon as the words leave his mouth, but by then the damage is done. He apologizes twice to Carolina sports information staffers, who deal with the media on a daily basis, and also mentions his regret to one of Carolina's academic counselors the next day.

In many ways, May is the most open of any of the Tar Heels. He is frank with the press, sometimes almost too much so. When he is frustrated on the court, it shows. When he is happy, it shows. Publicly, however, he maintains a consistently pleasant personality. In some ways, he is the polar opposite of McCants. No matter what happens, he always seems to have a smile, and he is always willing to talk to the press for five more minutes, even after a defeat.

Part of that personality is due to his background. His father, Scott May, won a national basketball championship at Indiana and played with Phil Ford on the gold medal–winning 1976 Olympic team. He played professionally both at home and abroad after his college career, enabling him to educate his son about the importance of savvy public relations.

Because Scott May had played for Indiana, the May family had a close relationship with the volatile Bob Knight. Of course, Knight usually had his own unique way of expressing his fondness for the family. Sean May vividly recalls standing in front of a summer basketball camp in Bloomington as an eighth-grader. Knight called him out in front of the camp to make a very important point.

"Kids, I want you to look at this guy," the legendary coach boomed. "His dad was an All-American, but this guy will never be anything. His dad worked hard in practice every day, but this kid doesn't love the game of basketball. His dad worked harder in one practice than he has worked in his whole life. That's why he'll never amount to anything in basketball."

The move was typical Knight, and almost a decade later, May still talks glowingly of the legendary coach known for his plainspoken critiques of players. But being Scott May's son, it is obvious, wasn't always easy in Bloomington, Indiana. Pedigree is important in this basketball-mad state, but it doesn't outweigh skill. That's why, as a kid, Sean was usually one of the last players picked for pickup games.

"When we went to play at the Y, I'd have to beg people to pick him for pickup," says Scott May Jr., Sean's brother, who began his college career at Indiana before transferring to the University of Southern Indiana. "He was really bad. He couldn't shoot, he couldn't do anything."

The younger May also struggled in football, where divisions were usually grouped by weight. Players over the weight limit were not allowed to carry the football, so Sean had to wear a strip of black tape on his helmet to signal that he was unable to carry the ball. In one of his last football games, he intercepted a pass and began rumbling down the field, only to be whistled down by the officials, who were unwilling to let the big boy carry the ball. His main talent as a youngster, it seemed, was with computers, something he still enjoys to this day. "I'm just a nerd," he admits.

He generally expressed indifference about working out with his father at the local YMCA. But around the time Sean entered high school, his father began to notice a change. Suddenly, Sean was tagging along. Suddenly, he seemed to want to play basketball.

That was all the interest his father needed to see to begin working more closely with him. He'd noticed that Sean lacked coordination, so he devised drills to help him improve his hands. The elder May held a basketball with Sean positioned about ten feet away, his back to his father. Suddenly, his father would call out "Sean!" and fire the ball at him. Sean's task was to turn around and catch the ball before it pelted him.

"I got a couple of bloody noses that way," May says. "Those were the worst. But those drills really helped me with my hands."

Scott May Sr. knew that his son was bigger than most boys his age and could score almost at will in the paint when playing within his age group. As a high schooler, Scott May had been in the same situation. His high school coach sat him down and said, "Scott, there are no six-five centers at the next level. You have to learn to play facing the basket, learn to pass and dribble."

It's a lesson he passed on to his son. During summer pickup games against lesser competitors, Sean May would ask his father how he could improve. The response? Work on your off-hand dribble, play facing the basket, learn to operate on the perimeter. The lesson was similar in back-yard one-on-one games against his brother. Scott May Jr. stands about 7 inches shorter than Sean, but he was too quick to allow Sean to post him up. The younger brother quickly learned that to score against Scott, who is eleven months older, he would have to develop a perimeter game.

As his skills began to come together, it was a foregone conclusion in Bloomington that he would attend Indiana. Being Scott May's son had its advantages—a police officer once let Scott May Jr. slide on a ticket when he recognized his famous name—and its disadvantages.

"A lot of people refer to your father, and sometimes you get tired of it," Sean says. "But it was great being Scott May's son, too."

Sean's desire to establish his own identity played a role in his recruitment, as did the fact that Knight was unceremoniously given the boot at Indiana. (He landed at Texas Tech, where the May family took a research trip before Sean made his college decision. The visit prompted wild conspiracy theories in Bloomington, since most IU fans were aware that Knight was not on good terms with his replacement, Mike Davis.) But the truth was that May grew up a college basketball connoisseur. He watched games from noon to night every Saturday with his father, and one team that always seemed to play in those games was North Carolina. Combine that knowledge of the program with his father's close friendship with legendary Carolina point guard Phil Ford, and it seemed like a good fit.

Despite his heritage, May is one of the few Tar Heels who understands much of the history behind the program. He is prone to bring up great comebacks of the past when the team makes a run, and when asked which Carolina basketball alumnus he'd most like to meet, he doesn't mention Michael Jordan or James Worthy or Vince Carter. Instead he picks Lennie Rosenbluth, the National Player of the Year in 1957, who led the Heels to a national championship.

While the rest of the UNC community heads home for the Thanksgiving holidays, the Tar Heel basketball team gathers at the home of their head coach for Thanksgiving dinner following an afternoon practice. The next day players and coaches board a charter plane for Cleveland, where they will face Cleveland State the following day.

The contest is a reward for junior Jawad Williams. Dean Smith made a practice of scheduling games near the hometowns of his players as a way for each player's family and friends to get to see him play in person. The tradition waned in importance as more and more games were televised, but Williams had carried it on at Kansas and wanted it to be a part of his Carolina tenure—with one adjustment. Smith usually tried to schedule the game during a player's senior year. But after a tough lesson with the Jayhawks, Williams likes the games to be played during the junior year or earlier. As Kansas coach, he scheduled a trip to Oakland to play Cal in a "home" game for star forward Drew Gooden. But Gooden bolted for the NBA the year before the game and left the Gooden-less Jayhawks to take a suddenly meaningless trip to California. With the Gooden incident still fresh, Jawad Williams's homecoming is scheduled for his junior year—a wise decision, since the lanky forward has been entertaining NBA thoughts.

After their arrival at the airport, the team boards the bus that will take them to their Cleveland hotel. Snow and sleet are falling sideways. Jawad Williams, who plays the role of sage to many of his younger teammates, duly receives plenty of good-natured grief about forcing the team to play in snowy Cleveland over Thanksgiving. "'Wad," one player says as the bus rolls toward the hotel, "this better be worth it." It's worth it for Williams, who has never adapted to the North Carolina interpretation of barbeque. To a Tar Heel native, barbeque is pork. To Williams, however, barbeque means ribs, and he enlists close friend Marvin Rashad to bring him a plate of ribs from his favorite restaurant, Open Pit, while the team is in town.

With 3 minutes left in Saturday's game, the ribs are looking like the best part of the trip. Supposedly overmatched Cleveland State has a 73–72 lead in front of 11,534 fans who came inside to try and escape the biting windchill. Carolina built an early lead but then hit a lull when Raymond Felton collided with Jackie Manuel late in the first half. Felton eventually returned to the game, but Manuel suffered a twisted knee and remains on the bench for the rest of the afternoon. The depleted roster is exacerbated by foul trouble, forcing Roy Williams to use some unexpected combinations. At one point in the opening half, the Heels have almost half the starting lineup of the 2003 Winston-Salem Reynolds High School squad on the floor, as Felton, junior Melvin Scott, Jawad Williams, and freshmen Reyshawn Terry and Justin Bohlander see action. Shortly after the Manuel-Felton collision, Carolina's lack of depth becomes obvious, as the Heels have to insert little-used walk-on Damien Price, who is primarily a practice player, into the action. The roster becomes even thinner when Williams benches Rashad McCants—who had two fouls and was trying to avoid a third—for playing matador defense and allowing Cleveland State's Victor Morris clear passage to the basket, a play about which the head coach will later say, "Every player I've ever coached would have taken the charge."

The juggled lineups allow Cleveland State to ease back into the game and take a 4-point halftime lead. The game remains close throughout the second half and becomes a nip-and-tuck affair in the final stages. After a missed CSU free throw, Raymond Felton fails to box out his man, and Vikings guard Percell Coles guns in a three-pointer to give his team a 4-point advantage with less than 3 minutes to play.

Down 4, 3 minutes to play. It is almost exactly the same situation Carolina practiced just a few days earlier, and the Tar Heels look calm in the face of nearly 12,000 screaming fans, most of whom expected to see a blowout. On UNC's next possession, Jawad Williams—whose main pregame task was securing tickets for forty-two family members and nine friends—muscles inside for a basket, prompting a Roy Williams timeout.

"This is the time when you guys become a good team," he tells his squad in the huddle. "If you want to be a good team, this is where you prove it. You have to stay together and figure this thing out."

They do. Cleveland State fails to convert on its next possession, and after a Viking foul Rashad McCants makes his first free throw before clanking the second. But Williams reaches up and tips the miss back toward midcourt, where it is recovered by Raymond Felton. As the Heels set up their offense, CSU's Omari Westley chooses to play in front of Williams to try and keep him from getting the ball in the post. Williams would not have been treated to this kind of respect in previous years, and he takes advantage of it. When Westley loses track of Williams, he slips unnoticed outside the three-point line in front of the Tar Heel bench, and when the ball is swung to him, the hometown Heel drills a three-pointer to give Carolina the lead at 78–76, an advantage they would not relinquish on the way to an 82–76 victory. Over the last 3 minutes of the game, the Heels reel off 10 straight points.

"It was just like practice," Jawad Williams says after the game. "That makes us more calm. When we got down we started rushing our shots, which is always bad, but then we realized we had to take our time and take good shots."

The game is a victory but the bus ride back to the airport is considerably more solemn than the arrival the previous day. Near silence envelops the team and their head coach, who makes it obvious that he considers the day's effort unacceptable. Even worse, it appears as though his biggest fear—that these Tar Heels are a talented group of individuals incapable of playing as a team—has reared its head.

"For a while there tonight we had five guys on the floor thinking they were still in high school and that they were God's gift to the game because they were McDonald's All-Americans," he says after the game. "We've got to know that the name on the front of the jersey, the North Carolina, is more important than the name on the back."

The coach is especially displeased with the way the Heels failed to share the ball, including three straight possessions on which McCants, Felton, and Terry tried to score on their own, resulting in two poor shots and a turnover. At Sunday's practice, Williams does something he has done only three times previously in his coaching career: he makes his team watch the entire game tape. Usually the coaches only show extracts of the footage to illustrate key points they want to emphasize, both positive and negative. This time, because of the overall lack of intensity shown against the Vikings, there is a full screening. The Tar Heels watch the complete first half and then take to the Smith Center court. One of the day's drills is meant to emphasize the importance of sharing the basketball and working for good, even great, shots instead of jacking up the basketball at the first opportunity. Williams hands the Blue team a 20-point advantage and announces that the team will scrimmage for ten possessions. If the starters score on every possession, they could tie the score, but just one Blue basket will put the game out of reach. Then the coach introduces the catch: for every pass the White team makes before a basket, they get one point.

Suddenly, the Tar Heels are a team of glad-handed passers. They rack up 10 points before one basket, 9 before another. No one goes one-on-one at the expense of his teammates. The ball is quickly worked around the perimeter, dumped inside, fired back out, and reversed across the court. It is crisp, up-tempo offense, but it is also patient offense—exactly the kind that Roy Williams favors. The message seems to be getting through: the more passes the starters make, the more the defense is broken down, and better scoring opportunities are created. The coach's point made, and the White team victorious, the squad returns to the locker room to suffer through the second half of the Cleveland State film.

The only problem that arises in the four-hour practice is the further depletion of the squad's talent. With Manuel already hobbling because of his knee injury, Jawad Williams takes a shot to his hip and suffers a hip pointer. If neither of the juniors can play, tenth-ranked Carolina's chances against its next opponent—eleventh-ranked Illinois, which pounded UNC by 27 points last year and has won their first three games by an average of 22 points—are slim.

The game against the Fighting Illini is part of the made-for-television Atlantic Coast Conference–Big Ten Challenge, which matches two of the most formidable basketball conferences in America. The two leagues work in conjunction with television behemoth ESPN to arrange the best possible matchups, and the conference that wins the most head-to-head battles gains a certain measure of conference pride. The event probably means more to ACC fans, who are already in the throes of their basketball obsession by early December, than Big Ten fans, who are primarily concerned with football's bowl season. Carolina has been entirely luckless in the Challenge, losing all four of its previous games. Because of their status as a national television draw, the Heels usually draw one of the Big Ten's best teams regardless of their expected strength; last year the Heels had to play on the road in Champaign when many other ACC schools enjoyed games at home or at neutral sites. This year, league officials send the Illini and Heels to Greensboro for their game, a "neutral" site where Carolina has won ten of its last eleven games and which will be heavily covered in light blue.

Earning a smidgen of conference pride, however, means absolutely nothing to Roy Williams. "I could care less," he says on the day before his team meets Illinois. "That's probably not the company line . . . I'll pull for the ACC schools, but I'm not going to get up and have an extra chocolate nut sundae if we win seven games."

It is exactly what every coach in the league is thinking, but it's not something any of them would say publicly. Williams is more concerned with his team than with conference superiority. The Heels stand 3–0 and are ranked tenth in the country, but Williams is in a unique situation. Fans have the luxury of viewing this year's team with last year's squad as prologue. They have already seen Rashad McCants lead the Tar Heels to a win over Duke, seen Raymond Felton play brilliantly in the final month of the season, seen Carolina upend highly ranked Maryland in the ACC Tournament. Williams, meanwhile, has only seen what has happened since practice began on October 17. The Tar Heel head coach has heard glowing reviews of Felton's play, but remains concerned about his point guard's ability to take care of the basketball—the sophomore had four turnovers against Cleveland State and seems to make at least one exasperating pass per game. Felton also has a fragile relationship with McCants. The two are supremely talented basketball players, but they occasionally wear on each other. The irony is that both are focused completely on winning, but their single-minded focus tends to cause some friction. A college basketball team is not a collection of thirteen clones, and Felton and McCants have very different personalities. Felton is the "yes sir, no sir" man who must encounter difficulty on the court before he will show emotion. McCants, meanwhile, shows emotion as he gets off the bus. The duo play seamlessly when things are going well, but they can snipe at each other when tribulations occur. When McCants calls a dubious foul in a preseason pickup game, Felton's team loses and he stalks off the court in disgust.

The petty disagreements are not yet a team chemistry issue. But Williams wants to see his team lose the egos and play basketball as a unit. At the press conference when he was hired as Carolina's coach, Williams used the analogy of a fist: five fingers working together that are much stronger in tandem than they are separately. At times, however, there are a couple of fingers sticking out of the Heels' fist.

It seems an unlikely time for Carolina to come up with a game that surprises and pleases their new coach, but that is exactly what happens. At the pregame shoot-around before the 9 P.M. tip-off against Illinois, Roy Williams approaches the injured Jawad Williams, who went through a very limited practice the day before and is questionable, at best, for the game.

"Well, Jawad, what do you think?" the head coach asks.

"About what?" Williams replies.

"'Bout playing," Roy Williams says.

"Coach," Jawad answers, "I'm playing."

The exchange seems to set the tone for the rest of the evening. Carolina has never been known as a particularly tough team. Its previous matchups in the Atlantic Coast Conference-Big Ten Challenge usually ended with the burly Big Ten opponent outmuscling UNC players in the paint, and the Heels have been outrebounded by a cumulative 154–124 margin in the previous four Challenge contests. Preseason news stories on Carolina focus on the team's athletic ability or the talent of the starting five, but—with good reason, since there was little evidence of it last season—never on its toughness or desire.

That changes in front of 16,211 rowdy fans in Greensboro. Both Williams and Manuel play despite their injuries. Felton goes down with a leg cramp late in the game, but returns to hit some key free throws. Both Sean May (23 points and 14 rebounds) and Williams (18 points and 12 rebounds) notch double-doubles, and the Heels turn in a first-half defensive effort that is the mirror opposite of their poor performance against the Vikings. Illinois point guard Dee Brown misses his first six shots against harassing defense from Felton and Jackie Manuel.

Brown leads a team that has averaged just 15 turnovers per game entering the contest, but they lose the ball 14 times in the first half alone. The Illini are so rattled in the stanza's final minute that they allow a Jawad Williams three-pointer with 34.8 seconds left and then carelessly toss away the ball. Rashad McCants recovers it and sinks another three-pointer to give the Tar Heels a 6-point advantage at intermission.

Illinois takes a 1-point lead after a brief spurt with 14 minutes remaining, and the game seesaws until the Illini's Roger Powell picks up his fourth foul with 6:19 left and the game tied at 69. It is the perfect illustration of Roy Williams's offensive philosophy. Work the ball inside often enough, he is fond of saying, and you will eventually get the other team in foul trouble, which enables you to play against substitutes rather than starters in the game's crucial minutes. That's exactly what happens: Powell's departure prompts a Tar Heel run, and they quickly stretch their lead to 8 points.

In a late-game timeout, the coach reminds his team of their offensive execution in practice two days before. "I want offense just like we had on Sunday afternoon," he says, referring to the drill that rewarded every pre-basket pass with a point.

That's exactly what he gets. Jawad Williams, who is becoming a master of the tip-out, once again tips out a Carolina missed free throw with under a minute to play, giving the Tar Heels a crucial extra possession. The Heels, who are occasionally spotty from the free-throw line, hit key shots from the charity stripe down the stretch to close out an 88–81 victory. The squad celebrates the victory in the locker room with a mosh pit, and even Roy Williams joins in the celebration.

After the game, the head coach looks nothing like the downcast man who seemed perplexed three days earlier in Cleveland.

"This is one of those moments in coaching you truly enjoy," he says. "Tonight we guarded people and we were unselfish. If we play like that, we've got a chance."

It is about as close as Williams will ever come to admitting that his newly 4–0 team could be special. The look on his face indicates that for the first time, he has seen a glimpse that this team might be able to fulfill his expectations, might be able to put aside their tumultuous history together and play as a unit.

The players understand what has happened in the Greensboro Coliseum. "I know Coach is a little unsure of what this team is capable of and how much fight we have in us," Sean May says. "This shows him we're ready to take the next step. We're ready to be not a good team, but a great team. This shows him we're ready to follow him."

The game is significant for another reason. Crowds at the Smith Center in Chapel Hill are notoriously laid-back. The loquacious Florida State point guard Sam Cassell famously (and somewhat unfairly) labeled the Carolina fans a "wine-and-cheese crowd" after the Seminoles upended the Tar Heels during the 1991–92 season.

The Tar Heels once enjoyed one of the most formidable home court advantages in all of college basketball. From 1966 to 1986, they played home games at Carmichael Auditorium, which with its metal bleachers, metal roof, and undistinguished exterior looked more like a high school gymnasium than a basketball palace. But somewhere in that venerable building some Tar Heel magic resided. Carolina lost just twenty games in twenty years on that court, and its home court comebacks became legendary. The quintessential Carmichael game took place on March 2, 1974, the annual renewal of the rivalry with Duke University. On that day, the Blue Devils built an 86–78 lead with just 17 seconds remaining. These were the days before the three-point shot, so an 8-point deficit required four possessions, an almost impossible feat in less than 20 seconds. But the Heels tied the game on a Walter Davis 30-footer at the end of regulation and eventually captured a 96–92 overtime victory.

Those were the kinds of breaks that seemed to happen for Carolina in Carmichael, where legend (and Maryland coach Lefty Driesell) held that Smith turned up the heat in the visitors' locker room. Although the Tar Heels engineered several memorable comebacks in the Smith Center—proving that they had at least as much to do with preparation and talent as with luck—the same magic never surrounded the building. It was enormous, seating 21,750 fans, more than twice Carmichael's capacity. Instead of uncomfortable metal bleachers that practically forced the occupant to stand, the first six rows are made up of cushioned seats that resemble first-class seats on an airplane. The most controversy, however, centered on the way the plush seats were distributed. When the Smith Center was being built in the mid-1980s, the new wave of publicly financed building had yet to begin. No one believed that UNC could build a privately financed 20,000-seat basketball arena without some creative financing.

The first option pursued was a hike in student fees that would have resulted in students retaining the rights to thousands of prime seats around the court. But the student body—including student Matt Doherty, who frequently recalled voting against the increase—rejected the proposal, forcing Carolina's booster club, the Rams Club, to explore other financing avenues. Their plan was to solicit donations from Tar Heel fans in exchange for permanent rights to seats in a designated area. The idea was a forerunner of the permanent seat license plan, which has become commonplace among professional sports teams building new arenas. In exchange for a donation of a certain amount, donors would be allowed into the building before the first game to select their seats. They would then have the rights to those seats for the life of the building, which was first known as the Student Activities Center but was christened the Dean E. Smith Center before the first game. Predictably, the donors snapped up the choicest seats, creating a situation in which a large number of courtside seats were occupied by those who had money in 1985—not the most vigorous group by 2003. The setup got little attention at the time, but as other schools, including Maryland and North Carolina State, built new arenas that handed over some prime courtside seating to students, Carolina students began to chirp. The final straw, however, was the increasing attention given to Duke's "Cameron Crazies." In Cameron Indoor Stadium, the sideline locations are given to students, who, thanks to Dick Vitale, became one of the best-known fan bases in college sports. In the late 1980s and early 1990s they frequently invented clever cheers and, although they had become a stale caricature of themselves by 2003, Vitale was still screaming their praises and the nation never had a clue that in the middle and upper rows of Cameron—where television cameras never ventured—rested a laid-back fan base even more staid than the one at the Smith Center.

The situation got renewed attention during the 1999–2000 season when a snowstorm blanketed the Triangle area and prevented many fans from attending the January 27 game against Maryland. After giving the regular ticket holders a grace period early in the game, organizers announced with about 15 minutes remaining in the first half that all unoccupied seats were being made general admission. The result was a sprawling, seat-hopping mass of humanity that crawled over seats in order to reach the choice midcourt locations. The Tar Heels responded with a 75–63 victory, and the seed was planted for seating changes.

To spark some student excitement, the Rams Club worked with the athletic department prior to the 2000–01 season to construct several risers on one Smith Center baseline. The risers were intended to be filled with the wildest, craziest Tar Heel students to be found, but a distribution policy that rewarded luck rather than dedication siphoned off some of the excitement. The risers were an improvement, but the perception still exists that Carolina crowds largely wait to be entertained before responding vocally. That's a foreign concept to the new Tar Heel coaches, who are used to the more Carmichael-like atmosphere at Kansas, where even non-marquee, non-conference games are 16,300-seat sell-outs. At preseason gatherings of the Rams Club, Roy Williams makes a regular part of his stump speech a challenge to season ticket holders to "take off their corporate hats" and come to the games ready to make some noise.

The win over Illinois, which was a game not included in the season ticket package and which included numerous fans unable to get tickets to games in Chapel Hill, had the most raucous crowd of the season. Roy Williams thanks those fans—and issues a backhanded challenge to the inhabitants of the Smith Center—by releasing a letter two days later that reads, in part, "I'd like to take this opportunity to thank the fans that made our basketball team's visit to the Greensboro Coliseum a memorable experience. The boisterous atmosphere in the arena helped to make the game an intense competition from the opening tip to the final horn."

Later that week, however, Williams's team does little to energize the crowd during the first half of a game against George Mason. The out-manned Patriots, who were the preseason pick to win the Colonial Athletic Association, follow the Cleveland State script, making their first seven shots and edging out to a 49–47 lead. The second half, however, is much different. Carolina opens with a 15–2 run and turns in a virtually perfect half. After a 5-assist, 3-turnover first half, Raymond Felton is exquisite in the second stanza, handing out 13 more assists on his way to a single-game school record total of 18. Most are passes to Sean May, who hits 10 of his 12 field goal attempts and displays his glue-like hands on one errant second-half Felton pass. After drawing the defense on dribble penetration into the lane, Felton sees two George Mason defenders closing on him. The best scoring opportunity is a pass to May, but the defenders seal all the passing lanes except for a tiny window behind the Tar Heel center and to his left. His options disappearing rapidly, Felton decides to throw the pass anyway, and zips a laser that appears headed for the third row of fans. But May sticks out a paw and reels in the pass one-handed, dropping it softly into the basket for 2 of his career-high 26 points and one of Felton's assists.

After the game, May chides his fellow sophomore. "You owe me one," he tells Felton with a smile. "That pass was terrible."

As Felton's assists begin to pile up, Roy Williams is made aware that his point guard is one pass away from eclipsing Jeff Lebo's school record of 17 assists. Unwilling to run up the score or risk injury to his floor leader, he immediately calls for a play that, if run correctly, will result in a Felton-to-Jawad Williams lob for an easy slam dunk. As with everything else in the second half, it clicks perfectly and Felton gets his record assist and is promptly removed from the game. Even the Tar Heel substitutes play flawlessly, and Carolina cruises to a 115–81 victory, scoring more points than any Carolina team since 1994. Even more important for a team that remains banged up—Manuel is still recovering from the sprained knee and Jawad Williams occasionally has to sit out certain drills during practice to rest his hip—the Heels make it out of the game with no serious injuries other than a late-game incident with their head coach. As he applauds a play by one of the Carolina substitutes, Roy Williams boisterously claps his hands together, causing the bulky ring on his right hand to smack a finger on his left hand. He winces noticeably and spends the game's final minute shaking his right hand in pain.

The offending ring is a Kansas University back-to-back Final Four ring. His Tar Heels are 5–0 and ranked in the nation's top ten. But they've not done anything to earn their head coach any replacement jewelry.

Reality soon intrudes on the Tar Heels' basketball season. The day after the George Mason game is the last day of fall classes for the University of North Carolina, which grants students two reading days before semester exams begin on Thursday, December 11.

Roy Williams counts it as a point of pride that he coached three Academic All-Americans during his tenure at Kansas. He brought one of them, Jerod Haase, with him from Kansas to join the coaching staff at Carolina. The new head coach's emphasis on academics will alter the Tar Heels' preparation for their next game, which is a week away against lightly regarded non-conference foe Akron. In a typical week with just one game, the Heels would usually practice at least five times. This week, however, they will have formal practices just twice. The team takes

Monday off and then on Tuesday goes through a "run and shoot" practice, which consists of approximately forty-five minutes of dribbling, shooting, and dummy offense. Wednesday is a full practice, but Thursday and Friday are back to the run-and-shoot format before the team goes through a full practice on Saturday in advance of the next day's game.

It's the way Williams has conducted practice during exam weeks throughout his career. Although he has yet to find any pattern in the way his teams perform during exams—some post blowout victories, others struggle against inferior competition—he believes this approach provides the best way for his players to balance schoolwork and basketball. The entire squad spends a significant amount of time during the week with the tutors provided by the Academic Support Center, including Wayne Walden and Burgess McSwain, who organize the academic side of the Carolina basketball program. Walden, who was at Kansas when Williams arrived before the 1988–89 season, is a treasured member of Williams's support squad. He was one of the first hires Williams made after arriving at Carolina.

"I've jokingly said—and my staff doesn't know if I'm joking or not, and I want to keep it that way—that I would rather lose every one of my assistant coaches than lose Wayne Walden," Roy Williams says. "He is the best I have ever seen about staying on top of things and on top of kids. He is totally devoted to our players and to what they are doing in the classroom. He is willing to give whatever time is necessary plus more, and he genuinely cares how the kids are doing in the classroom."

This first exam period is slightly more difficult for Walden and the coaching staff than when they were in Kansas because they are still not entirely acquainted with the players' various study habits. At Kansas, Williams made academics a key part of his recruiting strategy. At Carolina, however, he has to make his system work with the players he was given, some of whom arrived in Chapel Hill unprepared for the level of work required at one of the nation's top public universities. The biggest academic advantage is enjoyed by players like Damion Grant and Rashad McCants, who attended prep schools that introduced them to the idea of time management.

Other players on the roster, like Jackie Manuel, attended good high schools but had virtually no experience with the amount of work that would be required of them in college. Walden pays special attention to Carolina's freshmen, setting them up with individual tutors and keeping close tabs on their reading to ensure that nothing is being put off until the last minute. The travel required of Division I basketball players means several missed classes per semester; players present a letter to each professor at the beginning of every semester detailing the expected dates they will be out of class for travel. The players are often in the stressful position of trying to make up for missed classes and prepare for upcoming tests.

"When I was a freshman, it was mind-boggling," Manuel says. "During exams that first time, I was like, 'What is going on?' "

The task for Walden and for Burgess McSwain, the associate director of the academic support center, is to cushion the potential shock of exams. For most of the year, McSwain is a confidante for the players. She is something rare in the experience of most Carolina basketball players: a person who doesn't care at all about their basketball talents. "She loves us more than basketball," Scott says. "Her heart is so pure. When you want to talk to somebody and let it all out, she's the one to talk to. Without her I couldn't have gone through everything I've gone through here."

The players' near-universal love for her added even more stress in the spring of 2003. In public, they were questioned constantly about the status of Matt Doherty; in private, they were even more concerned about McSwain, who was fighting cancer and in dire health during the coaching transition. She recovered over the summer, and during exam week, McSwain's ordinarily tough love turns tougher. The academic contact on the coaching staff—an eclectic bunch that includes Academic All-American Haase, and pre-med major C. B. McGrath—is Holladay, a former law student who has served in that capacity for nearly a decade. The staff wants the players to see Walden as the good cop, so it's Holladay who sometimes has to assume the role of bad cop when classes are cut or academic work is otherwise neglected.

"I make sure the players do what they are supposed to do," Holladay says. "As long as they are putting their best foot forward, going to class, and studying, I'm a constant source of encouragement."

If something other than encouragement is needed, there are various methods. The first step is usually to require the player to come to the

Smith Center at 7 A.M., books in hand, for an early-morning supervised study session. Further disciplinary measures, if required, can include extra running—something no player wants to do given Williams's already strenuous practices.

Walden travels with the team and organizes at least one study session per road trip; earlier this year, although they were just over two hours from home, the Heels had a study hall on the day of the Davidson game. Walden and McSwain oversee a staff of eight tutors who work with the players on an as-needed basis. The amount of time they're needed varies, but the team is encouraged to follow one of Roy Williams's favorite sayings: "Smart people need tutors."

"One thing I know is that I don't have all the answers," Williams says. "That's why I'm always asking questions, and why I tell my team that smart people need tutors."

Students taking exams also need tutors, which is why their importance rises during the exam period. Beginning with the first reading day, McSwain begins working with players every morning at 11 A.M., sessions that sometimes stretch until the day's practice or run-and-shoot session kicks off at 4 P.M. The Heels practice for a couple hours and then some return to study hall at 7 P.M.

The study halls are not cramming sessions, and Walden prefers an approach that focuses on several subjects over a period of days rather than focusing exclusively on the next exam. For him, this semester was different than any he's experienced in the past ten years because he was dealing with players who were completely new to him. Just as they had no idea what to expect from him, when he came to Chapel Hill on August 4 he had no idea of their academic backgrounds.

"It was difficult, because at Kansas we were able to give them some freedom after their first year and we had some idea of what to expect from them," Walden says. "Here, I didn't know anyone or know their strengths and weaknesses or how they learn. Burgess has been a tremendous help. She knows how the system works here and she knows those kids."

McSwain should know. She's been around the Tar Heel basketball program exclusively for the past twenty years, and around Carolina athletics in general since the 1950s, when she was an undergraduate. Her experience has been that basketball players—who are used to performing under pressure in front of thousands of people—can often transfer that talent to test-taking. Of course, making a free throw in front of 15,000 screaming fans and solving a quadratic equation are two very different things.

Many players have exams after the team's 10 A.M. practice on Saturday, and all have at least one exam remaining after the Akron game. It's one of the few times all season that basketball is not the number-one priority for the players. "They are mentally drained," Holladay says. "Because of that, they look physically drained."

It shows against Akron. If Cleveland State was a lethargic performance, this one is downright lackluster. The Tar Heels pull out a 64–53 victory, but their sixth straight win is so ugly it inspires long faces in the postgame dressing room. The victory is almost entirely attributable to the Tar Heels' superior physical talent—the Zips are a mid-major opponent who will be lucky to make the NCAA Tournament.

Roy Williams's postgame comments are pointed.

On the win: "It's very, very disappointing."

On the team's effort: "We stunk. It was pathetic."

On Sean May's 21 rebounds, a record for the Smith Center: "Twenty-one rebounds shows great effort, but a lot of those rebounds were his own misses. You pad your rebound total, you hurt your field goal percentage."

On the last time he was so disappointed in the performance of one of his teams: "I coached ninth-grade football one year. The quarterback got down behind the guard instead of the center. I felt sort of stupid at that point. That's the way I feel today."

Then, taking note of the day's major news—earlier in the day U.S. forces captured Saddam Hussein in Iraq, where the former dictator was discovered hiding in a hole—the Tar Heel head coach adds a final coda.

"Some great things happened in the world today," he says. "We got Saddam. I'd like to find one of those dad-gum holes he was living in and go there for a little while myself."

It is vintage Roy Williams, who so far has coached six Carolina victories and seemed fully pleased after exactly one of them—the win over Illinois. Williams is known for his competitiveness, but in fact he isn't happy just to win; he is happy only when his team wins and performs well. Ugly wins will be acceptable in the ACC Tournament or the NCAA Tournament, but right now it is mid-December and he once again seems perplexed about his team. In response to the halting victory, he adjusts the week's practice schedule. Instead of a day off on Wednesday, the last day of exams, he schedules a full practice on Wednesday, Thursday, and Friday in advance of Saturday's Atlantic Coast Conference opener against Wake Forest.

The players expect the adjustment. Nearly all treat the Akron game as a defeat, especially Sean May, who despite making over 60 percent of his field goals on the season, hits just three of his eighteen shots. The final miss, a point-blank layup that rolls off the rim, causes him to pause before getting back on defense and stare blankly at the orange cylinder, which has suddenly turned unfriendly. May is not alone in his offensive struggles: the only starter to hit more than 50 percent of his field goals is Raymond Felton, who makes five of nine shots but commits five turnovers. Felton's performance does nothing to alleviate Williams's concern about his point guard. Coming into the season, people within the program promised Williams that he had never had a point guard like Felton. The comment was meant as a compliment—that is, he'd never had a point guard with such raw talent, with such flare.

But Williams doesn't care about flare. He values the point guard more highly than any position on the floor and wants a player in that role who is an extension of himself on the court. Through the first month of the season, Felton has not been that type of point guard. He has made some head-scratching passes and has also been slow to get adjusted to some of the demands placed on him by Williams's offense and defense. For fans, it is an easy assumption: Roy Williams plays an up-tempo style, Felton is fast, so it must be a perfect match. But the ACC opener looms in just six days, and although there is no friction between the two, neither is entirely comfortable with the other. Felton's assist/turnover ratio is just slightly over 2:1, the baseline for what Williams considers acceptable from a point guard.

"The biggest thing he has to understand is the primary goal of winning games by getting the ball inside first," Williams says. "He can push the ball harder and defend better. He can keep the guy in front of him a little better. Penetration down the court really breaks down our defense and that starts with him. He can get more consistent in the way he builds out our defense by pushing the other guy out to halfcourt."

The team spends the evening at a local Wal-Mart shopping for Christmas gifts for local underprivileged families, continuing a tradition that Williams began in Kansas. Just a few hours after the sluggish win, the players have already forgotten most of that afternoon's disappointment. The way they interact off the court mirrors their on-court relationships: Melvin Scott is the designated jokester, Jawad Williams shops seriously, and Rashad McCants shops alone while many of his teammates pair up. As they check out after nearly two hours of shopping—and several autograph requests by surreptitious Wal-Mart employees who circumvent Roy Williams's request that the team not sign autographs, since they are doing charity work—Jawad Williams returns to the Smith Center to study for a mathematics exam the next day. Jackie Manuel has two papers due the following afternoon, and even team manager Eric Hoots has academic responsibilities, a ten-page paper due later in the week that he hasn't yet started.

By Wednesday afternoon, all the exams will be finished and the practice schedule will be back on a regular rhythm. Standing 6–0 and ranked fourth in the country, the Tar Heels are about to begin the season in earnest.

The 2003–04 campaign marks the Atlantic Coast Conference's fifty-first season of basketball, and all fifty-one have been fraught with intrigue, rivalries, and some of the best college basketball in America. According to the Associated Press poll of December 15, the league boasts three of the nation's top five teams. Duke, which spent a week at number one before losing to Purdue, is slotted third. Carolina is fourth. Georgia Tech—which after winning the Preseason NIT and beating preseason number one Connecticut is the league's best story of the opening month—is fifth. Wake checks in at fourteenth, and even Maryland, which brings up the rear of the poll at twenty-fifth, boasts an impressive win at formerly number-one-ranked Florida the previous week. Expansion is on the horizon, with Virginia Tech and Miami joining the league next season and Boston College coming in 2005, all to bolster the conference's football reputation, which lags significantly behind basketball. The additions will mean the end of the league's beloved round-robin schedule, which requires each team to play each league foe twice—once at home and once on the road. The current schedule provides perfect symmetry. Lose to a team in the first half of the season, and there remains a chance to get it back the second time around.

The UNC athletic department and Chancellor James Moeser actively opposed expansion for three main reasons: concerns over missed classes for Olympic sport athletes facing increased travel demands, financial concerns about moving from nine to twelve schools, and the impact expansion would have on the basketball schedule. Among the schools that favored the expansion, perhaps none was more perplexing than Wake Forest. A tiny private school first located in Wake Forest and then moved to Winston-Salem thanks to an influx of tobacco money, the Demon Deacons were participants in the first college basketball game ever played in the state of North Carolina (on March 2, 1906, against Duke) and are long-standing members of the storied "Big Four" quartet along Tobacco Road, which also includes NC State, Duke, and North Carolina. They first met the Tar Heels on the hardwood on February 3, 1911, and have since established one of the longest-running rivalries in the South with the Heels.

But one of the byproducts of expansion is the potential end to the home-and-home basketball series between the Deacons and Tar Heels. The teams have met 207 times, a colorful history complete with on-court brawls, shocking upsets, and record-setting individual performances, but that twice-a-year rivalry is on the verge of extinction. The new twelve-team ACC will have too many members to play a round-robin schedule, since the NCAA limits teams to twenty-eight games and no one wants twenty-two to be league contests. To aid in scheduling, the ACC assigned two "primary partners" to each school—Carolina's are Duke and NC State; Wake's are NC State and, somewhat inexplicably, Georgia Tech. Home-and-home series are not guaranteed with any schools other than the primary partners, which means that in the very near future the Tar Heels and Demon Deacons will meet just once a season on the hardwood.

As if to prove the sheer folly of that plan, the two teams engage in one of the greatest regular season games in Atlantic Coast Conference history. Outside the Smith Center 30 minutes before tip-off, fans are swarming the sidewalks holding up two fingers, the universal signal for wanting to buy a pair of tickets. One woman is overheard to remark that she has been buying tickets out front for over ten years, and she has never seen a tougher game to purchase than this one. That's heady praise for a decade that has seen matchups between nationally first- and second-ranked teams, titanic clashes with rival Duke, and a pair of games against marquee national opponent Kentucky. A half hour before tip-off, the cheapest tickets that can be found have a face value of $35 and are being sold for $100 apiece.

Inside the Smith Center, there is little early indication that an instant classic is on tap. Wake Forest forward Vytas Danelius is out with an injury, but Carolina received good news earlier in the week when 6-foot-6 forward David Noel was medically cleared to play against the Deacs, ending his recovery from the torn ligament in his hand suffered in an early-season practice. Noel returned to full speed practice during the week and although Roy Williams was coy with the media earlier in the week about how much the athletic sophomore would play, Noel fully expects to return to the Tar Heels' rotation, where he can provide rebounding, scoring, and energy that has been sorely lacking. The most criticized aspect of Carolina's team has been the bench, and Noel's return immediately enables Williams to confidently call on his first seven men, and pushes walk-on freshman Justin Bohlander to the less-demanding eighth spot in the rotation, a role he better fits at this stage of his career. If he is the third man off the bench, any contribution from Bohlander becomes a bonus rather than a necessity.

Early in the game, it appears the Heels may get to use plenty of their bench. Raymond Felton scores 7 of his team's first 15 points on a combination of spinning moves into the paint and perimeter jumpers, and by the time Sean May hits a jumper with less than 6 minutes gone, Carolina has a 19–8 lead and Wake Forest coach Skip Prosser is using his first timeout. Prosser, a relative ACC newcomer in just his third year with the Demon Deacons, has already had a profound impact on recruiting in the state of North Carolina. Traditionally Wake has rarely recruited against Duke, North Carolina, and NC State for the state's very best players. Instead, its coaches recruited creatively, mining unknown prospects like Tim Duncan, who arrived from the Virgin Islands almost entirely overlooked by the college basketball elite, and overseas talent to remain viable. Prosser has changed that strategy. Under him, the Demon Deacons have made a habit of identifying the state's best players very early and securing commitments from them before other schools have a chance to get involved. The team he brings into Chapel Hill features a staggering eight scholarship recipients who are North Carolina natives, compared to three scholarship Tar Heels— Rashad McCants, David Noel, and Reyshawn Terry—who are in-state players. Wake already has a commitment from the class of 2004's Cameron Stanley, a highly touted prospect at Raleigh's Millbrook High, and Prosser has also secured verbals from high school juniors Kevin Swinton and David Weaver, both of whom are North Carolina natives. Swinton and Weaver won't be eligible until the 2005–06 season, seemingly decades away in the fast-paced world of college basketball, but their early commitments enable Wake Forest to turn their sights to even younger players, widening the recruiting gap on other schools that are still going after high school juniors. Wake's proficiency on the recruiting trail was a significant roadblock for Carolina's new coaching staff in their first months on the job. Instead of trying to make inroads with in-state players who could make an impact relatively soon, the Tar Heel coaches targeted younger players who are still several years away from contributing.

Prosser's North Carolina–heavy bunch is full of players who were overlooked by the other area schools. Sophomore center Eric Williams was virtually ignored as an overweight high school player, but has lost fifty pounds in the past fifteen months and now is an ACC force. Sophomore guard Justin Gray has relatives who attended NC State, but the Wolfpack paid him scant attention and he enrolled at Wake and will be an All-ACC selection this season. Freshman point guard Chris Paul's slight stature scared off some suitors, but he eventually became a highly touted prospect. Carolina got involved too late, however, and he rejected Doherty's offer of a walk-on position and instead accepted a scholarship from Prosser.

Wake's sizable in-state contingent looks nervous early. Eric Williams is listless in the paint during the first half, and Carolina makes 65 percent of its shots. But somehow, Wake hangs in, largely by stifling UNC's transition game. Prosser prepared his team for Carolina's up-tempo style by telling the Wake scout team not to take the ball out of bounds after made baskets during practice—the subs simply grabbed the ball and ran with it. That defense eventually leads to offense, as the Deacs get a banked-in three-pointer from Trent Strickland that seems to energize them, and they close their deficit to 3 points with 3 minutes left in the half. At that point, a seemingly insignificant play occurs that will have serious ramifications. Sean May, the only Tar Heel with the bulk to defend Williams, gets the ball on the block with his back to the basket and begins to make his move. As May moves, Wake freshman Kyle Visser, who is defending him, goes down in a heap. May is called for a charge, his second foul of the game. It is the one play May will later wish he had back.

Strickland gives the Deacs their first lead on a leaner, and with 6 seconds left, Roy Williams calls timeout. The play is simple: give the ball to Raymond Felton and let him scoot down the court. The sophomore point guard does exactly that, swishing a baseline jumper as time expires to forge a 47–47 tie at the break.

The teams battle evenly through the early minutes of the second half, with Carolina seemingly always on the verge of breaking the game open. The final 27 minutes of action, which begin when Rashad McCants slams home a vicious alley-oop dunk on a pass from Felton to give Carolina a 62–60 lead with 12:30 left, are some of the most remarkable ever played in the Smith Center. The Heels eventually stretch their advantage to 66–60 after Jackie Manuel, not known for his ballhandling, improbably gathers in a 60-foot May pass and lays it in left-handed with less than 11 minutes to play. May converts a three-point play 2 minutes later that gives Carolina a 7-point advantage with 9:30 left.

Roy Williams is not accustomed to his team losing 7-point leads in conference games at home. The 7-point bulge is not comfortable, but it also should not be as perilous as it seems. Just 2 minutes later, Carolina has lost the lead, as Paul converts a three-point play to give Wake a 70–69 lead. It is the kind of slip Williams abhors, and it is the first sign that he does not yet have this team where he wants it mentally. There are more signs to come.

After Sean May makes a brilliant one-handed catch of a bullet pass from McCants and ties the score at 75, Felton commits a defensive lapse and allows Paul to dribble the length of the court for a basket, prompting the Tar Heel head coach to brutally slam down his right hand on one of the folding chairs that make up the Carolina bench. Williams turns back to the court with his teeth gritted. It is obvious from his face that Felton has committed the gravest sin a Williams-coached player can commit: too much celebration of an offensive play at the expense of defense.

The point guard redeems himself with 3 minutes left, as he sinks a pair of free throws to create an 82–82 tie. McCants also makes two-of-two charity tosses, and Felton hits another pair to give the Heels a 1-point lead with 1:36 left. May blocks an Eric Williams shot attempt and the ball trickles out of bounds to Carolina, giving them the ball with an 86–85 lead and just over a minute left. This is the moment when the head coach expects his team to out-execute the other squad, for his point guard to seize control of the game. After a timeout, Carolina sets up a play to squeeze some precious seconds off the clock and create a good scoring opportunity in the paint. The five Tar Heels who take the floor assume their proper positions—with one exception. Rashad McCants, who is busily jawing with a Wake Forest player in the UNC frontcourt, apparently forgets that he is the player designated to throw the ball inbounds. No other Tar Heel notices the problem and takes the initiative to make the easy pass inbounds, so the official places the ball on the floor and begins his 5-second count. Roy Williams is forced to call a timeout to avoid a turnover.

Once the ball is correctly inbounded, Eric Williams blocks a May shot, and the previously unheralded Strickland makes his second huge play by scoring while being fouled by Felton. He makes the bonus free throw, giving Wake an 88–86 lead with 46.2 seconds left. For one of the first times in the game's closing minutes, Carolina executes its next play perfectly. Following a timeout, Jawad Williams sets a screen for Melvin Scott that appears designed to free Scott for a game-clinching three-pointer. Both Strickland, who is supposed to be guarding Williams in

Wake's man-to-man defense, and Chris Paul, who is assigned to Scott, follow the Tar Heel guard out beyond the three-point line, and Felton whips a bullet pass to Williams for a two-handed dunk that ties the score and forces overtime.

In overtime, the battle of attrition truly begins. Wake's Justin Gray is the first to foul out, leaving with 1:34 remaining in the first overtime. After Rashad McCants hits a pair of crucial three-pointers to give Carolina a 1-point edge with 32 seconds left, David Noel retrieves a missed trifecta by Taron Downey. Once again, Roy Williams's Heels are in a plum position. Raymond Felton, who is 5-for-5 from the free-throw line in the game, is fouled and has a chance to stretch the lead to 3. His first attempt clangs off the front rim before bouncing off the back rim. The second hits only the front rim.

Unbelievably, Wake almost hands the game back to the Heels. Chris Paul dribbles the ball out of bounds with 9.7 seconds left, and the Deacs have to foul Jawad Williams with 8.4 seconds remaining. Once again, Carolina has a player at the line with a chance to stretch the lead from 1 point to 3. Once again, the player misses the first, but Williams hits the second for a 104–102 advantage. Paul takes the ball the length of the floor, but David Noel rejects his shot across the Wake Forest baseline. With 3.1 seconds left, the Demon Deacons have to inbound the ball from the baseline. During a timeout, Roy Williams instructs his team not to foul a jump shooter. Once the teams come back on the floor, there is a miscommunication as Paul is designated as the player to take the ball out of bounds. The most dangerous player on any inbounds play is the man throwing the initial pass, because defenders frequently forget about him and allow him to step inbounds after throwing the pass, get the ball back, and then score an uncontested basket. That's exactly what happens: Paul triggers the play and then steps into the corner behind the three-point line. The rookie gets the ball back and is beginning to fire a potentially game-winning three-pointer when Melvin Scott crashes into him, sending him to the line for three foul shots. Paul makes two of three, sending the game into a second overtime. Roy Williams will later describe the fouling of the three-point shooter as the most discouraging moment he's ever had in coaching.

The second extra session begins ominously, as May misses an easy layup and is then disqualified after picking up his fifth foul. The Deacs can't find Williams inside to take advantage of May's absence, however, and both teams go scoreless through the first 3 minutes. Jawad Williams finds Felton on a backdoor cut—something the team practiced extensively in the days before the game—to give the Heels a 2-point lead with 1:45 left, and when Paul throws the ball away with under a minute remaining, Carolina once again has the game firmly in grasp. The Tar Heel point guard brings the ball up the floor with Paul right behind him. There is minimal contact, and Felton goes down in a heap with Paul whistled for a foul. Felton leaves the floor with a twisted ankle, forcing Roy Williams to select a player from his bench to shoot the crucial free throws. He selects McCants, who clangs both of them, opening the window for Wake to tie the game when Eric Williams finally scores inside with 13 seconds left.

Carolina's last possession of the second overtime, which takes place with Felton still on the bench, is frenetic, as Melvin Scott takes his time before jacking up a 21-foot three-pointer that rims out. It is not the kind of shot Roy Williams expects his team to take with the game on the line, even with Felton and May on the bench, and it is at least the fifth avoidable error in the last 15 minutes of action that could cost the Tar Heels the game.

After so many missed opportunities, the Smith Center crowd is virtually silent during the intermission before the third overtime. It is not a bored quiet—not the type of silence that typically earns criticism for Carolina fans—but rather the quiet of fans who have been completely sapped. Virtually the entire crowd has been standing ever since McCants rammed home his alley-oop dunk almost an hour earlier. It is the first time in twenty-one years that Carolina has played a three-overtime game, and there is a growing sense that these two teams might play forever. The tickets that earlier seemed outrageous at $100 apiece now seem like a bargain.

The Smith Center crowd rouses early in the third overtime as Noel hits a three-pointer and Scott perfectly runs a three-on-one fast break that leads to a Williams two-handed dunk. Carolina's lead is four, an advantage that seems luxurious given the tenor of the game. The Heels play tenacious defense on Wake's next possession, as the Demon Deacons seem disorganized without Paul, who fouled out late in the second overtime. Without their freshman leader, the reins go to Taron Downey, an unheralded left-hander who, of course, is a native of North Carolina. With 32 of 35 seconds having ticked off the shot clock, Wake Forest still hasn't gotten the ball below the three-point line. Downey moves two steps to his right, elevates over Scott, and drains a head-shaking desperation three-pointer that is the biggest shot of the game. Downey's trifecta cuts Carolina's advantage to 111–110 and seems to indicate that no matter what the Heels do—even after Felton returns from his twisted ankle with 1:41 left—Wake will have an answer.

The Heels' final possessions are a case study in what Williams does not want his team to do. Jawad Williams hoists an ill-advised three-pointer, two easy shots are missed in the post, Manuel misses a pair of free throws, and Noel misses a three-pointer, a shot the coaching staff does not want him to take, his earlier success notwithstanding. Even when Melvin Scott hits a three-pointer from the top of the key that ties the score at 114 with 1:04 left, it almost seems as if he is prolonging the inevitable rather than giving Carolina a chance to win.

Eventually, the inevitable happens. After a timeout, the Demon Deacons run some clock and then find Williams inside, where he has been virtually unimpeded since May fouled out, for a basket. Jackie Manuel beats his man down the floor, but his shot is blocked by Visser and Wake recovers. Downey hits one of two free throws for a 117–114 Wake lead, and the Tar Heels have one last chance. During a timeout, Williams designs a play in which Jawad Williams is intended to set a screen for McCants. But when the ball is inbounded to Felton, both Williams and McCants are setting screens and thus are completely out of the play, forcing Felton to try and create something on his own. The Deacons steal the ball, Eric Williams makes a pair of free throws, and Wake opens the ACC season with a 119–114 triple-overtime win that will be called one of the greatest games in ACC regular season history in most newspapers the next day. Wake's North Carolina natives score 96 of their team's 119 points and play 75 percent of the available minutes in the game.

The Carolina coaches aren't ready to be as generous as the newspapers in their assessment of the game. Asked how often he wins a game like this one with one of his Kansas teams, Williams says, "Ten out of ten." Especially in the overtime sessions, Carolina occasionally played individually rather than as a unit, something that does not escape Roy Williams's notice.

"We have to pull together and make sure we're focusing on what's going right and what's going wrong with our team, not with each one of us," he says. "Learning how to win is playing with poise and making plays regardless of the score or how much pressure somebody may be feeling."

Shoddy defense and poor shot selection again cause problems. Upon reviewing the film, the staff is also perturbed at the amount of time Felton and McCants spend waving their arms to encourage the crowd— time the coaches feel their star duo should have devoted to playing defense.

The coaches agree it has to stop. However, enforcing the ban could be tricky; it was when Matt Doherty began to tell McCants to be less demonstrative on the court that the talented guard first retreated into his shell last season. As recently as two months ago, McCants was still seething about the perceived attempt to silence him.

"When I wasn't able to be emotional on the court, I didn't play well," he said. "In games where I was emotional, we won and I played really well. When somebody tries to change the way you've been playing all your life it's a hard adjustment."

Roy Williams sends his players home for a five-day respite, the longest such break he has ever granted as a head coach, unsure of when they will learn how to win a game. He has lost his only Atlantic Coast Conference game as a head coach, one that was played at home. He is the coach of the ninth-ranked team in the country, but he has a point guard who has been slower than expected to grasp his full role in the new system, a shooting guard whom he will have to persuade to play in a way he does not want to play, one member of the bench who can't be in the game when the Heels have the ball late in the game because he is a free-throw shooting liability, and a scholarship freshman whose minutes have dwindled to virtually nothing.

He has exactly one week to solve all those problems, because beginning January 3 with a trip to top-ranked Kentucky, Carolina's schedule includes seven games against teams ranked in the most recent Associated Press top ten.

Merry Christmas.

6

Putting together a non-conference schedule at the University of North Carolina is a difficult balancing act. The athletic director and basketball coach have the final authority in making a schedule, but nailing down twenty-eight workable games involves numerous other entities. Despite missing the NCAA Tournament for two straight seasons, the Tar Heels are still a significant television draw, so the program is frequently approached by television networks trying to pair two squads that will draw big ratings. Carolina tries to play at least two or three marquee non-conference games each year, games that put the team on national television in front of a full country's worth of fans and recruits. That's how the University of Connecticut, a Big East school that regularly resides in the nation's top ten, landed on the schedule—the Huskies will visit Chapel Hill in January as part of a four-games-in-four-years series that airs on CBS. Likewise, the Heels will road-trip to Lexington the first weekend in January for a game at the University of Kentucky, the fourth installment in a six-game series between the two winningest programs in college basketball history.

Those two contests are the gems of this year's schedule, which has received some criticism for not being as strong as usual. The Atlantic Coast Conference games are always treacherous, but the true measure of a quality schedule are the non-conference games, and these are given great weight by the NCAA Tournament selection committee. Other than Kentucky, UConn, and the ACC-Big Ten Challenge game against Illinois, the 2003–04 slate is light on big-name opponents. The road game at Cleveland State was scheduled as a favor to Jawad Williams, and Akron landed on the schedule when it was called about being Williams's "home" game. (The Zips didn't call back soon enough to get that slot, but they still wanted a game, even if it was played in the Smith Center rather than in Cleveland, and Carolina agreed.) The season opener against Old Dominion was part of a three-game contract that called for two games in Chapel Hill and one in Norfolk, where the Heels helped inaugurate ODU's new arena during the 2002–03 season. The Davidson game occurred largely because of Matt Doherty's ties to the school, where he had served as an assistant coach before moving to Kansas to work under Roy Williams.

Williams acknowledges that this year's schedule does not include as many high-quality opponents as he would like. "The schedule will get better," he said before the season began. "We're going to play a big-time schedule. It's something that's coming, but it's not here now."

The Tar Heel head coach has already initiated discussions with Arizona about a home-and-home series that will help keep Carolina on the minds of prospects on the West Coast, which was fertile recruiting territory for Williams while at Kansas. Games with Texas and Southern Cal are also under discussion.

One of this year's games, however, wasn't open to discussion. When Raymond Felton was being recruited, Doherty promised that the Heels would play a game close to the point guard's hometown of Latta, South Carolina. That game was, not coincidentally, scheduled for

Myrtle Beach—about an hour from Latta—during a weekend tournament known as the Beach Ball Classic organized by the chief of Felton's AAU team, John Rhodes. It was at that tournament that Felton first burst upon the national scene, leading his tiny high school to a win over national power DeMatha in 2001.

Almost nothing about the game made sense. The venue for the contest, the Myrtle Beach Convention Center, was listed as holding 6,750 for the game but probably held significantly fewer. The game also caused Carolina to take a major financial hit. Typical home games at the Smith Center bring in approximately $350,000 in revenue for the athletic department. The game against UNC-Wilmington, although listed as a home game on the schedule, will bring in exactly zero dollars and will deprive thousands of Carolina fans the opportunity to see the Heels play.

"Playing at Myrtle Beach is unusual," Williams said. "We have a chance to lose a lot of money right there. I probably would've just told Raymond that I would come and eat dinner at his momma and daddy's every time I go to the beach instead of taking a home game to Myrtle Beach."

Exactly how unprepared the organizers were for a major Division I basketball game was illustrated even before tip-off. Carolina officials checked on the availability of a tape of the national anthem four hours before the game and were assured that a tape was on hand. And as a backup, Convention Center honchos assured UNC, there was someone in the building who could sing the anthem if needed.

Just before the 1:00 P.M. tip-off, the two teams complete their warm-ups and stand next to their respective benches for the playing of the anthem. Despite the earlier assurances, however, no tape can be found and no singer located. After an awkward pause, the game proceeds without a national anthem.

Once it begins the game doesn't do much more to alleviate Roy Williams's trepidation about giving away a home game. After 90 seconds of play, as Jawad Williams defends Wilmington's Taylor Lay in front of the Carolina bench, Lay gets the ball and swings his arms through—in basketball parlance, "rips through." His elbow catches the Tar Heel flush on the jaw, flattening Williams and leaving him prone on the hardwood for nearly a minute. After Williams is helped to the bench, just 30 seconds pass before Sean May goes down in a heap after twisting his ankle while battling for an offensive rebound. In less than a minute, UNC's only two legitimate post presences are out with injuries. Williams tries to return later in the first half but remains woozy—"I couldn't remember where to go on offensive plays, I had to ask somebody," he will say later—and May makes a couple of unproductive attempts to return before being benched for the rest of the game early in the second half. Team doctor Tim Taft evaluates Williams at halftime and allows the forward back into the game after he passes cognitive tests. In the end, Williams plays only 22 minutes and May just 12, both season lows.

The rest of the Tar Heels appear to be almost as woozy as their junior leader. After Rashad McCants hits a three-pointer with 16:38 left in the first half to give the Heels a 6–2 lead, Carolina doesn't muster another basket for nearly 7 minutes. Such a drought would be fatal against a better team, but Wilmington is almost as hapless offensively as Carolina, and UNC trails just 7–6 by the time Melvin Scott finally discovers the bottom of the basket with a twisting layup with 8:57 left in the half.

Less than a minute later, McCants is removed from the game. It is a reaction to another defensive lapse by the mercurial sophomore that occurred earlier in the half. With just over 11 minutes left in the first half, Williams threw a zone at Wilmington. Almost entirely a man-to-man aficionado, the Tar Heel head coach plays zone only sporadically, but when he does, he expects it to be played well. McCants gets out of position in the zone and allows the Seahawks' Anthony Terrell to make an uncontested jump shot from the corner. A substitute is immediately sent to the scorer's table to replace McCants, but the next dead ball doesn't occur for another 3 minutes. When McCants arrives at the bench, he receives a tongue-lashing. Williams doesn't rip into McCants as soon as he is removed; instead, he gives him a cushion before kneeling down in front of him and informing him in plain language that his defensive effort was poor. Myriad factors have combined to put the Carolina head coach in a foul mood. First is the fact that the game has to be played at all. But if it must be played, he wants to play well, and his team is muddling through yet another disappointing half. Now McCants, whose defense has been a topic of discussion throughout the young season, has made another error.

So the sophomore is already in treacherous water when the Seahawks bring the ball in front of the Carolina bench with just over 5 minutes to play. The Heels have gone back to man-to-man. Wilmington guard John Goldsberry tries to hit Halston Lane on a backdoor cut, but walk-on freshman Justin Bohlander jumps into the passing lane to deny the pass, a solid defensive play that has been emphasized in recent practices.

Another recent point of discussion is team enthusiasm. When Roy Williams gathered his squad at the hotel in Myrtle Beach the night before the UNC-Wilmington game, he showed the players a tape from the loss to Wake Forest. Among the clips was a shot that showed the Tar Heel bench after an exciting Carolina play. Most of the players are standing and cheering, but freshman Reyshawn Terry remains seated, barely stifling a yawn.

Less than twenty-four hours later, Carolina has made another impressive defensive effort. Williams turns to his bench to point out Bohlander's play and discovers his entire team standing and applauding . . . except for McCants and freshman Jesse Holley, who are seated. Holley, a scholarship wide receiver for John Bunting's football team, is a newcomer to the hoops team. He was a virtual unknown to the basketball staff, but he is trying to make a place for himself with defense and energy. Later, Holley's teammates will explain that he had been standing and had sat down only the instant before the coach spotted him. McCants, however, has no such excuse. A look somewhere between disbelief and disgust on his face, Williams grits his teeth and says, "If you guys can't cheer, get your asses to the locker room." Both stare back at him, apparently believing they have just been given a choice. They have not. "Go to the locker room," their coach says. "Right now." The chastised duo walks off the Convention Center court. It is the first time in his coaching career Williams has had to discipline a player in that way.

The entire exchange takes place in less than five seconds and is noticed by virtually no one. Even when the coach is asked about it by a reporter after the game, the questioner doesn't realize McCants left the court for disciplinary reasons. But it is exactly the kind of extracurricular distraction that Williams abhors, and part of the reason Rashad McCants plays for Carolina and not for the Kansas Jayhawks. Through his Asheville connections, Williams was well aware of McCants as a high schooler. But he chose not to pursue him, and McCants became a Tar Heel.

McCants's banishment lasts only for the first half, and his second half is magnificent. Williams benches him for the first 4 minutes of the second half, but when he is finally inserted into the game, he nails four of six shots and scores 11 points, propelling the Tar Heels out to a 17-point advantage less than 8 minutes into the second half, after leading by just 5 at halftime. It is the type of offensive explosion that endears him to fans and makes him an ESPN favorite. Less noticeable are his two second-half turnovers, one of which occurs with virtually no defensive pressure when he is careless with the basketball while dribbling and is called for a double dribble. More perplexing is his decision to wave his arms boisterously after sinking a three-pointer, causing Wilmington coach Brad Brownell to call a timeout late in the half. The arm-waving is a topic that miffs the coaching staff; during the previous two practices Williams asked his star sophomore to eliminate it. Now, just a day after agreeing to shelve it, McCants is doing it again. Williams doesn't immediately see it, but Joe Holladay points it out to him as the team approaches the bench for the timeout. Williams immediately grabs McCants and leans close to his ear to once again remind him that such theatrics will not be tolerated.

The Tar Heels eventually grind out a 71–54 victory, running their record to 7–1 in a very unartistic performance. After the game, Roy Williams is frank about his decision to send the two players to the locker room: "If you are very bored, you shouldn't be on our bench."

The unusual schedule continues as Carolina has just two days before their next game, a Tuesday night tilt at the Smith Center against Coastal Carolina. CCU is located just outside Myrtle Beach, meaning that the Heels drive almost four hours from Chapel Hill to Myrtle Beach in order to play a "home" game against UNC-Wilmington, and then drive four hours back to Chapel Hill to play a game against a team that just drove four hours from Myrtle Beach. Roy Williams has little time to dissect the schedule. Much more troubling is his team's injury situation. Jawad Williams is diagnosed with a mild concussion when he wakes up Monday morning with a headache—something he did not have during Sunday's game—and will be held out of the Coastal game as a precaution. The medical staff is also being careful with Sean May, who will join Williams on the bench to give his tender ankle more time to heal.

Even without two of the team's three leading scorers, Coastal is little more than a glorified practice. The Tar Heels put together their most efficient offensive performance of the season, handing out 29 assists on 38 field goals, and make a solid defensive effort in cruising to a 105–72 victory.

With classes suspended for the winter break, Roy Williams has three days to prepare his team for Saturday's game at Kentucky. Carolina and Kentucky have a fierce rivalry, which is rare between non-conference foes. Usually it takes close contact for two schools to build hatred, but the Heels and Wildcats have done it while playing just twenty-five games against each other. In Chapel Hill, there's the lingering suspicion that those folks from Lexington have never quite been on the up and up, and around Rupp Arena there is the sense that those who favor the lighter shade of blue consider themselves somehow superior.

Although both schools have local rivals that they play every year—UK-Louisville and Carolina-Duke are two of the showcase games in college basketball—fans view the rivalry with the bitterness usually reserved for a neighborhood foe. The two programs have waged a see-saw battle for the title of college basketball's winningest program, a fight that has occasionally involved one program or the other "discovering" uncounted victories. Kentucky came close to getting the NCAA death penalty for recruiting violations; under Smith the Heels never had a whiff of impropriety.

In 1997, Carolina missed the chance for a championship game showdown with the Wildcats in Indianapolis by suffering a Final Four semifinal loss to Arizona. As the Heels left the court, some Kentucky fans in the boisterous Wildcat contingent at the Hoosier Dome held up signs that read "Another Carolina Choke." The scene repeated itself a year later, as Utah prevented a championship game for the ages by dispatching Vince Carter, Antawn Jamison, and the rest of the Heels in the semifinals. Once again, Wildcat fans seemed almost as delighted with Carolina's loss as with their own squad's victory.

Almost six years later, the Kentucky fans were more concerned about their own team. The Wildcats opened the season with seven straight wins, but lost to Louisville and struggled against Austin Peay. In Lexington, that qualifies as a major slump.

"How do you think the game will go?" one local store owner was asked on the eve of the game.

"Oh, we'll get killed," said the merchant, a big Kentucky fan. "We're playing terrible."

"Haven't you only lost one game?" she was asked.

"Well, yes," she said, "but a couple of our wins have been really ugly."

Such are the standards in Lexington, where simply winning isn't always enough to pacify the rabid fan base. Over 23,000 fans will pack into Rupp Arena on Saturday, making it the most cavernous venue the Heels will play in during the regular season. Even a couple of the Tar Heel players, who play their home games in the 21,750-seat Smith Center and are therefore ordinarily unimpressed by opposing facilities, comment on Rupp's vastness as they go through a shootaround after arriving in Lexington on Friday afternoon. Both Jawad Williams and Sean May participate in the brief session intended to get the team familiar with the shooting backgrounds in the arena, and both expect to play in the next day's nationally televised contest.

If Rupp was impressive when empty, it is even more intimidating when packed with thousands of Wildcat nuts in royal blue. Their trip to Lexington two years before made such an impact on members of the Carolina program that Athletic Director Dick Baddour accompanies the team to get a firsthand look at the Rupp atmosphere, the pregame introductions, and the use of video boards. Before Kentucky's starting lineup is introduced, the arena is darkened. When the lights are cut at exactly noon, the arena is in total darkness except for the pulsating, siren-like blue light coming from team earrings worn by hundreds of female Kentucky fans. Roving spotlights and fireworks are also employed. Not coincidentally, when Carolina plays its next home game four days later in Chapel Hill, the Tar Heel marketing department has tweaked their pregame routine: thumping rap music now plays from the time pregame introductions are finished until the tip-off.

Whether it's the music, the fans, the flashing earrings, or just a simple lack of preparation, Carolina begins the game atrociously. The first sign that something is amiss comes when the usually velvet-handed Sean May fumbles a pass from Raymond Felton out of bounds in the game's first 10 seconds. The next 3 minutes are a snapshot of how not to play Roy Williams-style basketball. Felton throws the ball away again on the next possession, which is followed by Kentucky's Kelenna Azubuike out-hustling Jawad Williams downcourt for an easy dunk. Felton loses the ball again; Rashad McCants lazily boxes out Erik Daniels and is beaten for a layup; Melvin Scott turns the ball over; and Azubuike scores on yet another offensive rebound. May caps the miserable series by throwing an inbounds pass to McCants, who is running upcourt and not looking at May. UK's Gerald Fitch easily intercepts the pass and nails a three-pointer, giving Kentucky a 10–2 lead in less than 4 minutes.

Roy Williams is undergoing a slow burn on the Tar Heel sideline as his team turns in its worst minutes of the season. Finally, when McCants jacks up an ill-advised three-pointer that caroms off the backboard, the head coach reaches for the hook. He sends in substitutes for May, Williams, and Scott. Then, when the referees pause before allowing the Wildcats to inbound the ball, the Carolina coach decides to make a wholesale change and sends in Reyshawn Terry for McCants and little-used Jesse Holley for Felton. It is the first time all season he has substituted five players at one time, and it leaves the Heels with a makeshift lineup that includes one junior, two sophomores, and two freshmen. At that moment, no player on the floor for Carolina is averaging more than 7 points per game. Holley, who is left to run the team in Felton's absence, missed over thirty practices at the beginning of the year because of football commitments.

The substitutes get off to an inauspicious beginning when Terry falls flat on his face with the basketball, Carolina's sixth turnover in just over 4 minutes. That turnover leads to a television timeout, during which Roy Williams is as animated in the team huddle as he will be all season.

Rather than spending time with his clipboard diagramming plays and strategies as he usually does during timeouts, Williams devotes the entire 2 minutes to an emotional plea for effort.

His bench players respond. When play resumes, Holley dives into the crowd to save a loose ball and Manuel blocks a jumper. Holley nearly gets another steal at midcourt, and by the time the starters return to the game with 14:27 left in the half, Carolina's deficit is just 8 points. During nearly 2 minutes of action, Williams's questionable lineup has played Kentucky evenly.

Suitably chastised, the Carolina regulars immediately begin to chip away at the lead. Jawad Williams converts a three-point play to draw the Heels within 1. The Heels launch an 11–0 run, capped by a Sean May dunk and David Noel layup, to provide a 15–12 cushion. Kentucky plays halting offense for the rest of the half, scoring just 8 points over the stanza's final 16 minutes after scoring 12 in the first 4 minutes. The Heels aren't much more efficient, but they slowly edge out to a 28–20 halftime advantage with 11 points from Melvin Scott. The main drama of the first half, however, surrounds McCants. After returning to the game with the starters, he is immediately benched after making lazy plays three more times during the first half. After the third occasion, Williams sits his star sophomore for 2 minutes and then reinserts him with a little over 1:30 remaining. Less than 30 seconds later, McCants throws the ball away, infuriating his head coach and earning his fourth benching of the half. It is, observers comment, almost certainly an unofficial Tar Heel record, and an extremely uncommon occurrence for a program in which the players ordinarily perform their on-court duties with machine-like precision.

Despite the sideline fireworks, the Carolina locker room is calm during halftime. Williams's regular routine is to give the players the first 5 minutes of the 15-minute break to themselves. Some change jerseys or get medical treatment. While the players are preparing for the second half, the coaches meet in a separate room to review the first half. With 10 minutes left in halftime, team manager Eric Hoots notifies Williams of the time. The head coach enters the locker room and delivers the points he wants to emphasize before asking assistants Joe Holladay, Steve Robinson, and Jerod Haase to add their input. As halftime runs out,

Williams sums up his message in an orderly way before sending his team back on the floor. While the Carolina staff calmly follow their normal procedures, down the hall UK coach Tubby Smith blisters his squad, berating the players for lackadaisical effort and poor offensive execution.

His Wildcats execute like a Texas jury in the opening minutes of the second half, aided by a complete Carolina defensive breakdown. One of the most basic plays in college basketball is the high pick-and-roll, which features a big man setting a screen near the top of the key for the point guard or shooting guard. The guard dribbles around the big man while his defender is impeded by the screen, forcing the defense to come up with a way of preventing the guard from dribbling straight down the lane. There are various ways to defend the play, but the method Roy Williams teaches is for the Tar Heel big man to step out around the screen and provide some interference for the dribbler. Stepping out usually causes just enough hesitation to allow the Carolina guard to get back into defensive position, and the move is thwarted.

But after the teams trade baskets to open the half, Kentucky's Gerald Fitch gets a high screen. Sean May fails to step out, Raymond Felton is occupied by the screen, and Fitch saunters down the lane for an easy layup.

"I think we've worked on covering the screen on the ball more than anyone in America," Roy Williams will say after the game. "But we didn't guard it very well. . . . We need to be able to guard people and not lose our man."

Sensing a flaw in the Carolina defense, the Wildcats score their next three baskets on layups. The Heels continue not to defend the high screen well, and after the flurry of point-blank buckets, Gerald Fitch hits two straight jumpers off of screens. McCants shows a flash of energy with a layup and a blocked shot that leads to a three-point play by Scott, but then suffers his fifth benching of the game when he pulls down an offensive rebound and then holds it too casually, allowing UK point guard Cliff Hawkins to swat it out of bounds off McCants's leg. The Tar Heel sophomore returns to the bench and hunches over, just feet from where his father is seated in the first row of fans, next to Roy Williams's wife, Wanda. James McCants spends most of the frustrating game yelling at his son and the head coach. After the game, he will shout at his son and the coach as they leave the court and then proclaim loudly into his cell phone that the Carolina coaches gave away the game by sitting their best player (in his opinion, of course, Rashad McCants) on the bench. His son agrees, and will later say that being yanked in and out of the game prevented him from getting into the flow of the game. A writer will opine in the next day's newspaper that Williams may have cost his team the game by leaving McCants on the bench; Williams believes he gave his team a better chance to win by benching an inconsistent player. Meanwhile, Fitch, who made just two of eight field goals in the first half, has caught fire against Carolina's ineffective defense; by the time he strokes another three-pointer with 13 minutes left, Kentucky has tied the game at 37 and the Rupp Arena crowd—which booed the team off the floor at halftime—is rocking.

His team completely unable to defend the screen on the ball, Roy Williams calls for a zone defense. It is a rare move for Williams, who does not consider himself a good zone coach and who feels that it slows the game down too much to be effective in his fast-paced system. But it also seems to be the only way the Tar Heels can stop the pick-and-roll. But Carolina does not play the zone very well, and Kentucky builds a 6-point advantage. UNC goes back to man-to-man, whereupon Hawkins almost immediately beats Felton with a high screen that provides him with an easy layup. When after the next Carolina basket Felton fails to signal the Tar Heel defense—a point that has been repeatedly pounded home to him—Williams clenches his fists and storms up and down the UNC sideline. He instantly replaces Felton with walk-on senior Damien Price, who will play the first meaningful minutes of his Tar Heel career. Price plays solidly in the extremely hostile environment, even capably defending the pick-and-roll and picking up an assist on a Reyshawn Terry three-pointer.

Felton returns to the game with 5:17 left after almost 4 minutes on the bench, but the game's closing minutes are a hodgepodge of missed opportunities, turnovers, and casual defense. McCants eventually is benched for the game's final 3:25, but he is hardly the only offender, just the most noticeable. The Heels close the Kentucky lead to 57–56 with less than a minute to play on a Felton three-pointer, but on the next possession the Wildcats go back to the play that has worked so well for them throughout the half—the high screen. As the game clock ticks below 20 seconds and the shot clock melts below 5, Gerald Fitch gets the ball as Chuck Hayes sets a screen for him. May steps out to defend the play, one of the first times all afternoon the Heels have executed their defense correctly. Jackie Manuel also extends his spidery arms to try and distract Fitch, but he is a breath too late, and Fitch fires a three-pointer over the two Carolina defenders that finds the bottom of the net, giving Kentucky an insurmountable 4-point lead with just seconds remaining. Just for good measure, the Heels commit a turnover on their final possession, as Felton's entry pass to May is swatted away.

The postgame press conference, by Roy Williams's standards, is profane. The Carolina coach utters five *frickin's*, three *damns*, two *craps*, one *hell,* and one *dad-gum* in less than ten minutes of describing his team's effort. He has coached his new team for ten games and has won eight of them. But as the Heels board their charter flight back to Chapel Hill, there is an air of uncertainty not befitting one of the best fifteen college basketball teams in America.

The next day's team meeting at the Smith Center takes place after the squad participates in another Roy Williams-imported tradition, when nearly 100 Special Olympics athletes arrive for a two-hour basketball clinic. At first, the timing seems awkward, since the previous day's loss is still fresh. But the clinic also serves to illustrate a point Williams makes after every game; part of the team's postgame routine includes a reminder from the head coach of how fortunate the players are to be college basketball players. At times, the reminder rolls off the squad as mere words, but today as the players watch the sheer joy of their guests at the chance to shoot a few hoops on the Smith Center court, smiles slowly begin to spread. Jawad Williams and senior walk-on Jonathan Miller are the team's best coaches, as they are on a first-name basis with all of their charges within minutes of meeting them. Even McCants, whose benching is the subject of several Sunday morning newspaper articles, flashes a few smiles.

There are no smiles, however, once the clinic is over. The Heels meet for over two hours to review the Kentucky game tape, a meeting Jawad Williams will later call "sad" because of the legion of missed opportunities they see on the video. Their head coach writes three points of emphasis on the board in the locker room: transition defense, failure to get to the boards, and pride. The first two are physical failures, and the cause of numerous Wildcat points the day before. The third problem is mental and will determine the course of the rest of the season. Four future opponents are ranked in the top ten in the latest Associated Press poll, in which the Heels have fallen to twelfth. The result of any further efforts like the one against Kentucky would be simple: numerous defeats and, by Carolina standards, a catastrophic season.

In addition to the team meeting, Williams and McCants get together for an individual session. The head coach knows that his hot-shooting sophomore is not a trusting individual. In some ways, it almost seems McCants has been testing Williams, trying to see how far he can push him before the head coach breaks. That's what happened last season, when Doherty snapped too often and ruined any chance of a decent relationship with McCants. But Williams handles it differently. He tells his precocious player that he believes in him and that if McCants stays four years, he'll accompany him to the green room at the NBA Draft, something he has never done before with any of his players.

It is exactly what McCants needs to hear. He can cite only rare instances from his basketball career—his prep school in New Hampton was one of them—when he felt that his coach cared about him off the court no matter how many points he was scoring. Although it sounds strange, he sees in his head coach a bit of a kindred soul. The two men have different ways of responding to losing, but more than perhaps anyone else in the program, they both abhor defeat.

"I think he thinks his competitiveness is greater than mine, and I think mine is greater than his. But you know how it is, you can't correct someone who is older than you about something like that," McCants says with a wide grin.

The talented sophomore follows the meeting with two of the best practices of his career on Monday and Tuesday. Last season, he likely would have retreated into his shell after a poor performance and a meeting with the coaches. Under the new staff, however, he blossoms.

While many in the outside world speculate about the relationship between Williams and McCants, their private talk has rendered that a moot point within the team. What is not moot, however, is the head coach's overall frustration with his team's effort the previous day. McCants was simply the most visible offender. The game tape reveals that almost every player on the team shares in the blame for dropping another winnable game.

"I've been fortunate, spoiled rotten, the past several years, because coaching has been an easy gig," Williams says in the aftermath of the UK loss. "Right now I'm as frustrated as I've ever been in my life. . . . It's not supposed to be easy. Sometimes we act like things are supposed to be given to us. I want my team to want to win. I want them to frickin' make something happen. I get tired of hoping the other team will screw it up. That's the most frustrating frickin' thing I've ever been around is hoping somebody will screw it up. That's what the crap we are supposed to do—make something happen. We better learn how to frickin' guard people. We can hope all we want to, but we're going to hope right on out of here."

Although much of the post-Kentucky media attention focuses on Rashad McCants, a different player holds much of the season's potential in his hands. Point guard Raymond Felton was selected by the media as the Atlantic Coast Conference preseason player of the year and was a member of several preseason All-America teams, prompting Roy Williams to point out to Felton that Chris Duhon struggled during the 2002–03 season after also receiving the ACC's preseason honor. The hopes around Felton were built up largely during a six-game stretch at the conclusion of the 2002–03 season when he handed out 59 assists, notched four double-doubles, and averaged over 15 points per game. The highlight was a 15-point, 14-assist performance against Wyoming in the second round of the NIT, perhaps Felton's best game of his freshman campaign.

After that season, expectations for Felton were astronomical in the fall of 2003. Few observers noticed that during that same six-game stretch, he committed 25 turnovers, including 8 in a win over Maryland. One of the best ways to judge point guard efficiency is the assist-to-turnover ratio. On the stat sheet, any pass that leads directly to a basket is an assist (although Carolina's coaches keep a more complicated set of statistics that awards an assist for any pass into the post), while any loss of the ball to the other team is a turnover. Under Roy Williams, assists are expected, turnovers forbidden. Most of his teams at Kansas featured two solid ball handlers in the backcourt, but among his new charges at Carolina, only two—Felton and Melvin Scott, who had just 36 assists and 27 turnovers in limited point guard duty as a sophomore—had assist/turnover ratios of at least 1.0 last season. During his freshman season, Felton's ratio was 1.82. Many of his assists were of the spectacular variety, like one particularly memorable play against Clemson at the Smith Center when he finished a fast break while falling down, delivering the clinching pass while horizontal to the hardwood.

It seemed like a perfect match: a coach who prefers an up-tempo style inherits a point guard with a perpetual motor. Forecasts for the numbers Felton might post in Williams's frenetic offense were giddy, and they seemed to fit perfectly with the point guard's unstated plan of leaving for the NBA after his sophomore season. But it takes more than just fast dribbling and alley-oop passes to take control of the coach's new team. Through the season's first ten games, Felton has struggled defensively and is still mired in an offensive slump, ranking fifth on the team in scoring. More than anyone on the roster, the Tar Heel sophomore is having trouble applying what his head coach tells him on the court. There have been occasions during the season's first month when Williams called Felton to the sideline, instructed him on a play or a defense, and then watched helplessly as his point guard ran something completely different. It's not a case of willful disobedience; it's a player who has experienced very little coaching in his career getting used to playing the game a different way.

"Talent-wise, Raymond is better than any point guard I've ever played with," Sean May says. "He can go on the court and do anything. But it's been a struggle for him this year because his freshman year, the coaches just let him go because the program was heading in the wrong direction and they needed something quick to put it back on its feet. This year, Ray is having to learn the little things Coach is teaching him."

The quiet kid from Latta, South Carolina, grew up shooting baskets with his father until late at night, sometimes well past midnight. Raymond Felton Sr. was a solid player for Latta High, a good enough shooter to regularly beat his son in shooting competitions until the younger Felton reached his late teenage years. The son would wait impatiently for his father to come home from work, dribbling a basketball in the family's grassy backyard. Grass has a funny way of being uneven, of spinning the ball in unpredictable directions. At the time, it was a hassle. But when Felton graduated to playing on hardwood, he controlled the ball like it was tethered to his hand.

"Once he was able to play on cement," his father says with a smile, "he probably felt like he was riding in a Cadillac."

But even Cadillacs can go unnoticed in tiny South Carolina towns that exist primarily as a thruway to Myrtle Beach. Ask town residents about the most famous person to come out of Latta prior to Felton, and a couple might mutter something about a major league baseball player who they think might have once lived there, but the rest just stare blankly. That's why the elder Felton, who was probably the best player in Latta history before his son, never played in college. It's why John Rhodes remembers that when he informed his coworkers with the Beach Ball Classic that he wanted to invite the Latta High School Vikings to play in the prestigious high school event, "they told me I had lost my mind."

Felton was obviously a good player by Latta standards. He signed his first autograph in the tenth grade, so taken aback by the request that he printed his name. That's how he signed it throughout his sophomore year, printing "Raymond Felton #20" until he switched to cursive as a junior. That wasn't the only thing that changed during the summer between his sophomore and junior years. Carolina head coach Matt Doherty went to an AAU event on the West Coast in search of big men. AAU tournaments are set up with numerous courts adjacent to each other, the better for college coaches to watch as many players as possible.

As he watched his post target, the Carolina boss would occasionally turn his head to a nearby court.

What he saw was what people in Latta had grown used to: Raymond Felton was controlling the game. He was scoring. He was passing. And more often than not, he was on the winning team. His scoring was proficient, his dribble penetration impressive. But what sent most college coaches scrambling for their cell phones was the way he saw the floor, the way he controlled the game and had an older player's sense of where all his teammates were at all times. Most AAU games are individual showcases. Over on the side court, however, Felton was sparkling while playing a team game.

"I see things happening before they happen," Felton says without a hint of braggadocio, trying to explain the way he sees the court. "I can get the ball on one end of the court and know something is happening at the other end. I pass the ball and all of a sudden, he's there. It's just a sense I have. It's nothing I can explain or that anyone taught me."

When Felton repeated that performance one weekend later at a tournament in California, he wasn't a secret anymore. Recruiting letters, which had been trickling in to the family home, now arrived from thirty different schools at a time.

Once Felton committed to the Tar Heels as a junior, Latta High games, already a hot ticket in the town of less than 1,600, became must-attend events. Fans stood in parking lots and peered through windows, all for the chance to see a teenager bounce a basketball. It bordered on madness, but the subject of all the commotion remained unimpressed.

"That's just the way he is," says best friend Jermichael Wright. "He's a people person. He's down to earth. If you give him the chance, he'll talk to you about anything. After our tenth grade year he went out to all those AAU tournaments and got all those big honors. When he came home it was just the usual. He never boasted about it. He never even told me he won MVP of the Gibbons tournament. I had to find out from someone else."

Felton's quiet good manners go mostly unnoticed. Few people know, for example, that when Akeem Richmond—a Sanford, North Carolina, native who has served as a ball boy for the Tar Heels for three seasons—celebrated his thirteenth birthday, one of the congratulatory phone calls he receives is from Raymond Felton, who excuses himself from a date to make the call.

Although Felton always had good coaches, they were hesitant to change anything about his playing style. His quickness and deceptive strength were more than enough to overwhelm most high schoolers, and any corrections to his play were usually suggestions rather than requirements. He arrived at Carolina as part of a heralded six-man recruiting class that included equally talented prospects Sean May and Rashad McCants, but it was Felton who got most of the attention. Tar Heel basketball fans have a special connection with their point guards, beginning with the patron saint of the breed, Phil Ford, who remains the school's all-time scoring leader. Ford, a Rocky Mount, North Carolina native, was the first freshman ever to start his first collegiate game for Dean Smith.

Ford was a UNC assistant coach from 1988 to 2000 and then served as a color commentator on Tar Heel basketball radio broadcasts, so his opinion still holds significant value in Chapel Hill hoops circles. He went to see Felton play for the first time with the perspective of a player who has performed at the college level and who knows how much high school prospects have to learn before they can contribute.

"Most times, when someone has gotten that much hype before you see them play, it's kind of a letdown when you watch them for the first time," Ford says. "That's not a slap in the face, it's just reality. Very seldom does someone live up to those types of expectations. But the first time I saw Raymond play, I was in awe. He is very talented for a young point guard."

Even Smith, who is notoriously tight-lipped about comparing players, and who as a coach rarely offered any glowing superlatives about underclassmen, threw some fuel on the fire.

"I hate to put this kind of pressure on Raymond, but he and Phil Ford are two of the finest college guards I've ever seen," said the game's all-time winningest coach.

Felton's freshman season earned him first-team All-ACC Freshman honors and he was a third-team overall All-ACC choice. His 236 assists were a Carolina freshman record, and when his teammates and coaches picked him as the squad's Most Valuable Player, it was the first time in the program's history that a freshman won that award.

There was, however, a lingering feeling among some of his teammates that he was the beneficiary of preferential treatment. Some of the sophomores on the 2002–03 team felt that their point guard never received the kind of harsh treatment that they got from Doherty. When, in the final days of the Doherty regime, Felton had very positive things to say about the coach to the media while some other Heels were rumbling about changes, some of his teammates privately said it was only natural that Felton wouldn't echo their sentiments—after all, he had never experienced the coach's wrath in the same way they had.

That ended with the hiring of Roy Williams, who himself played point guard and demands more from that position than any other slot. His favorites at Kansas were steady players like Jacque Vaughn, who wasn't especially flashy but treated the basketball like a newborn infant. During his senior season, when he missed ten games due to injury and therefore played only against the Jayhawks' toughest opponents, Vaughn committed just 64 turnovers the entire season, posting an assist/turnover ratio of nearly 4:1. Felton already has 34 turnovers in ten games, some of which have been against inferior competition. For the head coach, then, the season's first third was less about the varying moods of Rashad McCants and more about the need to get on the same page with his point guard. Preseason reports to Williams about Felton from friends and other coaches were glowing, but in early January, Williams had yet to see much of the substance of those raves. His sophomore is the ACC leader in assists, with over 8 per game, but he is shooting just 41 percent from the field and, after a summer spent working primarily on his perimeter jumper, he has seen his three-point percentage drop from 36 percent as a rookie to 24 percent through ten games. More important to Williams, Felton isn't applying what he is told by the coaches. He still sometimes forgets to signal the defense; sometimes he is instructed to run one play but then executes another. If the Tar Heels are to be competitive in the tough ACC, they need Felton to read the defense properly and kick-start their offense.

"This team doesn't have that person who gets us ready to attack for forty minutes," Sean May says. "I think that guy is Ray. He has so many things he has to control throughout the game."

That control of the game was lacking against Kentucky. When the team gathers in the Smith Center the following day everyone in the room understands that Williams has given them a strategic foundation that should have resulted in a win in Lexington. He has been in games like that before, has won them on numerous occasions. Some small adjustments, such as defending the pick-and-roll the way he teaches it, would have changed the outcome. Williams's preseason fears are coming true. He inherited a team with four McDonald's All-Americans who have been told how talented they are for most of their careers. Those same All-Americans have a grand total of zero NCAA Tournament appearances among them. Most members of the media and most Carolina fans underestimated the challenge of getting those touted players to buy into their new coach's system. Williams did not. He saw, almost from the first day of practice, that he had a team whose reputation vastly exceeded their accomplishments. He brings that point up again to the team on Monday, trying to persuade them that individual accomplishments will mean very little if the team falters.

"We're going to try and do it," May says. "Rather than saying, 'Coach is right,' and then doing it our own way, we're trying to buy into his system. We're young and immature, and it is taking some time. We don't have that senior who has been through it and has been to the tournament. We don't know what it takes. We have to understand Coach knows what he is doing."

The first evidence that the team believes in their head coach begins to show against Miami, a quick team that will join the ACC for the 2004–05 season. The Hurricanes have plenty of athletic talent but very little fundamental execution—exactly the type of squad that a Carolina team usually carves apart. Miami's best player is Darius Rice, a lanky forward who has been compared to Kevin Garnett of the Minnesota Timberwolves. Rice, who hit a buzzer-beating three-pointer to beat Carolina last season, will be the defensive responsibility of Jawad Williams. The Heels prepare their junior for the task by forcing him to chase his man through double- and triple-screens in practice the day before. When Jackie Manuel, the team's designated defensive stopper, commends Williams on his defensive effort late in practice, Williams says only, "I learned it from you."

It is apparent 65 seconds into the game, when Miami is forced to call timeout because it is unable to inbound the ball against Carolina's defensive pressure, that this is not the same team that played Kentucky. Tight defense forces 11 Hurricane turnovers in the first half, including three in a row during one stretch that seems to ignite the home team. Any screens on the ball are met with loud yells of "pick right" or "pick left" as the Heels communicate perfectly against the pick-and-roll. Carolina's base defense is a harassing man-to-man, but Roy Williams goes to his "Scramble" defense early in the game, a frenetic double-teaming defense designed to force opponents into hurried decisions and create turnovers and easy scoring chances. After the game, Dean Smith will remark to Williams that it is the most he has seen of the Scramble all season.

It works. The 'Canes look unprepared for the pressure and the fast break opportunities seem to jump-start the Carolina offense. "It's the first time this year that I've felt like our defense controlled part of the game," Williams says later. "Against some other teams we've played, our athletic gifts controlled the game, because we were just more athletic and talented than they were. But our defense against Miami controlled the game."

The fast tempo created by the Scramble leads to steady offensive execution. Jawad Williams pulls down two early offensive rebounds and is the recipient of a crisp outlet pass from Rashad McCants that leads to a dunk. Against the Wildcats, the offense occasionally bogged down as McCants methodically evaluated his options. Tonight, there is less evaluating, less thinking, and more reacting. By the time McCants dives headlong on the floor chasing the ball at midcourt, the Tar Heels are on the verge of opening a double-digit lead.

But Miami has too many talented players to get blown out in the first half. Thanks largely to three three-pointers by Robert Hite, Miami stays close throughout the first 20 minutes despite minimal contributions from Rice, who is being pushed around in the paint by the newly bulked-up Jawad Williams. Eventually, an errant Rice elbow opens a nasty cut on Williams's eyelid, forcing the son of the Golden Gloves boxer to the locker room for some Tyson-like treatment. After receiving three stitches in his left eyelid to close the wound, Williams returns to the court and joins forces with David Noel to hold Rice to 3 points, although Rice never leaves the game during the opening half.

The second half eventually turns into a Carolina clinic, as the Tar Heels race to a 60–43 advantage on the way to an easy win. As a team, Carolina hands out 24 assists on 35 field goals, an impressive ratio that reflects the type of team basketball Williams wants to play. Five players score in double figures, including Jackie Manuel, who notches 15 and also hits his first three-pointer of the season, after which Williams turns to his bench and says, "I still don't want him shooting that shot," with a wry smile. After missing his first three shots, May is treated to some early time on the bench, but he responds to Williams's advice to "be positive" with 23 points and 16 rebounds, the first time in nearly a month that the self-critical Tar Heel big man feels he has played up to his capabilities. Jawad Williams's concussion got most of the attention against UNC-Wilmington, but May's sprained ankle from the same game has hampered him ever since. It's not just hurting him on the floor; it's also limiting the amount of running he can do in practice, which is causing his body to get out of shape.

Jawad Williams, who deservedly earned some criticism for soft play as a freshman, looks like an enforcer against Rice, whom he holds to just 7 points. Perhaps more impressive than that total is Rice's field goal attempt total, which is a meager 8. It's not that the Miami star wasn't making his shots; Williams's defense—pushing him off the block and muscling him out to the perimeter—was preventing him from getting the ball at all.

"I was just trying to keep the ball out of his hands," says Williams, who, despite his postgame modesty, was motivated to face a player considered superior to him by national experts. "I figured he can't score if he can't get the ball."

The 89–64 win is the best example so far of Roy Williams-style basketball. A key component of that type of game is a point guard intent on distributing rather than scoring. Raymond Felton takes just three shots, a statistic that remains burned in his brain for the rest of the season. He has been a point guard all his life, but he has also always been the primary scoring threat. He keeps a happy face publicly but is still having difficulty learning how to be a true point guard.

"It's hard averaging so many points in high school or getting as many shots as I did my freshman year here and then only getting three shots in a game," Felton says.

But it's undeniable that the approach resulted in a solid win for the Tar Heels. After spending several days talking about wanting to implement more of their coach's teaching, the players actually do it this time, and the results are impressive.

"I think we're starting to trust him and believe in what he's saying," Melvin Scott says. "He's a new coach. You can't just say, 'Oh, we love him.' He can't just say, 'Oh, I love them and I trust them.' We've just got to believe in each other, and each and every game we've got to learn about each other."

The Heels are becoming Williams's team off the court as well. The three days since the Kentucky game have seen a swirl of media stories and Internet message board posts about the player-coach friction in Lexington. McCants was very visibly benched on several occasions in the game against UK, and his father provided a couple of juicy postgame quotes to the Asheville newspaper, which prompted many to ask if the Doherty-McCants issues from last season had now become Williams-McCants issues. Last season, the player discontent became a running storyline that was addressed after almost every game. The team's three biggest wins of the 2002–03 season—Connecticut, Duke, and Maryland—were accompanied on the very same day by newspaper or television stories about player unrest.

While Williams is not oblivious to the history, he did not experience it firsthand. His patience for media questions about the moods of Rashad McCants and his teammates is slim, and when a television reporter, who is stumbling through a postgame question about team chemistry, appears to become flustered and then blurts out that some people consider this Carolina team to be full of "spoiled brats," Williams responds with a nearly four-minute answer.

"You know, I think you guys have standards that you've got to go by whether it be print media, TV media, radio, whatever it is. But there's so much in today's society that people don't have to go by.

"I used the phrase on my radio show—and I probably shouldn't have—I said, 'Any wino on the streets of Raleigh can do a Web site and a chat room and put it on the Internet and people think they're experts.' So that part of it is damaging. And things that are being said are damaging.

"I know what kind of kids we have. I know the problems we have, they know the problems we have. I can go in that locker room right now and look at every kid and tell them that I love them. I don't have any problem saying that whatsoever. My son and my daughter, I don't love anything in the world as much as I do them. But you know what? I've gotten mad at them before in my life because of their behavior, because of something they did. If they continue to do it, then it gets to be habits. And I do get really, really upset at that.

"But to say I know what Coach Doherty went through and that we've got a bunch of spoiled brats or whatever terminology you used, I think that's not right. I think what we have to do is you have to get teams to focus.

"Every one of you guys in here, and girls, you know what? You're as selfish as you can possibly be. You want what you want. You know who the most selfish player [is] I've ever been around in my life? Michael Jordan. But he did everything he could do for his team to win. And everybody's got to fight it off. I mean, if Michael had 40, he wanted 50. All right? But he wanted to beat you. And every player I've ever coached has been selfish to some extent. Great players are the ones that fight that selfishness off if it's hurting their team. And that's the challenge of what we've got with this team.

"I don't think they're doing whatever terminology you used—spoiled brats or whatever—but we have been focusing too much on our own individual self. And that's nothing unusual. One of the greatest players I ever coached at Kansas, Rex Walters, I told him a million times, 'You're the most selfish player I've ever coached.' And I've got as much respect for him as anybody could. By God, he was tough. And he wanted to beat your tail.

"So we've just got to do a better job of fighting it off. I don't think we've got a locker room full of bad kids. And what happened to Matt, they're sorry about it. I'm sorry about it. I hate that it happened. They got a bad rap on the press conference when they walked down the hall and somebody told them to come down the hall to a press conference. And Steve [Kirschner] himself said that he should have given them more warning. Every one of you guys look sloppy half the time yourself. Somebody comes and says, 'Get in front of a camera in ten minutes,' you're not going to go primp around, especially if you're not at home. But they got a bad rap and they're still getting a little bit of that. We still have some problems. I'm not saying it's—Green Apples, Green Acres, what was that farm where everybody was so nice? Green Acres—but we're not the Oakland Athletics of the old days, either."

It is a stunning pronouncement for a postgame press conference, which are usually bland affairs full of compliments for the other team and generic answers. It is the first time Williams has publicly talked of his love for the Carolina players, something he regularly did at Kansas. It seems that, in the eyes of the head coach, the Tar Heels are slowly transforming from "the players" into "my players."

8

Roy Williams has many virtues, but subtlety is not one of them. Asked by a reporter to comment on Carolina's upcoming opponent, eighth-ranked Georgia Tech, he responds this way:

"The biggest thing for me when I look at them is that you look down the line at their players and they are a team. I think that is the most difficult kind of opponent you can have, one that is truly a team. They have four guys averaging in double figures, the players know their roles, they are competitive as all get out, they guard you and cause teams to shoot 35 percent against them from the floor."

The implication is clear. Eventual national finalist Georgia Tech plays as a team. Carolina, so far, has not. The Jackets lost last season's ACC Rookie of the Year, Chris Bosh, to the NBA Draft, but have replaced him with an interchangeable lineup of speedy, athletic, high jumpers who run the floor and pressure the ball defensively. Carolina's coaching staff expect to see plenty of defensive pressure on Sunday night in the Smith Center, something their squad has not handled well so far. In true Roy Williams fashion, however, the head coach intends to turn up the tempo rather than scale it back. The practices before the Tech game focus not just on surviving the press, but on attacking it. It is the perfect opportunity for Raymond Felton, who began the season with NBA aspirations, to have a breakout game. His plan—it's not a secret, as roommate David Noel casually admits during the season—has always been to play two years at Carolina and then go to the pros. Felton's family has done preliminary research on his professional future and potential income.

The Carolina point guard is the Tar Heel who has had to make the biggest adjustment since the coaching change. During Felton's freshman season, Sean May went down with a foot injury, leaving the Heels without an inside scoring presence. That caused Doherty to rely heavily on Felton for most of the offense, giving him the freedom to score and penetrate at will. With May back this season, that freedom hasn't always been available.

Against Tech, he needs to outperform Yellow Jacket sophomore point guard Jarrett Jack, who was less highly touted coming into the season but who is among the ACC leaders in several categories. When Williams writes out three keys to the game on the board before the game, one of them—attack and make good decisions when you get there—is almost exclusively Felton's domain.

This night is to be his showcase. Carolina races out to a 9–0 lead in the first 90 seconds, hitting its first 4 field goals and stunning Tech by slicing through defensive pressure. Yellow Jacket coach Paul Hewitt calls a timeout after a Jackie Manuel putback gives the Heels a 26–14 lead with 12:08 left in the first half, but it is just a momentary breather. Less than 3 minutes later, the Tar Heels have stretched their lead to 34–16. Manuel scores 12 points in the first 11 minutes, and for the first time all season, Felton looks like the player many fans expected him to be. He fast-breaks when the opportunity is there and runs the half-court offense when it isn't. More important, he controls the game exactly how

Williams has instructed him. As Carolina surges out to a nearly 20-point advantage, the sellout Smith Center crowd begins to roar; it is a moment when, in the past, Felton might have turned to the crowd and waved his arms. This time he simply claps his hands for his teammates and hunkers down on defense, eventually initiating a fast break that ends with a Sean May basket.

The first half ends with a 53–39 Carolina advantage; it is a nearly flawless stanza marred only by a lapse in the final 90 seconds that included a David Noel turnover and 4 Tech points in a row, which keep the margin from being even uglier. Still, it is a fairly stunning half. Georgia Tech entered the game giving up an average of 57.6 points per game, and Carolina has nearly equaled that in the first 20 minutes.

In the second half the Jackets eventually cut the deficit to 9 points on a Will Bynum dunk, which the Arizona transfer punctuates by getting in Felton's face and yapping. Tech coach Paul Hewitt immediately walks down the sideline and silences his post guard with a zipping motion across his lips. But the second half is notable mostly for yet another Jawad Williams head injury. This time it's his nose, as he takes an elbow from Jack and goes down in a heap at midcourt. He is helped to the Tar Heel locker room on wobbly legs, obviously in severe pain.

Even without Williams, Carolina stretches its advantage to 98–84 by the time Melvin Scott goes to the free throw line with 2 minutes remaining. As the officials prepare to hand him the ball for the first of his shots, a muffled cheer begins in the student section behind the Tar Heel basket. Eventually their words become clear: "o-ver-rated," they yell derisively at the Tech players. It's a cheer that has become a staple of any college football or basketball game when a highly ranked team loses.

It is also a cheer that Roy Williams never wants to hear again. He bolts down the Carolina sideline toward the student section and waves for them to stop immediately. Later he will explain that he does not want his fans belittling other teams or the accomplishments of his team. It is a move straight out of the Dean Smith playbook. For years, as crowds at NC State's Reynolds Coliseum held up folding chairs to distract freethrow shooters, and as Duke's Cameron Indoor Stadium crowd got more and more creative with their freethrow distractions, any Carolina fan brazen enough to so much as wave his arms during an opposing freethrow attempt received a disapproving glare from Smith. The Tar Heel legend believed in boisterous cheering, but not in mistreating the opposition.

Carolina rolls to a 103–88 victory, the first time since 1993 that UNC has scored 100 or more points in back-to-back ACC games. Felton narrowly misses a triple-double, finishing with 25 points, 9 assists, and 7 rebounds. He also engineers an offense that notches 22 assists and just 14 turnovers, the first time all season that a Georgia Tech opponent has registered more assists than turnovers.

Roy Williams notes his point guard's stellar game, but instead of singling out his scoring, he makes a very public note of another statistic he considers more important. "I thought it was Raymond's best game of the year," Williams says. "He was more aggressive and he had a seven-to-zero assist-turnover ratio in the first half."

The head coach is pleased with every aspect of Felton's game— except his defense. Continuing a season-long trend, Georgia Tech has good success with dribble penetration, as Jack continually beat his defender and darted into the lane.

"We have got to do a better job guarding the basketball," the head coach says. "Melvin and Raymond have great quickness and should be able to do a better job guarding the ball."

Jawad Williams is beginning to wonder if he'll ever catch a break. The junior forward added some muscle in the offseason, but that's not enough to protect him from the errant elbows he seems to find on a regular basis. Already this season he's taken three shots to the head, and the most recent elbow from Jarrett Jack caused a small fracture on the left side of his nose. While doctors don't think Williams has suffered another concussion—a second concussion in less than a month would be extremely serious and would perhaps jeopardize his playing status for the rest of the season—he is exhibiting some signs of a "post-traumatic headache," a symptom probably caused by the force of his nose breaking but that could be a concussion indicator. Either way, it's not good for the Tar Heels, and it seems extremely unlikely that he will play Wednesday night when Carolina travels to College Park to take on the

University of Maryland. Later on Monday, he is privately ruled out for the game, although on the injury report he is still listed as questionable.

That changes on Tuesday, when his headaches clear up and he indicates a strong desire to play. Team doctors evaluate him and find no reason why he shouldn't at least make the trip with the team, so when the Heels board their Tuesday-evening charter, Williams is with them.

Recent trips to College Park have not been kind to the Heels. In 2002, Maryland delivered a 112–79 shellacking; last season's 96–56 loss to the Terps was one of the most significant defeats of Matt Doherty's final season. On that trip, almost everything went wrong. Long accustomed to the finest in travel, the Tar Heels traditionally stay at the Watergate Hotel in downtown Washington, D.C. when playing at Maryland. On the day of February 22, 2003, however, what should have been a 45–minute drive turned into a traffic nightmare, and the team bus arrived at the Comcast Center less than 20 minutes before tip-off. The team might have been there physically, but mentally they never arrived; they absorbed one of the worst beatings in program history. But what really indicated the state of the program happened after the game. The bus ride from the Comcast Center to the airport after the game was marked by laughter and joking. No one, it seemed, cared that the program had just been embarrassed in front of almost 18,000 ticket-buying fans and a much larger audience on national television. Some close to the program were stunned by the players' demeanor, but it underlined something that had been true for almost a month: most of the players simply didn't care anymore.

One year later, the intensity of the players has changed significantly. It is matched, however, by the frenzy inside the Comcast Center, a new building that opened prior to the 2002–03 season and features a ring of students around the court and a seating section climbing up the west wall at a 35-degree angle that holds the "Red Army," as the Terps have named their student section.

It is an enviable setup, and it illustrates the difficulty of winning on the road in the Atlantic Coast Conference. At Kansas, Roy Williams usually got at least one or two teams that were pushovers even when playing at home. The Jayhawks have defeated their in-state rival, Kansas State, twenty-two straight years at the Wildcats' home arena. At Carolina, such a road streak over a rival is unthinkable. Of all Dean Smith's statistics, perhaps his most impressive is his over 70 percent success rate in ACC road games. His low-key, steady style was perfectly suited to the road, and it kept his players from getting caught up in the frenzy of the opposing fans. That advantage disappeared in recent years: under Matt Doherty, the Heels won just two of their last fourteen road conference games. That lack of success has dimmed some of the intensity that used to accompany any Tar Heel road game; some of the hatred once reserved for UNC by rival fans is now applied to Duke.

Cameron Indoor Stadium gets most of the publicity in the ACC, but NC State and Maryland remain the two toughest places for Carolina to play. At Duke, the cheers are creative but rarely mean-spirited. At Maryland and State, however, they usually involve some variation on the word "suck" and frequently contain at least some personal tidbit. Sean May, as is his custom both at home and on the road, comes out for the pregame shootaround with his iPod plugged into one ear, but even that isn't enough to drown out the commentary of the Terp students. When Carolina's starting lineup is announced, the routine goes this way:

Public address announcer: "Starting at point guard for the Tar Heels, 6-foot-1 from Latta, South Carolina, Raymond Felton. . ."

Students, in unison: ". . . SUCKS!"

The rowdy crowd—which will be the subject of national discussion later in the season when it taunts Duke's J. J. Redick with a profane chant, prompting University of Maryland administrators to explore the constitutional feasibility of limiting free speech in a college sports arena—is tamed somewhat by Carolina's 10-point first-half lead, but it is still boisterous enough to cause at least one Tar Heel turnover, as Rashad McCants doesn't hear Raymond Felton's play call and goes the wrong way, causing Felton's pass to sail out of bounds. With less than 7 minutes remaining, the Heels' 10-point advantage looks safe, but it is frittered away in less than 4 minutes. The Terps, unranked at 9–3 and with a roster heavy on new players, cut their deficit to 45–44 when freshman Ekene Ibekwe easily dribbles by Sean May for a layup.

It is the kind of perplexing play that May makes far too many of in this game. Maryland senior Jamar Smith, who is listed as almost thirty pounds lighter than May, abuses him throughout the game, consistently setting up anywhere he wants to on the blocks and then powering past his opponent for easy baskets. May's help is inadequate in the paint because, although Jawad Williams is playing—Roy Williams gives the junior 12 minutes of action after holding him out of the starting lineup—he is extremely limited, partly due to a bulky mask he's wearing to protect his nose.

Almost as soon as the second half begins, Maryland takes off on a 12–0 run and eventually builds a 62–55 lead. The spurt is aided in part by Carolina going over 5 minutes without a field goal. Felton sprinted past most of the Georgia Tech defenders on Sunday; tonight Maryland makes a point of getting back in transition and stopping the Carolina fast break. Even when it looks like the Tar Heels have a numbers advantage, two or three Terrapins suddenly materialize to halt the assault. While Maryland is swarming all over the court on defense, Carolina isn't quite as enthusiastic. Smith is having his way in the post and after two good performances last season, sophomore point guard John Gilchrist is having his third straight stellar game against the more-heralded Felton.

Down 8 points with 7 minutes to go, Roy Williams finally gives in to Carolina's lackadaisical man-to-man defense and calls for a trapping one-three-one zone. It pays immediate dividends. Maryland turns the ball over on two straight possessions against the unexpected strategy, and a 3-point play by May closes the Terps' lead to 72–68. With 5 minutes left, the Terps widen the gap to 6 points, but back-to-back Carolina three-pointers, one by Williams and one by McCants, send the Tar Heel bench into a frenzy. This appears to be the type of comeback that fans in College Park have come to expect. Before Maryland moved to the Comcast Center, Carolina amassed a 29–19 record at Cole Field House, usually in a fashion that was extremely frustrating to Terrapin fans.

The boiling point came in 1996, when Maryland was riding a twenty-one-game winning streak at Cole. The Heels built three separate 10-point leads in the second half, but Gary Williams's Terps tied the game with less than 6 minutes to play. Duane Simpkins missed a three-pointer that would have won the game in regulation, and Keith Booth's baseline shot with 4 seconds left wouldn't fall, sending the game into overtime. That's when UNC freshman Antawn Jamison took over. On his way to a game-high 31 points, he scored 25 after halftime. With the game tied with less than 30 seconds remaining in overtime, Tar Heel point guard Jeff McInnis missed a jumper. With the clock under 8 seconds, the ball fell into the hands of UNC's Dante Calabria, who was sitting in the middle of the lane after falling down attempting to box out. He caught the ball and hooked it toward the basket, where it bounced harmlessly off the backboard without touching the rim. It fell straight into the hands of Jamison, who laid it into the hoop as time expired.

Carolina had won, literally, by the seat of its pants. The buzzer-beating loss sent Gary Williams into a frenzy; he demanded that courtside television commentators show the last play again on their TV monitors to determine whether Jamison's shot had been released before the final buzzer. But Dick Vitale's monitor revealed what Dean Smith already knew: the shot was good.

That's the kind of comeback Tar Heel teams used to make with great regularity in ACC road games. No other league team seemed to have such a knack for frustrating opponents at home. No other squad could put together such miraculous comebacks. Opponents seemed to implode at the mere sight of the light blue road uniforms.

This Carolina team, however, is not yet ready to make that kind of comeback, and this time it's the Tar Heels who do the imploding. Trailing 80–78 with less than 2 minutes left, Carolina puts together perhaps its best 25 defensive seconds of the game. But with the shot clock under 10 seconds and Maryland showing little inclination to create a good shot, David Noel commits his fifth foul to bail out the Terps. Travis Garrison makes both free throws, boosting the lead to 4. Maryland misses just enough free throws down the stretch to keep the game close, and when McCants hits a three-pointer with 3.6 seconds left, Maryland's lead is only 86–84. It's a minimal amount of time, but with the Terps forced to inbound the ball under the Carolina basket, it's plenty of time to force either an errant pass or a 5-second violation and then score on the ensuing possession. It's the kind of play the home crowd almost expects to see. Even though the Terps hold a 2-point lead and have possession of the basketball with under 4 seconds left, the Comcast Center is strangely subdued as Nik Caner-Medley takes the ball from the official after a timeout. Caner-Medley looks briefly downcourt, where Carolina has blanketed every available Terp. Then he turns to his left and delivers a pass to teammate Chris McCray, who has stepped behind the baseline to receive the pass—a legal play in the college game. Once he gets the ball, McCray will then have to make the inbounds pass without the benefit of a new 5-second count.

Except that the ball never reaches him. McCants, who is guarding McCray, first comes to a stop when McCray crosses the baseline, realizing that he is not permitted to cross the line. But then, instinctively, he reaches across the out-of-bounds line and swats the ball away. It is a flagrant violation of NCAA Rule 7, Section 6, Article 5(b), which states, "Until the thrown-in ball crosses the plane of the sideline or end line no opponent of the thrower-in shall have any part of his or her person over the inside plane of the sideline or end line." If McCants didn't make contact with the ball, the officials probably could have overlooked the error in such a critical late-game situation. But when he bats the ball, they have little choice but to call him for a technical foul, giving Maryland two free throws and possession of the ball. McCray makes both free throws and, after the second one, crisscrosses his arms twice and mouths "It's over" at the ESPN camera under the basket. He is right—Caner-Medley makes a meaningless layup at the buzzer and the Terps take a 90–84 decision.

The Tar Heels have now played three razor-close games in their last seven contests. They have lost all three. May blames himself for the loss, saying, "I played like a little baby out there and my teammates had to pay the price for my inconsistent play." Some of his teammates agree, chastising him for soft play. Although he shoots 3 of 10 in the second half, he's not the only one with problems: McCants made 2 of 8 shots in the final 20 minutes, Felton was continually burned by Gilchrist's penetration, and Jawad Williams was ineffective.

But it's not the lack of execution that most concerns Roy Williams. The Carolina head coach makes it clear to every player on the roster at the beginning of the season that he does not believe he should have to coach effort. North Carolina is a top-tier basketball program, and he believes effort should be a given at all times on that level. His job is to coach execution, to install the offenses and defenses needed to defeat top-flight opponents. With this team, though, he periodically finds himself coaching effort, finds himself asking his players to try harder, run faster, sacrifice more. It is a type of pleading he is not accustomed to doing. The team's listlessness shows up in the box score; other teams have little trouble making a high percentage of their field goals—Maryland sank 54.4 percent of its shots.

The seeming lack of aggression perplexes Williams. The bus ride to the airport is considerably more solemn than it was the last time the team lost in College Park, but no one is as despondent as Roy Williams. A light snow is falling at the Baltimore airport, which forces the team to sit quietly on the plane while it is de-iced. By the time the jet lands at the Raleigh-Durham airport, it is close to 2:45 A.M., and the team bus pulls back into the Smith Center parking lot at 3:15.

Despite the hour, Roy Williams can't sleep. Instead of going to bed, he pulls out a legal pad and goes through old box scores from his tenure at Kansas. He wants to find out how many times his Jayhawk teams allowed opponents to shoot 50 percent from the field. The results are about what he expects: only three Kansas opponents in the past two years made half their shots or better. In three ACC games, Carolina opponents have already done it twice.

"To go up there and defend like that is not what we want to do," he says. "You can't allow teams to shoot 50 percent against you if you want to win in college basketball. We didn't do a good job of guarding them, nor of getting shots when we got turnovers."

The team has just one day of practice before the top-ranked University of Connecticut team visits the Smith Center on Saturday for a 3:30 P.M. tip-off that will be nationally televised by CBS. The head coach had doubted from the opening day of practice that his team was as good as it thought it was. Now it seems that the players are starting to agree with him. Sean May, always an aficionado of game tapes, views the Maryland tape three times. The last viewing is with his father, Scott, who tells his son, "You played like you were in high school." Father and son, both talented players, agree that May is not finishing plays the same way he did earlier in the season. In December, he was following through; now he appears to be simply throwing the ball at the basket and hoping it finds the net.

"I'm starting to double-pump on my post moves," May says. "I'm not as fluid right now."

Connecticut isn't exactly the perfect remedy for that problem. Its center, Emeka Okafor, is clearly the best center in college basketball and the eventual second overall pick in the 2004 NBA Draft. He blocked 9 shots in a recent outing, and his intimidating presence in the middle is exactly what Carolina doesn't have—and exactly what the Heels' struggling offense doesn't need. Coming off the difficult loss to Maryland, players are beginning to express some doubt for the first time.

"I'm concerned," David Noel says. "Maryland is the third one we've lost that has been so close. When you lose three games like that, especially two in league play, it's tough. They're so devastating. I can't even explain it."

The Huskies saunter into the Smith Center with the nation's top ranking, which they were handed in the preseason and have lost just once since then—to Georgia Tech when Okafor played sparingly because of an injury. After watching film of Connecticut and admiring the way the team plays cohesively on defense and offense, Roy Williams tells his coaching staff that the Huskies are one of the best teams he has seen in college basketball since he became a head coach. That makes them a daunting opponent, but despite the fact that Las Vegas oddsmakers install his team as a one-point betting favorite, Williams believes he has one of his favorite motivational platforms: the role of the underdog. While he's boosting UConn to the media, he's rallying his players around the idea that they are an overwhelming underdog, that only the players and coaches believe they can win the game.

"I preached about how we can win this game but no one else believes we can," Williams says. "I love being the underdog if we're really good. If we're not any good, I don't like it. It's a great weapon if you can make a team that is really good feel that everyone is against you or they're the underdog."

As he did with Georgia Tech, Williams sees some traits in Connecticut that he would like to see in his own team. All five Husky players on the floor remain consistently committed to defense, and their transition from defense to offense is lightning-fast. Point guard Taliek Brown and shooting guard Ben Gordon are certain to present formidable challenges for a Tar Heel defense that has shown minimal ability to stop dribble penetration. Williams and Connecticut coach Jim Calhoun are good friends, and Williams feels comfortable enough with his counterpart to walk onto the Smith Center court during UConn's Friday practice, but that doesn't ease the Carolina coach's concern about the way his team matches up.

There is, then, an understandable bit of tightness as the Tar Heels gather for their pregame meal. The mood is broken, however, when junior shooting guard Melvin Scott shows up sporting a pink suit, pink silk shirt, and pink shoes with a bright pink strip along the toe. The outfit, which is probably better suited to Scott's hometown of Baltimore than Chapel Hill, was custom-made for his high school prom. He'd broken it out at pregame meals during past seasons, most notably before last season's home game against Maryland, when he promised his team-mates he'd wear the suit out of the locker room to meet with the media if the Heels pulled the upset.

Carolina lost, sparing cameramen across the state the challenge of balancing their color levels with a rarely seen pink ensemble. But Scott is at home filling the role of team prankster. He's the player most likely to break into a freestyle rap on the team bus, the most merciless player when it comes to ribbing his teammates. One summer day before the season, the Tar Heels were finishing a workout with strength coach Thomas McKinney when Jackie Manuel began feeling woozy. He threw up in the locker room just across from Scott and then retreated to the training room. To most people, it would have been a sign to leave him alone. To Scott, it was a sign to relocate.

He strutted into the locker room and found Manuel leaning against a wall, looking very pale, and not appearing as though he wanted to think about food any time in the next hour.

"Hey Jackie," Scott said with a devilish smile, "how about a big ol' Big Mac with a large order of fries?"

That's the Melvin Scott his teammates usually see. The one who took to wearing a headband that tied in the back, Sylvester Stallone-style, around the Smith Center during the summer and was immediately dubbed "Rambo" by assistant coach Joe Holladay. Ask Roy Williams about him and the response is a shake of the head.

"Your relationship with your players changes when they graduate," Williams says. "Except for Melvin. He thinks he has already graduated. He thinks he can say anything he wants to say right now."

That devil-may-care attitude can occasionally land Scott in trouble. He received deferred prosecution in July 2002 after police charged him with assaulting a nineteen-year-old woman at Player's, a popular Chapel Hill nightclub, on May 2. After Scott complied with court orders that included a $100 fine and a Student Health assessment, the charges were dismissed. Last season, Scott was held out of Carolina's game against Iona at Madison Square Garden following another episode of poor judgment. Wintery weather was blanketing the East Coast in the days before the game, which was played on December 27. The Tar Heel players and coaches had scattered to their homes for the Christmas break and were to reassemble in New York City. Most of the players got there on their own, but Scott's flight from Baltimore to New York was canceled. So was the flight scheduled to take the North Carolina natives and coaches from Chapel Hill to New York, so the team bussed to the Big Apple. Scott was told to meet the bus in front of his Baltimore home in the early hours of the morning on December 26, but when the bus stopped, there was no sign of the player most of his teammates know as "Pelle." It was almost two hours before he showed up, by which time Matt Doherty was on full boil, leading the head coach to deliver the one-game suspension.

Scott's occasional lapses and constant smile can fool some outsiders, who assume he's a clown. They don't realize he's been known to make unannounced visits to a nearby elementary school, delighting the children there, and he'll sometimes reveal another side to his personality. In fact, it's plainly visible to everyone. On his left shoulder is a tattoo of a pair of praying hands with the words, "Keep the Faith." There is another tattoo over his heart, where you can't see it unless he wants to show it to you. It's a tattoo of a cross, and the phrase, "In Memory of Claude."

Claude is Scott's father. When Melvin was ten, Claude died due to complications from diabetes. That left Bridget Scott as both the mother and the father to six children.

"With six kids in the home, the only thing to do was make sure they did the right things," she says. "I always stressed to stay in school and be the best person they can be. I made time to be there for them."

Before his death, Claude wasn't completely immersed in Melvin's life, but he wasn't an absent father either. In some ways, that in-between relationship made his death even tougher. If he hadn't been involved at all, Melvin would have had no sense of what was missing; if he had been a constant presence, Melvin would have had that quality time. "I always questioned it when I was younger," Scott says. "My mother and big brothers have helped me understand. But it feels like I missed out on some experiences. Other guys have a mother and a father.

"I just wish he could be here now. I want him to see me playing here and say, 'Dang, that's my son out there.' "

Scott isn't physically imposing like Rashad McCants. He doesn't have the natural gifts of Raymond Felton, or the rare combination of height and skill seen in Jawad Williams. He realized early in his career at Southern Baltimore High School that to get where he wanted to go—the University of North Carolina, the alma mater of his lifelong hero, Michael Jordan—he needed to outwork everyone else. Once when he was a freshman, Melvin overheard the basketball coach at Southern, Meredith Smith, talking about how early he got to school. Traffic was bad in that part of Baltimore, so the veteran head coach, who had spent twenty years at Southern, started getting to school before 6 A.M. to beat the traffic. He didn't plan on having a companion. But it wasn't too long before he had a regular carpooler.

"He said he wanted to come with me," Smith says. "We'd be in here in the morning before the janitors. We always had to call security and let them know we were in the building so they'd know what was going on. Melvin did this religiously."

"Guys were in their beds sleeping and I was working, and that was the key," Scott says. "I had to work on my game and get better."

He was never averse to doing extra work. Southern had a drill that involved running the length of the court ten times in 1 minute, with five sets of the drill spaced 45 seconds apart. Completing the running was never a problem for Scott. It was what he did during the break periods that was strange. Other players grabbed their shorts or even lay down during their 45 seconds of rest. Melvin Scott jogged. And then, when players who had failed to complete the drill had to do it again, he ran with them too.

"All of the rest of the kids saw what was going on," Smith said. "I told him that if he would always work like that, he would always be ahead of the pack, because no one else was going to work like that.

"He hates to lose. In pickup games he would take the worst players and expect to win. Sometimes just by his sheer force of will, he would win games he had no business winning. But when he would take those guys and lose, he might kick the basketball up in the air. I could beat him in table tennis, and we always had to play until I let him win."

That competitiveness even extended to sports with which Scott was unfamiliar. His senior year at Southern, the school fielded a tennis team for the first time. A teacher asked Melvin to be on the team because, well, he was Melvin Scott and everybody knew Melvin, so why not get him to play?

Why not? Because he had never picked up a racket, for one thing. Because he didn't know much about the game, for another thing.

Scott joined the team and does about average. About average for him, that is. He went undefeated in the regular season and made it to the playoffs before losing to some kid who probably spent most of his time cutting the crust off his cucumber sandwiches. He was not, however, a big tennis strategist. Asked for his official tennis approach—about whether he was a Stefan Edberg, utilizing the serve-and-volley, or perhaps a more Agassi-esque player, whacking from the baseline, Scott just smiles.

"Nah, I just charged it," he says. "I just tried to come at you. At first, I wasn't going to take it seriously. But then I decided that if I'm going to do it, I'm going to do it right, and I'm not going to embarrass myself."

Embarrassing himself was the cardinal sin, which made his freshman year at Carolina even tougher. Carolina went 8–20, of course, the worst record in program history and an absolutely unthinkable catastrophe for the players and coaches involved. Scott also struggled individually as the team's makeup forced him to spend significant time at the point guard position. Coming out of Baltimore, he was heralded as a shooter. As a freshman, though, he was asked to be a ball handler and fill the most dif-ficult role on the floor. The results were not pretty. He finished the season with more turnovers than assists and hit only 40 percent of his field goals.

Inconceivably for Scott, his role dwindled as a sophomore. Raymond Felton arrived to shoulder most of the point guard responsibilities, and Doherty never really got comfortable with a role for the sophomore guard. Scott's minutes increased late in the season as Jackie Manuel's dwindled, but the overall result was a year in which his shooting percentage, assists, and steals decreased, while only a late-season shooting outburst increased his freshman scoring average of 6.2 points per game to 6.3.

Shrewdly, Roy Williams realized early in the season that a starting position meant much more to Scott than it did to Jackie Manuel. Scott was inserted into the starting lineup for the season opener against Old Dominion and has held onto that slot throughout the year, even through an early-season shooting slump that impacted everything from his free throws to his three-pointers. By the time he entered the pregame meal in his pink ensemble on the afternoon of January 18, however, he had scored in double figures in six of his last seven games and defensively was probably more advanced than the more touted Felton.

His contributions against the Huskies will come mostly from the free-throw line, as he hit all six of his first-half attempts. The game does not begin auspiciously for the Tar Heels, as Emeka Okafor gets a wide-open dunk on the Huskies' first possession, and Sean May fumbles the ball out of bounds a few seconds later. Studying game film with his father does not appear to have helped May. He looks heavy-legged on several rebounds and chooses to jack up an ill-advised three-pointer midway through the first half rather than run through the other options of Carolina's secondary break.

Although their center is not playing particularly well and Okafor is on his way to a 12-point first half, the Tar Heels prove to be as athletic as the top-ranked Huskies at other positions. UConn's Charlie Villanueva rams home an alley-oop slam dunk to give his team a 29–26 lead with 7:30 left in the first half and immediately begins woofing at Carolina's David Noel. On the Heels' next possession, Noel sets a pick for Raymond Felton and rolls to the basket, elevating just in time to receive Felton's pass and slam it through the basket with two hands. As is his style, Noel declines to return the trash talk.

The effort that Williams so badly wanted to see in College Park is evident against Connecticut. Jawad Williams, who is wearing a new, custom-made mask to protect his broken nose, looks considerably more comfortable despite a pesky head cold that is complicating his recovery. Williams even takes a charge on Connecticut's Denham Brown late in the half after Carolina builds a 38–36 advantage with under 4 minutes to play. At this point in the game the Heels have let several previous opponents work their way back into the game: Cleveland State closed the first half with a rush, as did Maryland. This time, though, the blitzkrieg comes from the other direction. Carolina closes the half on a 12–0 run, punctuated when Williams sinks a jumper with 26.7 seconds left and is fouled by Rashad Anderson. Williams makes the free throw, and the Heels enjoy a 50–36 halftime advantage over a team their head coach considers one of the best in college basketball over the past decade.

It doesn't last long. Anderson hits a three-pointer on Connecticut's first possession of the second half, and the Huskies patiently chip away, eventually drawing within 1 point 7 minutes into the second half. Calhoun has emphasized something to his team at halftime: the Tar Heels can't guard Emeka Okafor. The 6-foot-10 center scores 6 of his team's first 8 points, posting up May at will. Roy Williams eventually yanks May for 2 minutes, during which Okafor is scoreless, and then removes him again for 4 minutes in the middle of the second half. This time, the Carolina coaches are not going to wait for their sophomore center to play himself out of his funk, as they did against Maryland. Despite the size disadvantage—Okafor has four inches and twenty-five pounds on David Noel—they go primarily with Noel and Jawad Williams in the post throughout the second half.

Eventually, Carolina proves unable to sustain its first-half momentum. After Noel gives up an easy basket to Okafor, Williams has seen enough and calls timeout.

"I thought we were feeling sorry for ourselves," Williams will say later. "I thought we were saying, 'Oh gosh, here we go again,' and you can't play basketball like that. You have to be aggressive."

His address to the team during the timeout illustrates that aggression. Grabbing a clipboard from a team manager, he slams it to the Smith Center hardwood as his team huddles around him.

"If you want to quit, go in the locker room and take off your jersey right now," he says through clinched teeth. "I'll get five guys out here who want to play. If you five want to quit, I'll just sit down and shut up and we'll get blown out. If you want to play, you have to show me in the next four minutes."

Although Connecticut builds a 3-point lead over the next 4 minutes, Carolina's effort is considerably better. But its post players can't get taller or stronger, which the Huskies have discovered, as they are going to Okafor at every opportunity. Calhoun rests him for one possession with 5 minutes left and a 1-point lead, and Carolina immediately takes advantage. Rashad McCants posts up on the left block, which is suddenly a much more enticing place without Okafor's long arms to bother shots. McCants is giving away an inch and ten pounds to his defender, Denham Brown, but he receives the pass in the post and quickly turns and drops the ball into the hoop with his right hand to give Carolina a 78–77 advantage.

Calhoun calls timeout to get Okafor back in the game. What follows may be the most important possession of the game. With May out of the game with four fouls, Jawad Williams draws the assignment on Okafor. A screen forces the Tar Heels to switch and leaves the under sized Noel on the UConn center. Unable to muscle him out of the paint, Noel has to front Okafor, daring the Huskies to throw an entry pass over his head. Ben Gordon gets the ball on the right wing a few feet outside the three-point line and looks in at the All-American. Noticing the height difference but aware of Noel's immense jumping ability, Gordon lofts the ball perhaps an inch or two higher than he would have liked. That added lift gives Rashad McCants just enough time to leave his man, swoop in behind Okafor, and swat the ball off the backboard. Noel recovers the loose ball, ending the Connecticut threat. When McCants perfectly seals his defender on the other end of the court—with Okafor defending Williams, who has gone above the foul line to draw the big man out of the paint—and rams through a slam dunk on a pass from Felton, Carolina has what seems like a sizable 3-point lead.

It lasts just over 2 minutes. After three Husky layups and an ill-advised Scott three-point attempt, Connecticut has an 83–80 lead with 1:30 left. Fifteen seconds later, Williams finds McCants with a sliver of daylight against UConn's man-to-man defense, and the sophomore guard calmly nails a three-pointer, giving him 7 straight points and tying the score at 83 with 1:14 left. The shot is a perfect example of McCants's classic shooting form, the same stroke that allows him to toss in fifteen or twenty straight free throws during practice while barely gazing at the basket. There is no hesitation in his game, as there occasionally has been when he bogged down the Carolina offense by taking tentative dribbles or holding the ball too long in the loss to Kentucky and several other games.

There is just McCants, the basketball, and the hoop. Catch. Shoot. Swish.

"I think the big adjustment for me was just to play," McCants says. "Just get out there and have fun and enjoy myself. I've been thinking too much and the game hasn't been very fun. When I think a lot, it hurts my game."

Although McCants's game-tying shot sends the Smith Center into a frenzy, there is still a minute left to play and a game to be decided. After Connecticut's eighteenth offensive rebound of the game, Charlie Villanueva misses a shot and the ball caroms off the left side of the rim. Using every inch of his wingspan, Jawad Williams outleaps Okafor to secure the rebound.

During a timeout, Roy Williams diagrams a play that Carolina calls "Long Beach." The Heels used it to perfection in the waning moments of regulation against Wake Forest when Jawad Williams got a game-tying dunk. They will try to do it again in a set they have not used all game.

Against Wake, Williams set a screen for Melvin Scott, and when both Williams's man and Scott's man followed the Tar Heel sharpshooter, Williams was free for a dunk. Against Connecticut, however, Williams sets the screen and Josh Boone stays with him, while Scott is blanketed on the perimeter. Raymond Felton dribbles just right of the key and sees that both the options on that side of the floor are covered. Meanwhile, Sean May is applying a hefty screen to Rashad Anderson, who is assigned to guard McCants. The pick opens just enough space for McCants to catch Felton's pass and fire it all in the same motion. There is no doubt about the shot from the instant it leaves his hand. It spins cleanly through the rim, and the much-criticized Smith Center crowd explodes.

Connecticut has one last possession, which ends in a missed Ben Gordon shot, and then everything is a blur. Raymond Felton—who has played extremely well, handing out 7 assists with just 1 turnover against a good defensive UConn team—rebounds the miss and cradles the basketball on his hip, running to midcourt with his index finger raised in the air, where he hands the ball to team manager Eric Hoots. Sean May finds David Noel and gives him a bear hug. "That's the way to step up," he tells his sophomore teammate, who finishes with 9 points and 8 rebounds. "I didn't do it, and you stepped up. I love you, man. I wouldn't want to be in any other position with any other player." The UNC student section empties in the blink of an eye, as hundreds of fans storm the Smith Center court and celebrate Carolina's tenth win all-time over a nationally top-ranked team. When the band plays the alma mater, the crowd sings along and the floor trembles.

The Carolina locker room is a mass of happiness. Even when the media enter, loud rap music can be heard thumping out of the adjacent dressing area. McCants emerges and heads straight for the door, waving his hand and saying, "Nah, I'm not talking."

Several of the regular reporters exchange knowing glances. This is the McCants they have come to expect, the moody malcontent who is unpredictable even in victory. But then something unexpected happens: McCants turns on his heel, uncorks his megawatt grin, and says, "Nah, I'm just kidding." He will sit and answer questions for almost a half hour, well beyond what is usually expected of a college player. For much of his freshman season, he was confused by the negative rap he seemed to get from the media. But his father and friends have finally persuaded him that for the media to portray another side of Rashad McCants, they have to see it. McCants delivers insightful answers when prompted with legitimate questions and even occasionally makes jokes.

"The press is important," McCants says after the season. "They make reputations. They can't make your personality, but they create how other people judge you and view you. I knew that as a freshman, but I didn't want to believe it. I knew it, I felt it, but I didn't want to believe it was as serious as it is."

It is an astute statement for a nineteen-year-old. He has made the winning shot to vanquish the top-ranked team in the country, the eleventh time a Carolina team has pulled off that feat. But he has also done something more subtle that will go largely unnoticed: he has matured.

9

Team	ACC Record	Overall Record
DUKE	5–0	15–1
GEORGIA TECH	3–1	15–2
NC STATE	3–1	10–4
WAKE FOREST	2–2	11–3
VIRGINIA	2–3	12–4
UNC	1–2	11–3
MARYLAND	1–3	10–5
FLORIDA STATE	1–3	12–5
CLEMSON	1–4	8–8

The glow from the Connecticut game does not last long. Thirteen games remain, all of them Atlantic Coast Conference clashes. In most conferences, a dominant handful of teams have emerged by mid-January and will spend the rest of the season thrashing everyone else in the league. That is rarely the case in the ACC, where even the best teams are usually challenged in every game, and teams move up and down in the national rankings as everyone in the league beats up on one another.

Looming two weeks away for the Tar Heels is a February 5 showdown with Duke. But for that game to have the meaning they want it to, the Tar Heels must win the next four games—against Florida State, Virginia, NC State, and Clemson. That quartet is, in most estimations, the less formidable half of the league; if Carolina wants to have a shot at a league title and potentially friendly first- and second-round NCAA Tournament placements in Raleigh, it needs to reel off four in a row and go into the Duke game at 5–2 in the conference. Georgia Tech does the Tar Heels a favor on January 20 by knocking off Wake Forest in Winston-Salem, bringing the Deacons back to the pack in the league. Duke, at 4–0 in the league and now the nation's top-ranked team after Carolina knocked UConn from the perch, looks like the best team in the conference, but slots two through seven are changeable. NC State stands 3–1 in ACC play, but their three wins have come against Virginia, Clemson, and Florida State, and they are coming off an ugly non-conference loss to future league foe Boston College, so very few observers expect the Wolfpack to maintain its spot in the top half of the conference.

The first stop on the must-win tour is Tallahassee, Florida. Of all the ACC schools, Florida State and Clemson are by far the least interested in basketball. The Seminole administration, led by school president T. K. Wetherell, spearheaded the recent conference expansion that resulted in the addition of basketball afterthoughts Boston College, Virginia Tech, and Miami. FSU's football home is the on-campus, 83,000-seat Doak Campbell Stadium, a brick monolith that underwent extensive renovations before the 2003 season and boasts skyboxes from goal line to goal line and one of the largest press boxes in college football. Their basketball home is the off-campus, 12,200-seat Leon County Civic Center, which is perhaps best described as "multipurpose." When the Tar Heels played there in 1999 the arena was undergoing a renovation that included a restructuring of the upper deck. Construction created areas at both ends of the arena that were open to the outside, and at tip-off time the temperature inside the building was in the 50s—with an occasional breeze. It was the kind of environment you might expect to find in a Division III school, not in the Atlantic Coast Conference.

The Seminole head coach for that game—which Carolina won by 18 points—was Steve Robinson, who lasted five seasons in Tallahassee before being dismissed. He came to FSU as one of the hot young coaches in college basketball after guiding Tulsa to back-to-back NCAA appearances, but left as a victim of the school's lack of commitment to the basketball program.

"I thought Steve did a great job at Florida State under very difficult circumstances," former Carolina head coach Bill Guthridge says. "It was almost impossible there."

As it turned out, he left Tallahassee with a reputation for running a classy program and refusing to take shortcuts. One student in the Thursday night crowd of 11,562 shows up sporting a "Robinson's Warriors" T-shirt from the late 1990s.

The night isn't as chilly as that breezy 1999 evening, but early in the game it looks like the outcome will be the same. Carolina makes ten three-pointers in the first half, tying the season-high for any game. The perimeter output is stunning, especially coming from a Roy Williams-coached team that usually emphasizes getting the ball inside first. But most of these trifectas, at least ten of the fifteen first-half attempts, are "good shots" by the Williams definition: the ball has been reversed, the guards have looked inside or even dumped it inside to a post player, and the defense has been broken down. The second three-pointer of the game—in which Raymond Felton uses dribble penetration and drops the ball inside to Jawad Williams in the post, who then hits Melvin Scott for an open three-pointer—is perhaps the perfect Roy Williams possession and gives Carolina an early 10–5 lead. Shortly after that, the Tar Heels take off on a 21–0 run, blowing out to a 36–13 lead 14 minutes into the game. Leonard Hamilton's Florida State team looks flat-footed, and Carolina beats them down the court for easy baskets almost at will.

The first crack in the Tar Heel attack appears when they are up 40–17. It is almost unnoticeable, but as FSU point guard Nate Johnson brings the ball across midcourt, McCants is supposed to double-team him after he crosses the centerline. But McCants hesitates, and the 'Noles work the ball inside and eventually get two free throws out of the possession. The first 15 minutes of the half have been a freewheeling exhibition of how good the Heels can be when they act on instinct rather than overthinking every move. The final 5 minutes are exactly the opposite.

On Carolina's next possession, McCants dribbles aimlessly into the lane and commits a turnover. Up by 20, the Heels' next defensive possession is abysmal—exactly what Roy Williams has in mind when he says he can't coach effort. Inserted for a brief moment, Reyshawn Terry allows FSU star Tim Pickett to drive easily past him to the basket. Sean May rotates over late, and instead of moving his feet to get into position, swipes at Pickett harmlessly as he takes a shot. The ball goes in, May is called for a foul, and suddenly the previously disinterested Leon County Civic Center crowd is paying attention again.

Florida State trims its deficit from 21 points with 2:30 left in the half to 16 points with 4.5 seconds to play. The time left on the arena clock seems insignificant, especially with the 'Noles inbounding the ball under the Carolina basket, which means Seminole point guard Todd Galloway will have to go the full length of the court. A similar situation happened earlier in the season in a Texas-Providence game at Providence, as Texas's P. J. Tucker (a North Carolina native who Roy Williams likely would have pursued) went the length of the court to win the game. After watching that highlight, Williams mentioned it to his team the next day in practice. "That will never happen against us," he told them. "Someone would run at him."

Galloway catches the inbounds pass roughly 91 feet from his basket and turns on the jets, dribbling fiercely up the right side. Felton, who never has time to get into a defensive stance and is too upright to make any kind of resistance, watches Galloway pull even with him and then, as he reaches the three-point line with a second remaining, take the ball forcefully to the basket. Sean May, Jackie Manuel, and David Noel all fail to provide any kind of help. The red light around the backboard comes on, Galloway lays the ball into the basket, and no one is quite sure what happened.

Technically, the red light is supposed to signal the end of the period in college basketball. But as official Ted Valentine reviews the television replay, which he is allowed to do in end-of-half situations, he notices that there is still time remaining on the clock when the light illuminates. ACC arenas are supposed to be the height of modern technology, but obviously something has failed—the light and clock are out of sync. If it's going to happen anywhere, it's bound to happen in Tallahassee. Valentine awards the Seminoles the basket, leaving Carolina with a 14-point lead at the break.

Roy Williams does not wait around to see the conclusion of Valentine's deliberation. The moment Galloway drops the ball into the hoop, he stalks off the court, as Felton swings his arms in frustration. Carolina boasts a double-digit halftime lead, but as the players leave the court, they look like a team in trouble. There is no screaming in the locker room, no berating the team for the poor defense that allowed Florida State to make 54 percent of their shots in the first half. But the frustration is evident.

As the second half begins, the perils of the three-point proficiency early in the game become obvious. Almost 50 percent of their first-half field goal attempts were trifectas, and the Heels have zoned in on a perimeter attack. McCants takes a three-pointer that is probably a good shot, but comes so early in the possession that a better shot might have opened up. Florida State cuts its deficit to just 10 points 2 minutes into the half, but Carolina appears to have weathered the storm when they stretch the advantage back to 69–52 with 11 minutes to play.

The next 660 seconds are unlike any ever played in Tar Heel basketball history. The 17-point advantage melts away, slowly at first and then in a rush. Byron Sanders misses a dunk that might have been the final dagger, and then David Noel, too unselfish with a fast break opportunity, passes to Jackie Manuel, who misses a wild layup. By the time Noel fumbles the ball out of bounds with 9 minutes left, FSU is within 12 and Pickett is egging on the Seminole crowd, which, lubed by liberal alcohol sales—the Civic Center is the only arena in the ACC where beer is sold—is coming to life.

Roy Williams, sensing the game is slipping away, brings his team out of the usual man-to-man into a zone defense, but Pickett hits a three-pointer to bring FSU within single digits. With 8 minutes left, the advantage is down to 7 and Carolina has the ball. The Tar Heels wait until the shot clock dwindles under 10 seconds, and then Melvin Scott penetrates into the lane. As the entire Seminole defense collapses on him, he dishes to Sean May with the shot clock down to 2 seconds. Instead of going straight up with the ball immediately, however, May cocks the ball behind his head for a more forceful slam dunk. That hesitation costs him—the shot clock expires before he can release the ball, and the basket is negated.

It is ironic, because for most of the second half May has been playing too soft, laying the ball up when he should have been dunking and allowing FSU freshman Alexander Johnson to push him around on both offense and defense. Although he publicly dismisses speculation that the ankle he sprained earlier in the season is causing him problems, the truth is that the injury is limiting his ability to lift off the ground, and that combined with his physical condition—the coaching staff limits his sprints in practice due to fears about him re-injuring the foot he fractured last season—has made him a very different player than the dominant force he was early in the season. Now, the one time that the Heels actually need him to lay it up instead of dunking, he goes with the dunk and the basket does not count.

Still, despite all the misplays and offensive and defensive struggles, a 24-point first-half lead and 17-point second-half advantage are too sizable to immediately dissolve. Even with 1:30 left, the Heels appear to have the game well in hand, especially after FSU throws the ball away.

Carolina ball, 3-point lead, less than 90 seconds to go. This is the kind of game a Tar Heel basketball team—and a Roy Williams-coached team—always wins. But the lasting effects of the early perimeter success, which Williams will call "fool's gold" after the game, have yet to inflict their final damage. Maybe Melvin Scott is still coasting off his four first-half three-pointers. Maybe he loses track of the shot clock. Maybe he is frustrated by May's inability to get open against Johnson in the post. Maybe he has a high school flashback to Southern Baltimore High. Whatever happens, it leads to disaster. Scott jacks up an extremely ill-advised, contested three-pointer from 21 feet away that doesn't come close. The ball goes out of bounds last touched by FSU, but things don't improve after a Carolina timeout. May does finally get the ball in the post on an entry pass from Scott, but he tries to lay the ball off the glass and Johnson swats it away from behind.

The game's final 20 seconds, by that point, seem preordained. Down by 3, Florida State's Galloway dribbles through the lane and then flares toward the right wing. His defender, Felton, falls down. May is the next-closest Tar Heel, but instead of helping on a three-point shooter—the only type of shot that can tie the game—he collapses inside on Johnson. Left with a remarkably open shot, Galloway drains it and ties the score. There are 7.2 seconds left, but unlike the Semi-noles—who got a layup in 4.5 seconds at the end of the first half—

Carolina settles for a three-pointer by McCants with 3 seconds left that bounds off the rim. Even after making the tying shot, Galloway has the presence of mind to harass Felton into giving up the ball rather than taking it all the way to the hoop. If it weren't so exasperating, the play would probably make Roy Williams smile.

The overtime almost seems unnecessary. Carolina takes nine field goal attempts in the extra session, all of them from beyond the three-point line. Only one of them connects, and FSU rides a tidal wave of adrenaline to a 90–81 victory. Williams breaks his second clipboard in as many games during a timeout with 1 minute left while delivering a "Don't give up" message to his team, but by then it is too late. Tim Pickett, who is guarded primarily by Scott—who had impressed the Tar Heel staff with his recent defensive improvements—finishes with 30 points.

It is one of the most stunning collapses in Carolina hoops history. The only immediate comparison is a home game against Maryland in 1997, when a Dean Smith-coached team that included Antawn Jamison, Vince Carter, Ed Cota, and Shammond Williams blew a 22-point lead with 14:24 left and were outscored 41–9 over the remainder of the game, losing an 85–75 decision. That Maryland team, though, was formidable. This is a Florida State squad that entered play having lost four straight games and appeared to be ticketed for the ACC cellar.

Even scarier: the Maryland loss was not the low point for the 1997 team. That came in its next game, when it lost a 75–63 game to Virginia and there was an shouting match audible to outside bystanders in the Carolina locker room after the game.

There is no shouting in the Tar Heel locker room this time. Roy Williams has been frustrated by this team, he has been disappointed. Now, he is simply mad. Florida State is the third ACC team in four games to shoot better than 50 percent from the field against his Tar Heels. When the team arrives at the Tallahassee airport, security screeners individually hand-scan every member of the traveling party before allowing anyone to board the charter flight, an extremely unusual step for a charter. Shoes are removed, belts are turned inside-out, and the entire process adds an extra half hour to the already gloomy trip home. As the team bus returns to the Smith Center, Roy Williams stands at the front of the bus and delivers a simple message.

"Go to class on Friday," he reminds his squad. "We've got to figure out a way to get this worked out, and we're going to."

Some of the players take it upon themselves to get it worked out. On the flight home from Tallahassee, walk-on senior Phillip McLamb sits with fellow walk-on Jonathan Miller and juniors Jawad Williams and Jackie Manuel. It is apparent to them that something is wrong with this team, that the whole is less than the sum of its parts. McLamb hatches the idea of a letter to each member of the team. He types it up and delivers it to every player. The gist is simple: too much talking has been done behind backs, not enough face-to-face. His teammates agree, and a players-only meeting is called for the next day. McLamb wants anyone who has something to say to arrive at the meeting ready to air any grievances.

After the shortest practice of the year on Friday, less than an hour, the entire roster gathers without the coaches in the Smith Center locker room. Everyone is given the opportunity to speak, and in the next 30 minutes, almost everyone does. When players address their teammates, they point out elements of the game that need to be played better, and most also critique their own games. The overwhelming theme of the afternoon is defense. In many ways, the players want to emulate the play of Jackie Manuel, who has consistently drawn praise from Roy Williams for his selfless dedication to team basketball. "More than anybody else on the team, Jackie Manuel has bought into what makes North Carolina's team do well," Williams says. "He's bought into all the little things. He's bought into complete intensity when he's out there. He's playing with a sense of urgency. . . He tries to do everything he's asked to do. On the defensive end of the floor, even when he makes a mistake, it's because he is trying to do too much. It's never a failure of omission." It has not been lost on the players that Manuel consistently gets the most praise from Roy Williams, and players are encouraged to perform with Manuel's selfless commitment to the success of the team.

As a group, the Tar Heels also decide to eliminate some of the theatrics that have accompanied their games and simply focus on playing basketball. In the past, the team has gathered in a circle around Rashad McCants before taking the floor prior to each game. McCants typically stalks around the circle, screaming motivation to his teammates. It's something the sophomore guard has done since high school, but now the team agrees that it's not necessary. Instead, the players decide to break their pre-warm-up huddle with the phrase they say at the beginning of every practice—"Hard work."

Saturday's game with Virginia is a noon tip-off, which means it is bound to restart the discussion over the Smith Center's atmosphere. At times Roy Williams has been disappointed by the Carolina home crowds. Ever since Florida State's Sam Cassell called the Smith Center a "wine-and-cheese crowd" in December 1991, the topic has been a sore subject in Chapel Hill; more fuel was thrown on the fire when VilCom, the company that owned the team's radio rights before selling them to Learfield Communications, decided to add enhanced crowd noise to the Tar Heel broadcasts. It was a tactic that had been used for years in pregame and postgame shows, but during the 1998–99 season, a VilCom executive decided to add extra crowd noise during the actual games, something the FOX television network did on occasion. (At one point a network engineer was yelled at to "turn it up" during a game.) It might have gone unnoticed except the radio network accidentally played it during an interview with Tar Heel standout James Worthy: listeners heard a regular interview with fans cheering madly in the background. Clued in by his readers, an enterprising newspaper reporter eventually exposed the story, which served to heap more ridicule on Carolina fans—who now, it seemed, needed artificial enhancement. Radio talk shows lit up with calls belittling the Smith Center crowds, angering the UNC athletic department and the Rams Club, the school's athletics fund-raising organization.

Five years later, there are still regular complaints about the Smith Center crowds. Roy Williams was not happy to see several hundred empty seats at the 7 P.M. weeknight tip-off of the Miami game, concerned about the way those vacant seats would be perceived by potential recruits.

It's just the latest example of the head-butting between the traditional presentation of Carolina basketball and the more glitzy pro-style environment many fans and administrators prefer. With Williams's blessing, some timeouts have featured popular music played over the PA system rather than the usual tunes from the band. The band is also now featured less prominently in the team's introduction. In years past, the band was the focal point before the team entered the playing floor in the minutes before tip-off. This season, a video produced by Learfield employees and the Tar Heel marketing staff is played as the team gathers in the tunnel, and then the band gives a short intro before the squad runs onto the court. The last music played before tip-off is House of Pain's "Jump Around," during which Williams can usually be spotted bobbing his head in time with the music.

"First his feet start tapping," talkative freshman guard Jesse Holley once remarked. "Then he looks down the bench and I look up at him, and it's like, 'It's game time.'

"Don't be fooled by Coach. He's been around for a while but his rhythm is still there. If you're around basketball for that long, you've got to develop some kind of rhythm."

Although it sounds trivial, the transition away from the band is not easy. The players and coaches enjoy the popular music, but the band has been an important part of Carolina basketball for many years and is loath to relinquish that role. Williams, especially, is aware of the role the band has played in the past and of the delicate balance between jazzing up the atmosphere and respecting the role of the band. But the desire for more PA music is not just a personal preference. The Smith Center is the only arena in the ACC where the home band sits next to the home bench; in most arenas, part of the home court advantage comes from placing the band next to the visitors, where they can provide a blaring distraction during timeouts. Instead, the Tar Heels have to shout over their own band at their home arena.

There is plenty to shout about in the game against Virginia, as Raymond Felton and Roy Williams struggle to communicate throughout the first half, a situation that peaks with under a minute to play and the Tar Heels holding a 42–38 lead. As the Cavaliers attempt a free throw with 50.7 seconds left, Williams instructs Felton that he wants to get "two-for-one," two possessions to Virginia's one in the closing seconds. With a 35-second shot clock, the Heels have time to take a quick shot before the game clock goes under 40 seconds, and then even if Virginia

uses all of the time on the shot clock, Carolina will get another possession. Felton nods his head, indicating that he understands the play and
the strategy.

Then, as he takes the ball down the court, he calls a different play. As
soon as he sees the play call, Williams drops his head. Felton's teammates
look perplexed, and the possession stretches out much longer than the
head coach wanted. Eventually, after plenty of standing around, Felton
drives into the lane and is called for a charge with 18.8 seconds remaining. Everything Williams didn't want to happen has happened: Carolina
wastes a possession, fails to score, and hands Virginia the last shot. His
mood does not improve when the Cavaliers' Elton Brown scores on a
layup at the buzzer. The head coach runs to the locker room, ferociously
ripping off his jacket before he is halfway to the tunnel.

Virginia shoots 50 percent from the field in the first half, the third
straight half that Carolina has allowed an opponent to make at least half
their field goals. The Tar Heels currently rank dead last in the ACC in
field goal percentage defense, an almost unthinkable position for a Roy
Williams-coached team. The halftime message is simple but intense:
Williams wants his players to guard someone. The team allegedly rededicated itself to defense at the previous day's meeting, and now it is time
to prove it.

Two minutes into the second half, Elton Brown, who at 6-foot-9
and 251 pounds is not a particularly agile player, gets a pass at the top of
the key. Sean May is guarding him. Brown takes one dribble, drops his
shoulder, and glides through the lane for an uncontested layup.

David Noel is stripping off his warm-up shirt almost before
Williams taps him on the shoulder and tells him to replace May. The
lapse earns Carolina's sophomore big man a seat on the bench for the
next 8 minutes of action, but it seems to wake up the Tar Heels. Coming
out of a television timeout with a 55–52 lead, the Tar Heel players huddle a few steps from the Carolina bench. "I'm about to take over," Felton
tells his teammates. "I need you all to come with me."

It is the kind of leadership that the team has been lacking for the
first fifteen games of the season. He hits Rashad McCants with a perfect
alley-oop pass for a slam dunk, drops in a pair of layups, whistles a pass
past UVA point guard Todd Billet's ear, and cranks up his defensive

intensity. In the first half, the Cavaliers were starting their offense 20 feet from the basket; now Felton is pushing them out almost to the midcourt stripe. Virginia commits twelve second-half turnovers and becomes largely a jump-shooting team. That suits the Tar Heels perfectly, as many of those turnovers turn into easy baskets on the other end. Felton plays the second half exactly the way Roy Williams wants. For the second time this season—the other was Miami—the Carolina defense has taken over a game and generated offense. A 26–6 second-half run ices the game, and the Heels avoid a home disaster with a 96–77 win. McCants, surprisingly, has become Carolina's most consistent player during May's slump. The sophomore guard scores 26 points and now leads the league in scoring during conference games at 21.8 points per contest. Quietly, he is also UNC's second-leading assist man behind Felton during league play, suggesting that he is doing a better job of deciding when to shoot and when to pass in a Williams-coached offense.

A winter storm dumps several inches of snow and then a thin layer of freezing rain on Sunday evening, forcing the cancellation of Monday's classes. The Tar Heels take advantage and go through a nearly three-hour practice on Monday afternoon. Their next opponent, NC State, plays perhaps the most distinctive style of offense in the conference. Wolfpack head coach Herb Sendek is one of a handful of coaches nationwide employing elements of the Princeton offense, a combination of cuts and screens designed to create easy layups and open three-pointers. When the offense works, it can be extremely frustrating to the opposition; the constant screening puts a premium on help defense, which has not been a strong suit of the 2004 Tar Heels. When it doesn't work (and it doesn't always work for the Pack under Sendek, who may be the most embattled coach in the conference despite having his team in second place), it can create interminable scoring droughts and very ugly basketball. State's 44.8 field goal percentage ranks eighth in the nine-team conference. Continuing a Sendek trend of road struggles, the Pack is just 1–4 on the road this season, although it is 2–0 in Chapel Hill over the past two seasons. In its five road games, State has hit just 42 percent of its shots, including a 24-of-60 performance in the most recent outing, an overtime loss to Boston College.

The Tar Heels have met and committed themselves to defense. State is not a fluid offensive team. This seems like a game in which Carolina's defensive intensity problems should go away. But then the Heels allow the Pack to shoot a staggering fifteen layups in the first half of the game.

Mercifully, State misses six of them, but they make just enough to take a 38–34 lead at halftime. As Jackie Manuel sits in the locker room after the game, he is told of the Wolfpack's first-half shooting percentage (57.7 percent). His jaw drops. "They shot *what?*" he asks incredulously.

Every player on the roster shares a bit of the first-half blame. Sean May plays well early, racing out to 7 quick points, but then tires and disappears. Jawad Williams gives up a dunk; David Noel and May don't communicate on a screen and give up a layup; and Noel allows State's versatile but non-athletic post man Ilian Evtimov to dribble around him for a layup. Roy Williams tries to rest his starters early in the game and puts a lineup of Felton, Williams, Manuel, Byron Sanders, and Reyshawn Terry on the floor, but the offensive possession is disjointed and ends with a hurried 24-foot three-pointer by Felton that misses, showing exactly why the Heels haven't developed a deeper bench. The only bright spot for Carolina in the first 20 minutes comes when Jackie Manuel picks off a pass and explodes to the basket, taking flight and jamming through a one-hand dunk over loquacious NC State junior Julius Hodge. Manuel, predictably, doesn't hang around after the ESPN-worthy slam to taunt Hodge, but McCants follows the play just closely enough to give Hodge a big smile as he retrieves the ball.

The play is a tangible example of Manuel's phenomenal progress. Under Matt Doherty, he was a hesitant player, shaky with the ball. The UNC student newspaper, *The Daily Tar Heel,* once published a cartoon ridiculing him. On at least two occasions, Doherty told Manuel that he wished he had recruited a different player. Had Doherty stayed for another year, Manuel almost certainly would have transferred. Instead, he has just thrown down a dunk over the eventual ACC Player of the Year, he has the highest shooting percentage on the team, and later in the season he will be the subject of a laudatory cartoon and column in the *DTH.*

The rest of the half, though, is not pleasant for the Tar Heels. Their defense, or lack thereof, has pushed their coach almost to the point of disbelief. "I can't do it for you guys," he tells them at halftime. "You've got to want to play defense. It's up to you. I can't do it."

They are words he has spoken before—words the players themselves used at their players-only meeting the day before the Virginia game. After that gathering, the players said privately and publicly that their intensity issues were behind them. Now they have surfaced again. It's not that State is more physically talented or quicker than Carolina. State is crisply executing its offense, functioning as a team, while the Tar Heels play like five individuals. Against a better opponent, the halftime deficit would certainly be in double digits.

Again it is Felton who ignites the Tar Heels. His on-the-ball pressure on State guards Mike O'Donnell and Engin Atsur helps kick in the Carolina fast break, which leads to better scoring opportunities. Pack coach Herb Sendek eventually has to turn to Hodge to do most of the ballhandling, because Felton has neutralized Atsur and O'Donnell. With 8 minutes gone in the second half, Noel swoops in and blocks an Evtimov layup attempt, kicking off a 10–0 Carolina run. Four minutes later, as the Heels are stretching their lead, Noel leaps out of bounds under the Pack basket to save a loose ball. He fires it back onto the court, where it caroms off a Tar Heel and rolls out of bounds. But just as it is crossing the sideline, Felton goes barreling after the ball and dives headlong in an effort to save it. He is unsuccessful, but it is a glimmer of hope for Roy Williams. He springs off the Tar Heel bench, appreciative of the effort his point guard has shown—and angry that the Smith Center fans haven't suitably saluted it. He gives three quick claps and casts a pointed glance at some of the seated fans. "Let's go," he says with a miffed look.

The State offense is methodical and not designed to come back from large deficits. State is never out of the game, but it never takes the lead again either. Up just 2 points with less than a minute to go, Williams again calls the familiar Long Beach play that won the Connecticut game. With Felton dribbling, Noel screens for Melvin Scott, but State defender Levi Watkins shadows Scott. May sets a down screen and instead of popping off the pick to shoot a three-pointer, as he did against

Roy Williams acknowledges the crowd at "Late Night with Roy Williams."

Raymond Felton shows off the explosiveness that made him the ACC Preseason Player of the Year.

His evolving relationship with Rashad McCants became one of the keys to the season for Roy Williams.

Raymond Felton's 20 points helped spark a comeback against Georgia Tech.

Always emotional, never dull: Rashad McCants against Illinois.

Carolina's students add an exclamation point for the coach.

Melvin Scott remained one of Carolin
best outside threats throughout most
the season

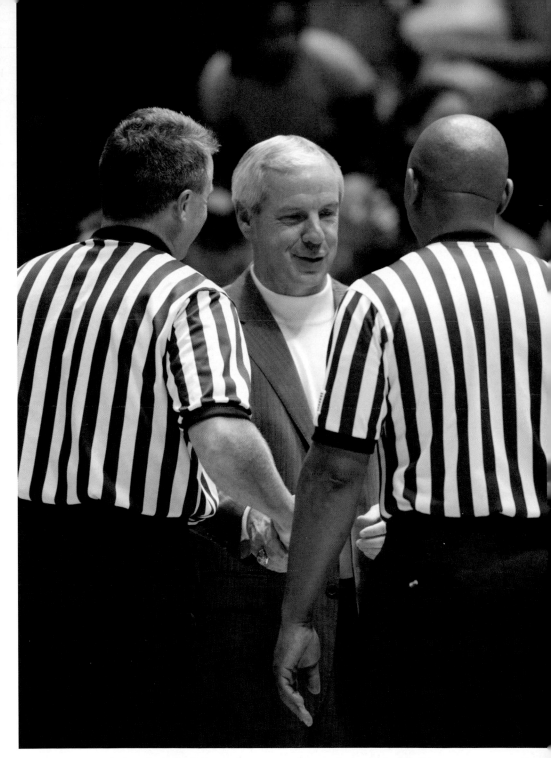

Coach Williams in a peaceful moment with officials.

Sean May put together 12 double-doubles during his sophomore season.

When healthy, Jawad Williams was one of the most productive players on the roster.

"Guard somebody!" Roy Williams exhorts his team defensively.

A common sight: Roy Williams on the move.

the Huskies, Rashad McCants jabs hard around the pick, swats Hodge's hands off him, catches the pass, and drives into the paint to score off the glass with 33.9 seconds remaining. The play gives Carolina a 67–63 lead, and although Atsur makes a meaningless three-pointer at the buzzer to trim the final margin to 68–66, the Heels have an important ACC win.

It is not, however, a work of art. In the aftermath, it's hard for the Carolina coaches to know if they should be discouraged about the first 20 minutes or encouraged by the final 20. It is late January and they still have not been able to develop any consistency in their team and are still having to reemphasize simple points that should have been learned in the preseason. That shows again the next day at practice, when Byron Sanders and Reyshawn Terry combine to botch a defensive drill. When Roy Williams asks him what he did wrong, Sanders attempts to explain away the mistake rather than admitting it.

That is not the response Williams wants.

"We have one very simple rule here," he says, his voice getting louder with each word. "Do what I tell you to do. I don't give a crap why you did it wrong. It's a very simple rule: do what I tell you to do."

For Roy Williams, who rarely turns a sour tongue so directly on his players, this qualifies as a profane outburst. It reveals what he has not yet said publicly: that this has become the most frustrating season of his coaching career. His team has ample talent but little depth and chemistry. Last season, the Heels bonded to get through a soap opera season. But without that bond to hold them together, this season has seen too much finger-pointing and placing of blame. For instance, McLamb, Scott, and Manuel all criticized May for soft play after the Maryland game, and while it might have been warranted, it wasn't what the highly self-critical and sensitive May needed from his teammates.

On a regular basis, the talented starters appear to go through the motions during games. Williams wants a team cut in his mold, a squad that dives on the floor every night, not just on rare occasions. After seventeen games, he does not expect his team to still miss assignments, run the wrong plays, and provide only sporadic intensity. He bases his expectations of his team on their best moments, on games like Connecticut when everything clicks. That makes the disappointment in games like Florida State even greater, and has even led Dean Smith to ask Williams if his expectations are too high.

Despite his frustration, Williams's competitiveness prevents him from blaming the players. He is the head coach. He is the one required to get through to them. That is the source of his frustration, and that is what prevents him from throwing up his hands and writing off the players as uncoachable.

One major problem is fatigue. Carolina has only seven reliable players, and even the best coaching won't make some of the reserves into superstars. Felton, especially, ends some games completely exhausted; his average of 37.7 minutes per game leads the conference by almost 3 minutes. Somehow, the Tar Heels must compensate for the lack of depth, so some of the pre-Clemson practice is spent installing the point zone, a less intense defense than the usual man-to-man that allows a tiny bit of rest. The plan is to sprinkle in that defense occasionally to give the starters one or two possessions of rest each half. Part of what has made Williams a great coach is his complete confidence in his system, which won him 418 games at Kansas. A coach with less confidence—some might say stubbornness—might be tempted to adjust his tactics to try to maximize this team's chances. A greater reliance on zone would provide more rest, and a less frenetic offensive tempo might keep Felton fresher in the game's final minutes. But Williams has won with shallow teams before. One of his first Kansas teams was so thin it dressed only eight players for one game, forcing him to suit up a manager. He has seen the system work. He knows it should work. But right now, it does not work, and that causes him some sleepless nights.

Even with all the problems, his team is within striking distance in the ACC and on paper seems capable of duplicating the feats of the 1997 Carolina team, which went 3–5 in the first half of league play and then reeled off sixteen straight wins on its way to the Final Four. The next game, at Clemson on Saturday, is eminently winnable, and with a victory there the Heels would be 4–3 going into the Duke game in Chapel Hill the next week. Win that one, and suddenly it's a four-game winning streak and Florida State seems like a distant memory.

The Tigers have lost four straight games, three of them by double figures, and appear nailed to the conference basement. New coach

Oliver Purnell, a close friend of Williams's, has nowhere near North Carolina's talent level. The Heels have been spotty on the road, but Clemson's Littlejohn Coliseum underwent a recent renovation that made it plusher and less formidable. Gone are the four rows of students who used to stand on the floor behind the baseline, making every out-of-bounds throw-in an adventure. It looks like a perfect opportunity: solve the road woes against Clemson and then get ready for Duke.

Roy Williams wants the Thought for the Day at Thursday's practice to warn his players against underestimating the Tigers. Printed at the top of every player's practice plan is the daily nugget of wisdom: "Overconfidence is that cocky feeling you get right before you realize you know better."

As Roy Williams sits on the bench 2 minutes before warm-ups conclude at Clemson, he scans the stands. His gaze wanders over to the Tiger band, up through the student section, and finally rests on a middle-aged blonde woman who is fixated on the Carolina bench and is holding a white poster board sign high above her head. The sign reads, "We miss you Roy. Thanks for the memories." A Kansas Jayhawk sticker adorns the upper left corner. Williams locks eyes with the woman and waves. Her duty apparently accomplished, the woman turns, walks up the Littlejohn Coliseum steps, and exits the arena. The Carolina head coach—the man who, when describing his hopes for the State-UNC crowd at the Smith Center a few days ago, said, "Those State people must get their tickets from Kans . . . uh, Carolina people"—watches her leave.

If the sign gives Williams a twinge of nostalgia, the game doesn't do much to cure it. Clemson's Olu Babalola goes backdoor on Rashad McCants on the game's first play, although Carolina gets 7 of its first 9 points off turnovers. When the defense is creating transition opportunities by forcing turnovers, the Tar Heel offense is very effective. But Williams's offense is designed to get the ball inside as a first option, and Carolina's inside presences—Jawad Williams and Sean May—are locked in slumps. As a result, when turnovers don't happen, the half-court offense struggles.

The Tigers enter the game making 29 percent of their three-point attempts. The first sign that something is askew comes with 9:30 left in the first half. Clemson has the ball with a 20–17 lead, but the Tar Heels play 25 seconds of very effective defense. As the shot clock ticks under 10 seconds, McCants knocks the ball away from Babalola. The Tiger forward has to go back to midcourt to retrieve the ball. He takes a couple of dribbles back toward the Clemson basket and just before the shot clock horn sounds, releases a desperation three-pointer.

It goes in.

The Tigers go on to make four of their five first-half three-pointers and 55.2 percent of their shots from the field. May, who was being touted as the nation's best big man in the season's first month, has regressed to the point of simply standing around on defense. Late in the first half, he is called for a 3-second lane violation by official Ted Valentine, the first time all year that call has been made in a Carolina game. In fact May had been in the lane for 6 seconds, standing aimlessly on the right side of the paint. One of Roy Williams's pregame points of emphasis to his team was that he didn't want his defense to continue their disturbing habit of trying to reach around post players for the ball rather than preventing them from establishing good position. May is eventually yanked for allowing Clemson's Sharrod Ford to post up and score 2 of his 11 first-half points; 7-foot Damion Grant replaces him. A fan favorite from Jamaica, Grant is a sophomore whose season didn't begin until the Connecticut game because of a bothersome left knee injury. As Grant goes to the scorer's table to check in, Williams tells him, "You've got to stay in front of him."

After Grant enters the game, Clemson tosses the ball inside to Ford, who has turned his back to the hoop and pinned Grant almost under the net. Ford, who weighs roughly 40 pounds less than Grant, turns, drops the ball into the basket, and is fouled by the Tar Heel sophomore. It is a 3-point play. Williams removes Grant from the game seconds later.

Carolina caps the half by miscommunicating on a Clemson inbounds play under the UNC basket, as Byron Sanders and Melvin Scott both follow Chris Hobbs after he sets a screen, allowing Shawan Robinson to score on an uncontested layup, giving the Tigers a 43–34 halftime lead.

Roy Williams was blunt in the locker room against NC State, telling his team that they had to decide to play better defense. This time, after an outmanned Clemson team outperforms his squad in nearly every aspect of the game, he is less levelheaded. The halftime speech is a high-volume affair that sends items skittering across the floor. The Tigers, a wounded team that came into the game with very little reason to believe they could beat Carolina, have been handed a coliseum full of confidence by Carolina's lazy first half performance.

That confidence continues, as Clemson makes 7 of 8 three-pointers in the second half, giving it 11 of 13 for the game. Some are extremely difficult shots made by a shooter with a defender's hand in his face, but most are not. In one particularly egregious play, Jackie Manuel and Sean May are double-teaming Robinson at the top of the key after he grabs an offensive rebound; inexplicably, both Tar Heels back away and allow him an uncontested shot, which he drains. It is the fifth trifecta of the game for Robinson, a Raleigh native who was not recruited by Carolina. Clemson stretches its lead to double figures in the second half and eventually pulls out an 81–72 victory that is not particularly challenging. Felton hands out 7 assists, but the only Tar Heel who scores reliably is Rashad McCants, who, in a dramatic departure from his early-season behavior, spends most of the second half encouraging his teammates to buckle down on defense. He finishes with 26 points and 4 steals, but he's the only Carolina player to make more than half his shots. Jawad Williams is so frustrated with his performance that after fumbling an easy pass out of bounds 1 minute into the second half, he takes off the protective mask he has worn to shield his broken nose and plays the rest of the game without it.

In nine of the last twelve halves of basketball, Tar Heel opponents have made at least half of their field goals.

"We're lost," Sean May says after the game. "We don't know what we're doing. There's something we're not doing and we don't know what it is. It's eating us alive."

"I'm very confused by this team," David Noel says. "One minute we're so high and the next minute so low. We've never been consistent with the things that we do. It's like, 'What are we?' There are so many things that go on with this team. We never get to sit back and say, 'Wow, we're on a good streak,' because we never get to that point."

At the next day's practice, Roy Williams attempts to fire up a team he believes may be getting desensitized to losing. "How can you not be chomping at the bit?" he asks Scott, Williams, and Manuel. "You guys have won two ACC road games since you've been here."

Jawad Williams has been especially tentative since his broken nose, shying away from contact in the paint and elevating less on his post moves to avoid physical play. The coaching staff hope he will play better without the mask. The Tar Heels simply must have better play out of their post players if they are to have any success in the ACC. May has turned into a shadow of his early-season self. The first missed shot, the first sign of bad luck in a game sends the sophomore center spiraling downward. He has made just 36 percent of his field goal attempts in the last six games after hitting 53 percent through the first ten games. As bad as he has been on offense, he has been even more of a liability on defense, where everyone from Jamar Smith to Sharrod Ford has enjoyed breakout games against him. Roy Williams has frequently talked about May's savvy, but his thinking approach to the game can also work against him when things are going poorly, because he obsesses over every detail. For the first time in his career, he has endured multiple, successive poor games, and he is not handling it well.

"I wasn't on anyone's scouting report at the beginning of the year," May says. "They only had ten games to scout me last year and in three of them I had a stress fracture. Now they've seen me. When teams throw double teams at me, I'm thinking when I catch the ball. My dad has told me that it has to be natural, that I know the game and have to just play, but it's easier said than done."

In an effort to increase their competitiveness, the head coach puts his players through five short scrimmages during Sunday afternoon's practice. Losing still tugs at Roy Williams, but he is concerned that some of his players have become desensitized to it. The stretch of four must-win games has ended with two losses.

Top-ranked Duke is next.

TEAM	ACC	OVERALL
DUKE	7–0	18–1
NC STATE	6–2	13–5
GEORGIA TECH	4–4	16–5
FLORIDA STATE	4–4	16–6
WAKE FOREST	4–4	13–5
UNC	3–4	13–5
MARYLAND	3–5	12–7
VIRGINIA	2–6	12–7
CLEMSON	2–6	9–10

Mike Krzyzewski fixed his eyes on the referee, giving him a stare of disbelief. Then the tirade began, the one designed to point out to the official the egregious error of his ways, the one that—if it worked—might be in the back of that referee's mind the next time he began to signal a call against Krzyzewski's Duke Blue Devils.

Roy Williams didn't see the beginning of the encounter. He had come onto the court to instruct one of his players as a television timeout was beginning. But when he finished with the lesson, he glanced down the sideline and spotted Krzyzewski in deep conversation with a referee. With his team huddled around their bench, Williams walked purposefully the length of the court to get in a few words of his own.

The arrival of the opposing coach, predictably, only infuriated Krzyzewski even more. The two engaged in a heated shouting match. It was the pinnacle of a Duke-Carolina moment. That it happened while Williams was still at Kansas only serves to underline the intense feelings between the two schools.

The above encounter took place in a 2001 NCAA Tournament game at Winston-Salem's Lawrence Joel Coliseum. Observers seated at the scorer's table that day are positive that at one point, Krzyzewski told Williams, "If you ever come to Carolina, I'll kick your ass." Both Krzyzewski and Williams decline to confirm the exact dialogue, but the gist was clear—these are not two men you'd expect to find in the same golf foursome. It's not that one believes the other cheats (Williams has a way of making it clear when he believes another coach is being unethical, as he once did with Florida's Billy Donovan) or that they don't respect each other's accomplishments. It's just that, frankly, they don't have very much in common. Williams is from the mountains of North Carolina; Krzyzewski is from Chicago. Williams learned his trade from the genteel Dean Smith; Krzyzewski cut his teeth under the more volatile Bob Knight. The best-known words to come out of Williams's mouth are "frickin' " and "dad-gum"; Krzyzewski has a reputation for being much harsher.

Williams has more in common with coaches such as Oklahoma's Kelvin Sampson or Clemson's Oliver Purnell, men he considers friends. It's doubtful that anyone would ever describe Krzyzewski and Williams that way. They are, at best, respectful rivals.

And that's how it is supposed to be in the Carolina-Duke relationship. College basketball rivalries exist on a sliding scale of hatred. Some, like the Missouri-Kansas rivalry Williams endured while coach of the Jayhawks, are based on pathological hatred and not a little bit of jealousy. Missouri's basketball program has always been overshadowed by the one at Kansas, so when the Jayhawks went into Columbia they were regularly treated to a shower of epithets and derogatory chants.

In its present incarnation, the Carolina-Duke rivalry is healthier than that. They are just eight miles apart on U.S. Highway 15–501, and that proximity has led to an assumption in the national media that the two schools somehow share a brain, that the similarities extend beyond their terrific basketball traditions to an overall outlook on life. That's not the case, as any Carolina or Duke student would be quick to tell you. The University of North Carolina has much more in common with fellow ACC member Virginia than with Duke. Of this year's freshman class at UNC, 82 percent came from the state of North Carolina. Duke's latest freshman class includes approximately equal numbers of students from the South and Northeast. Duke's total enrollment is 10,800; Carolina's is 25,494. Cameron Indoor Stadium is a sweltering bandbox that only recently received air conditioning, seating just over 9,000 spectators. The Dean E. Smith Center is an expansive monument to basketball that comfortably seats 21,750.

The 1980s saw a new participant in the rivalry, as Duke hired a little-known coach named Michael Krzyzewski before the 1980–81 season. He struggled initially, losing eight of his first nine games to Smith and the Tar Heels. Only a game-tying Gene Banks jumper in the last second of regulation and a Banks offensive rebound and putback in the extra period in 1981 kept him from starting out 0–9 against Smith.

In 1984, the intensity reached its current levels. Carolina was on the verge of becoming just the sixth team to finish the ACC regular season unbeaten when it played host to Duke on Senior Day on March 3. Matt Doherty dribbled the length of the court and hit a 14-footer over Dan Meagher with 1 second remaining to force overtime, and the Michael Jordan–led Tar Heels eventually prevailed 96–83 in double overtime.

Around that same time, Krzyzewski made his legendary "double standard" comment to the media, implying that there were two sets of rules in the ACC: one for UNC and one for every other team in the league. That was the first salvo in a battle that continued until Smith's retirement in 1997. Carolina and Duke played one of the most heated ACC Tournament finals in history in 1989, but it was almost overshadowed by the off-court battle between the two coaches. After taking offense at "J. R. Can't Reid" signs at Cameron that he felt were racially motivated, Smith pointed out that the combined SAT scores of Reid and fellow Tar Heel Scott Williams were higher than those of Duke's Christian Laettner and Danny Ferry—Reid, in fact, scored well above 1300. That incited Blue Devil fans, who felt Smith was using confidential information to his advantage.

With that as prelude, the 1989 final was a classic—an ugly classic, but a classic. At one point during a heated exchange, Krzyzewski looked down the sideline at the Omni in Atlanta and shouted, "Fuck you, Dean," at the Carolina head coach. Reid and Ferry banged under the basket all afternoon; Phil Henderson drew a technical foul as emotions rose and then kicked over a chair on the sideline; and the game wasn't over until Steve Bucknall and King Rice converted key free throws down the stretch. Actually, it wasn't over even then. At the buzzer Danny Ferry almost threw in a nearly 75-foot shot that would have tied the game.

"I don't know if this old man's heart could have taken it if Ferry had made that one," Smith said after his team's 77–74 triumph.

The battles—both between the coaches and the players—would continue. Smith and Krzyzewski would later disagree about the cleverness of the Cameron students, beer ads on ACC telecasts, and several other issues. But the memorable moments between the two teams continued. In 1995, it was Duke overcoming a 17-point first-half Carolina lead (and Jerry Stackhouse's incredible one-handed reverse thunderdunk over Eric Meek) at Cameron to build a 12-point second-half advantage. The Tar Heels built an 8-point lead in the first overtime before Jeff Capel hit a running midcourt shot to tie the game and force a second overtime, during which Carolina eventually prevailed, 102–100.

Three years later, the two teams split their regular-season meetings and were clearly the class of the conference. They met in the ACC Tournament final for a game that showed the true capabilities of that 1998 Carolina squad, which featured Antawn Jamison, Vince Carter, Shammond Williams, and Ed Cota. Jamison was dominant in the third meeting between the two teams, posting 22 points and 18 rebounds in Carolina's 83–68 victory.

Matt Doherty appeared to signal his entry into the rivalry with Carolina's win in his first Duke-Carolina game as head coach. The Tar Heels claimed an 85–83 win at Cameron Indoor in 2001 behind 24 points and 16 rebounds from Joseph Forte. That game was fraught with tension, including the beginning of harsh feelings between the Blue Devil assistants and Doherty. The Duke coaching staff felt that the Carolina coaches exaggerated a late injury to Ronald Curry after a foul, which allowed the Heels to remove the poor-shooting Curry and replace him with Max Owens, a much more reliable shooter. Owens hit both clutch free throws and 7-footer Brendan Haywood also hit a late pair to ice the game.

Doherty's arrival seemed to bring an air of nastiness to the rivalry that hadn't been present since the 1960s. The teams met three times during the 2001–02 season with little incident, due primarily to the fact that Carolina was enduring an 8–20 season and wasn't very competitive until Doherty implemented a slow-down strategy when the teams met in the first round of the ACC Tournament, a game Duke won by just 12 points after winning the two earlier meetings by 25 and 29 points. But with the talent level replenished for the 2002–03 season, things heated up. Doherty and Duke's Dahntay Jones exchanged words on the sideline in the first meeting of the season, a 9-point Duke win. Then, in the regular season finale in Chapel Hill, after Jones popped Felton in the face, Doherty left the Carolina bench to check on his player, who was bleeding from the lip near the Blue Devil bench. Suddenly, the Tar Heel head coach and Duke assistant Chris Collins were in a screaming match, a dust-up that eventually ended with Blue Devil scrub Andre Buckner pushing Doherty. In the ACC Tournament semifinals the next week, Duke assistant Johnny Dawkins refused to shake Doherty's hand before the game.

Although 132 straight games have been played in the series with at least one of the two teams ranked, that level of enmity had been missing in recent years. Duke and Carolina fans despise each other, and the players on the opposing team, but the players were increasingly becoming part of the same elite fraternity—college basketball superstars. They attended the same AAU basketball camps, they were counselors at the same summer camps, sometimes they even went on the same recruiting visits. Many of the players get their hair cut at a local barbershop, 40 Below, operated by one barber who is a rabid Duke fan and another who supports the Tar Heels. It's a long way from the old days, when Larry Miller could make himself a marked man simply by choosing one school over the other.

The Carolina marketing department picks the Duke game as the designated blitz for their "Turn It Blue" campaign, designed to encourage

Tar Heel fans to wear school colors to games. To aid in the promotion, a local merchant supplies 9,000 Carolina blue T-shirts, which are placed on every lower level seat. By the time the Blue Devils take the floor for pregame warm-ups, most of the courtside fans are clad in Carolina blue, and the ones who haven't yet put on their shirts are quickly singled out on the arena jumbotrons and then plastered with a "Turn It Blue" logo. It's peer pressure, but it's effective: by tip-off, only the small section of fans behind the Duke bench is wearing anything other than light blue.

They have very little to cheer about in the game's first 105 seconds. Carolina turns the ball over four times during that period, and top-ranked Duke has built an 8–1 lead by the time Jackie Manuel enters the game with 16:39 left in the half. His task is simple: shadow J. J. Redick, the deadliest outside shooter in the Atlantic Coast Conference and a three-point marksman who almost single-handedly led the Devils to the ACC Tournament championship last year with a 30-point performance in the title game against NC State. Fifteen seconds later, the Heels get their first field goal of the game, a Rashad McCants jumper, and then Manuel takes over. First he blocks a Redick three-pointer, takes an outlet pass from Sean May, and jams home a two-handed dunk. On the next Duke possession, Manuel and McCants trap Redick and Manuel rakes the ball away and fires a pass to McCants for a left-handed dunk. In 61 seconds, Manuel's defense changes the tone of the game and reignites the blue-clad Smith Center fans.

It is a development that nine months ago, even Roy Williams could not have foreseen. For two seasons under Matt Doherty, Manuel was an offensive liability. His awkward shooting form and hurried style of play contributed to a career field goal percentage of 38.3 at the outset of his junior year, and he had six more turnovers than assists during his Tar Heel career. Those are numbers that made Williams wince. Manuel was the first player offered a scholarship by the Doherty regime—an offer that was extended without anyone ever seeing him play in person. In high school at Cardinal Newman High in West Palm Beach, he was quicker than all his opponents and could simply glide by them for easy baskets. In college, the wild dashes into the lane usually ended with a turnover or a blocked shot.

Williams met with Manuel during his first month on the job and gave the rising junior a simple task: play defense and shoot when you're wide open, preferably close to the basket. It was not a glamorous role, and even the head coach thought that it might provoke his player—who as a freshman had said, "When I get my offense going, I'm going to be unstoppable"—to look into a transfer. "If you want to transfer," Williams told him, "I'll help you look for a school." Manuel briefly considered that option, but then decided to stick it out in Chapel Hill. Around that same time, his parents, who had moved with him from Florida to Chapel Hill, moved back to Florida. The senior Manuel had had some occasional tension with Doherty, who he believed was too hard on his son. The situation boiled over in the ACC Tournament during Manuel's sophomore year, when Doherty blistered Manuel for a mistake. His father was seated behind the Tar Heel bench. Later in the evening the father could be heard loudly informing the coach that he should never talk to his son that way again.

But there was an illness in the family, so Jackie and Stephanie Manuel moved back to West Palm Beach. They still made it to occasional games, but their absence seemed to force their son to mature. He arrived back in Chapel Hill in August a more confident, assertive basketball player. In the past, he had looked afraid to make a mistake; now he seemed to know exactly what to do. His dedication to doing exactly what his coach asks of him endears him to Williams, who sees in Manuel what he wants to see in the rest of his players. It leads the coach to look out for his defensive-minded junior. On one occasion in the second half of the Duke game, both Noel and Manuel go up for a tip-in and it's clear that the official scorer isn't sure who got the tip. Williams takes several strides down the sideline and yells, "That was Jackie!" After the win over Coastal Carolina, Williams noted that Manuel was mistakenly credited with a missed three-pointer that should not have been charged to him. He points out the error to Carolina's statistician, who makes the change. It's the least he can do for a player who has transformed his game. "I'm proud of the way Jackie has adapted his game," Williams says. "He's done a better job than anyone on our team of buying in to what we ask them to do." Those types of comments do not go unnoticed by other players. "When I first heard Coach say that, I was like, 'Dang, do

you think I've bought in?'" Raymond Felton says. "I felt I was sacrificing more than anyone on our team, because I was sacrificing my scoring. To hear him say that about Jackie was tough."

Against Duke, any offensive sacrifices from Manuel are secondary.
His primary role is to shadow Redick all over the court. Duke sets endless screens for their sharpshooter, twirling him around at least two picks
on each possession. Manuel follows right behind, a cyclone of long arms
and legs just an inch behind Redick. Against most opponents, the Blue
Devil sophomore needed just an inch to get his shot off. But with
Manuel defending him, he catches the ball and appears to have that
inch, only to see Manuel's spidery reach instantly close the gap. Redick
scores 8 first-half points, but he never goes on the type of three-point
streak that has buried several Duke opponents. The Devils ease out to a
12-point lead later in the half as Sean May battles cramps, but Melvin
Scott hits two free throws with 2 seconds left on the clock to narrow the
gap to 42–37 at halftime. It is as much as Roy Williams could hope for.
Duke is shooting 50 percent from the field and has gotten 11 Carolina
turnovers, and no Tar Heel is in double figures, but they are down just 5
points. The 21,750 blue-draped fans in the Smith Center are still optimistic enough to be into the game.

The Duke advantage evaporates almost immediately after halftime.
The Devils are missing shots and struggling to get powerful center
Shelden Williams involved in the game, which enables Carolina to run
their fast-break offense more effectively. The Heels are not effective with
their half-court offense, but when Felton gets a chance to dash down
the court and create opportunities, they are much more dangerous. A
Manuel layup on the break ties the score at 49 with 5 minutes elapsed,
and then McCants gives the Heels a 51–49 lead with 13:50 remaining.
The teams are separated by just a sliver over the next 5 minutes. Duke
senior point guard Chris Duhon picks up his fourth foul with 9:10 left,
and 30 seconds later, with the Devils holding a 62–60 advantage, David
Noel accidentally drops Luol Deng with an elbow while going for a
loose ball in front of the Duke bench. The Heels dash the other way, and
McCants ties the score again with a layup. Meanwhile, Mike Krzyzewski
has rocketed off the Blue Devil bench. He yells, "He knocked him out!"
to the officiating crew of Karl Hess, Duke Edsall, and Bryan Kersey,

furious that a foul was not called on Noel. During an ensuing media timeout, while assistant coach Steve Wojciechowski stomps around the perimeter of the Duke huddle and screams epithets, Krzyzewski spends most of the 2-minute timeout talking to Hess, who has run across the court to join the Blue Devil huddle. At that moment, nine fouls have been called on Duke during the second half, four on Carolina.

Over the next 10 minutes of game clock, no fouls are called on the Devils, while the Heels are whistled for six. It is that type of occurrence that convinces ACC fans that there is some sort of conspiracy involving Duke and league officials. The suspicion is especially rampant in College Park, where Gary Williams fuels it at every opportunity. It even extends to television announcer Dick Vitale, who is mocked as "Dook" Vitale by some fans (and even, occasionally, by fellow broadcasters) for his constant mentions of Duke, Cameron Indoor Stadium, and Mike Krzyzewski. Later in the season, while shooting an ESPN promo for the rematch in Durham, Rashad McCants is asked to name the three things he thinks of when he hears the word Duke. His response: "Cameron Crazies, Coach K, and . . . Dick Vitale." The ESPN producer gets a sick look on his face and says, "Uh, I don't think we can use that." Duke has won five straight league tournament titles, they seem to punch their NCAA Tournament ticket before Christmas every year, and Krzyzewski reels in top-rated recruiting classes year after year. Everyone is looking for a reason to hate the Devils.

With 6 minutes left, Duke is in trouble. Raleigh native Shavlik Randolph—who picked Duke over Carolina and NC State in a heated recruiting battle—misses a layup, allowing Felton to go 94 feet for a basket and a 64–62 Carolina lead. Then Felton hits a three-pointer, prompting a Krzyzewski timeout. It is so loud that some of the metal stairs in the Smith Center are shaking.

And then the Smith Center explodes. Redick misses a jumper and Felton claims the rebound. At first, it looks like Duke is back in transition to stop the fast-break opportunity. But then Felton, at his full-speed best, jets past Daniel Ewing on the fly to create a three-on-two advantage. After screaming past the three-point line, he drops a bounce pass to McCants on the right wing; McCants soars, double-pumps, and rips through a two-handed dunk.

Some will say later that it is the loudest it has been in the Smith Center since George Lynch's steal and dunk capped the memorable comeback against Florida State in 1993. The sheer force of McCants's dunk gets the net hung on the rim, so officials stop play in order to correct the problem. This allows the Smith Center videoboards to replay the dunk several times, inciting the crowd even more.

Carolina has a 69–62 lead over the top-ranked Blue Devils. There are less than 6 minutes left. The crowd is a blue sea of noise.

And the next four Tar Heel possessions are among the worst of the season. In the huddle during a timeout, David Noel thinks to himself, "I think we made our run too early." He is right. With the team up 7 after a Duke miss, Felton turns the ball over. The next time down the court, Felton loses the ball again, and on the next possession, Sean May misses an ill-advised 18-foot jump shot. It's a shot he can make, but it's not the type of high-percentage play his team needs at that juncture of the game. Duke closes the gap to 69–66 on a pair of Deng free throws. May travels, and Deng hits a layup to virtually erase what seemed like an unsinkable advantage just 3 minutes earlier. Duhon hits two free throws to give Duke the lead with 2:19 left, and then Deng hits another pair at the 1:06 mark to cap the 10–0 run. It has been almost 5 minutes since Carolina put a ball through the hoop.

May finally breaks the shutout with a follow shot, but then Redick makes a miraculous, twisting double-pump shot over Manuel's outstretched arms. With 20 seconds left, Carolina gets the ball to Jawad Williams at the top of the key, where he is most comfortable from the perimeter. He gives a pump fake that loses Duhon and fires a three-pointer over Redick that goes straight through the net.

The game is tied.

Daniel Ewing misses a late three-pointer, and a 5-minute overtime period begins. The Heels, though, are once again stymied by an ineffective half-court offense. They miss three early scoring opportunities in the extra stanza, one of which is a May layup that is contested by Shelden Williams. Duke edges out to a 79–76 lead after Deng scores on the baseline with 3 minutes left. Carolina gets the ball to Scott on the right wing with the shot clock winding down, but he holds the ball too long while waiting for McCants to post up Redick. With the shot clock at 4, Scott flings a 26-footer that bounds off the rim. Even in the heat of the most important game of the year, against their mortal rival, the Tar Heels have trouble executing the offense the way Roy Williams desires.

It happens again with under 1 minute to play, as the Heels are charged with a shot clock violation while trailing by 1. On the ensuing inbounds play, Duke gets the ball to Redick, a 97 percent free throw shooter, on the sideline in the backcourt. David Noel appears to have him pinned, but then reaches around and fouls him. It is a mental break-down, as it virtually assures the Devils 2 points rather than forcing Redick—who is not a flawless ball handler—to bring the ball up the court or get it to a teammate. Predictably, Redick makes both free throws for a three-point Duke lead.

But Duke-Carolina games are rarely decided without an extra bit of intrigue. After inbounding the ball with 22.1 seconds to play, Carolina works the ball to McCants, who is at the right wing at a 45-degree angle to the hoop. He pump-fakes to lose Deng, relocates a step to his left, and nails a bull's-eye three-pointer to tie the game.

Pandemonium ensues, both in the stands and on the court. Roy Williams has a timeout remaining but chooses not to use it. The clock stands at 13.5 as the Devils inbound the ball. Tar Heel players scramble to find their man. Blue-clad courtside fans are euphoric at McCants's three-pointer.

Duhon gets the ball 92 feet away from his basket. Just one month earlier, Williams had told his team that they would not let an opponent go the length of the floor for a hoop, only to watch Todd Galloway do it at Florida State. Surely this would be different. Surely a Roy Williams-coached team would not allow another last-gasp basket. Most college basketball players underestimate how much can be done in 13.5 sec-onds. Ordinarily, they rush a shot with several seconds remaining—as Scott had done earlier with 4 seconds left on the shot clock.

As Duhon starts up the court, however, trouble appears. Felton is the man assigned to guard Duhon. David Noel comes over to help pressure the ball, but instead of helping, he cuts off Felton and allows Duhon to zip past midcourt unimpeded. Duhon zooms in front of the Duke bench, now working on an open court and with several scoring options. Jawad Williams runs at him from the weak side as Duhon leaves the floor, but the Duke senior simply swoops under the rim and emerges on the other side. Returning to earth, he banks the ball off the backboard and watches it fall into the net with 2 seconds left. He has, in reality, left too much time on the clock. Carolina has a set play for this situation designed to create a good look at the basket in a minimal amount of time. Felton pushes the ball to Scott on the right side. The play breaks down and Scott jacks up a three, which isn't close. Duke claims an 83–81 victory and makes it through the first half of the ACC season undefeated in league play. Carolina falls into a tie for sixth in the league.

After the game, the Carolina locker room is a somber place. Roy Williams addresses the team briefly and mentions the 1997 Tar Heel squad that went 3–5 in the first half of the ACC season and then made the Final Four. When he leaves the room, most players remain in the cushioned chairs in front of their lockers, some with towels over their heads, a couple with tears in their eyes. It is the kind of moment most fans never see—an exhausted group of college basketball players trying to accept failure. And then, something that would have been unthinkable just one month ago happens. Rashad McCants gets up from his seat and tours the locker room, stopping to speak to each member of the regular playing rotation. The sophomore star, who has just scored 27 points, pulled down 9 rebounds, and led the team with 3 steals—when the coaches evaluate the tape the next morning, they will give McCants credit for forty defensive good plays, double his previous season high—looks each player in the eye and whispers a few quiet words to each one.

Meanwhile, in the coaches' locker room, assistant coach Joe Holladay tells Roy Williams that his son Mathew, who has been deployed in Iraq for the past ten months, is on the way home. Holladay went home after the pregame meal, around 6 P.M., and found his wife on the phone. "Someone wants to talk to you," she said.

"Hey Coach," said Mathew, an Army Ranger who had been in a very dangerous area. "Got any tickets for the Duke game?"

He was calling from Italy, his last stop on the way back stateside; he would return the first week of March. Holladay, who had for the most part only communicated with his son by email since March of the previous year, was overjoyed. He decided not to tell his players or fellow coaches until after the game. The plan was simple: win the game, break the good news, celebrate twice.

The news drains the last bit of emotion out of Roy Williams, who meets the media with tears in his eyes—not from the loss, but from the impact of learning that Holladay's son is on the way home. Noel is asked how the team will be able to bounce back and play at Wake Forest in less than thirty-seven hours. "I don't know how," he replies. "After a game like this I don't see how there's any way to get back up."

May leaves the locker room with a downcast expression despite his 15 points and 21 rebounds. He is intercepted by Holladay in a back tunnel of the Smith Center, who pounds him on the chest.

"I am so proud of you," the assistant coach says. "You gave everything you had. I used to tell my teams that if they could untie their shoes after the game, they had cheated, because they still had something left. You had nothing left. And I'm so proud of you."

"Thanks, Coach," May says, not cracking a smile. In less than two days, he must battle Wake's Eric Williams, who dominated him in their previous matchup.

Holladay watches his sophomore center walk down the hall and turn the corner. The former Oklahoma high school coach is one of the fiercest competitors on the team, a man who usually doesn't smile after a loss for at least a day. He feels a powerful mix of emotions—joy at the news about his son, disappointment over the loss. But he is able to flash a tired smile as he thinks about the way his boss reacted to the news about Captain Mathew Holladay.

"This job can make you forget about everything," he says. "Especially for a head coach like Coach Williams. Most coaches get tunnel vision. But he sees the whole picture. One of these days, we'll win one of these. I don't know when. But we'll win one."

11

TEAM	ACC	OVERALL
DUKE	8–0	19–1
NC STATE	6–2	13–5
GEORGIA TECH	4–4	16–5
FLORIDA STATE	4–4	16–6
WAKE FOREST	4–4	13–5
UNC	3–5	13–6
MARYLAND	3–5	12–7
VIRGINIA	2–6	12–7
CLEMSON	2–6	9–10

Roy Williams stands on the Smith Center sideline on Friday afternoon, fists clenched, eyes flashing. "Get in your stance!" he yells. "Stance!" And then: "Box out! Box!"

His players do not listen. But that's predictable, because it's not the real Roy Williams screaming at them; it's Melvin Scott, the team's designated jokester, doing his best impression of the Tar Heel head coach. The Duke game was the first in a series of three games over six days against three of the top sixteen teams in the country. In less than twenty-four hours, the Heels will play against Wake Forest in Winston-Salem, a place where they have lost three of their last four games, the last two by an average of 19.5 points. Carolina's road woes against ACC schools are reaching a critical point: the team hasn't won a conference game away from Chapel Hill since December 22, 2002. A loss to Wake would drop UNC to 3–6 in the conference going into the Georgia Tech game. In that case a 3–7 record is a real possibility, and such a record would seriously jeopardize any NCAA Tournament hopes.

So Williams decides it is time to loosen up. Instead of an intense practice to prepare for the Demon Deacons, the team has a light shootaround, and then the head coach divides the ten most infrequently used substitutes—Damion Grant, Damien Price, Jonathan Miller, Phillip McLamb, Wes Miller, Justin Bohlander, C. J. Hooker, Byron Sanders, Reyshawn Terry, and Jesse Holley—into two teams. The seven members of the regular rotation are assigned coaching duties. Some don't take the role seriously, like Melvin Scott, who spends most of the session pretending to be Williams, complete with fist clenching and his trademark phrases. It is, Williams will later admit, a fairly accurate portrayal.

Others, like Jackie Manuel, actually do try to dispense a little coaching to their charges. Frustrated after one of "his" players botches an assignment, Manuel walks over to Williams.

"Coach, I see what you mean," he says. "They don't listen to me either."

As practice is about to conclude, the Blue team, coached by Jawad Williams, Rashad McCants, and Manuel, forces a shot clock violation against the Whites and gets the ball out of bounds with 6 seconds to play. The winning team will earn "plus points"—valuable commodities that can be used by a player to excuse himself from conditioning drills—so the competition is intense. McCants diagrams a play, but the Blues end up freelancing and unexpectedly win the game when walk-on Jonathan Miller banks in a 35-foot three-pointer at the buzzer.

"That's the play I drew up," McCants says with a smile to his head coach.

The mood is still light the next day before the 1 P.M. tip-off against Wake. Melvin Scott is the first Tar Heel out for the pregame shootaround, joining most of the Demon Deacon roster with a broad smile on his face. The Deacs—who have significant chemistry issues of their own, including a practice scuffle between Eric Williams and Vytas Danelius earlier in the season and head coach Skip Prosser's decision later in the week to leave Trent Strickland at home during a road trip—

eye Scott with a bit of surprise. They have been handed a seventeen-page scouting report on the Tar Heels (Carolina's is barely two pages), which doubtless mentions that their opponents have just played a draining rivalry game forty hours earlier. The Heels were supposed to be flat. And here is Melvin Scott, shooting and smiling.

The junior's attitude catches the eye of Joe Holladay, who approaches Scott. "You're going to have a good day today," he says. "I can just tell."

It is the loosest Carolina has been before any road game this year. Team manager Eric Hoots even takes a pre-tip-off moment to phone in an order for six barbecue sandwiches, no slaw, from a nearby barbecue restaurant. A fellow manager will go to pick them up at 3:15 P.M. sharp. They are intended as a victory snack for the coaches.

Privately, the coaches would admit that they have very little idea what to expect in this game. Their players seem loose, but that has not always been a positive indicator this season. At Kansas, this staff went into every game expecting a win or, at worst, a narrow loss. This year, those expectations have changed—anything from a narrow victory to a blowout defeat now seems possible.

Outwardly, however, Roy Williams is the picture of confidence. After the starting lineups are announced, coaches are supposed to be able to address their teams for about 90 seconds before the tip-off. But CBS is televising this contest to a national audience, and when Williams sends his team out for the start of the game, they spend over 3 minutes just standing around due to a mistake on the pregame timing sheet. The Carolina head coach, thinking CBS is dictating the delay, motions for his five starters to come back over in front of the Tar Heel bench, where he has a grave look on his face. It appears he has just remembered an important point of strategy. His starters form a tight huddle around him, Felton draping his arms around his teammates. Their head coach looks them in the eye and says, "I don't really have anything to say. But let's just mess with CBS and make them wait a little while."

Felton and Scott crack toothy smiles. The grins only get bigger when Scott drains two three-pointers in the opening minutes of the game on his way to 16 first-half points. As Holladay predicted, he is having a good day. Williams buys his starters some rest and plays Terry,

Grant, and Sanders in the first half. At halftime the Heels hold a 38–33 advantage despite a lengthy offensive slump late in the half.

The drought continues in the opening minute of the second half, but Rashad McCants draws an intentional foul on Wake's Justin Gray while sinking a layup. McCants hits both free throws, Carolina gets the ball back as part of the intentional foul penalty, and Felton hits a foul-line jumper to complete a 6-point possession. Wake draws within 2 points with 2 minutes left and has a chance to tie, but Kyle Visser misses a point-blank shot. On the next possession, Felton dribbles the ball up the court while Scott runs down the right side, nearest the Carolina bench. Suddenly, Scott breaks into a wide smile, the kind he flashed before the game during shootaround. Asked later what prompted the smile, which seemed rather inappropriate with a key ACC game hanging in the balance and absolutely no evidence that the Heels could close out a road win, he just grins.

"I knew something the crowd didn't know and the Wake Forest guys didn't know," he says.

Which was?

"That we were going to pull this one out."

He is right. David Noel sets a high screen for Felton at the top of the key, and Taron Downey—following the instructions in the seventeen-page scouting report—goes under the screen instead of over it. That allows Felton a sliver of daylight to trigger his shot, and his three-pointer rips through the net for a 73–68 lead and, essentially, the victory.

On the bus for the ninety-minute ride back to Chapel Hill, the barbecue sandwiches taste perfect. A .500 record in the ACC is within sight, and with it a virtually automatic NCAA bid. Maybe the team has turned the corner. Felton did not have a turnover against Wake, and the Heels have put together two straight solid performances. If they can steal the game at Georgia Tech Tuesday night, a five-game winning streak going into NC State—a team exceeding preseason expectations and battling for the ACC lead—on February 29 looks like a real possibility. That would enable them to play for seeding over the last week of the regular season and in the ACC Tournament, rather than scrapping for enough wins to make the field. Any mention of the NIT is almost heresy. The Tar Heel coaches are led by Roy Williams, who has been to fifteen straight NCAA Tournaments. The NIT, they feel, is for mid-major teams looking to earn name recognition for their programs. It is not for major college powerhouses. Not for Kansas.

And certainly not for North Carolina.

With the win over Wake still fresh, the game at Georgia Tech on Tuesday night suddenly looks much less imposing. No longer is Carolina a reeling team. Now it is a team poised to make a second-half push into the top of the Atlantic Coast Conference standings. The Jackets rocketed into the top ten earlier in the season on the strength of a Preseason NIT championship, but have since returned to earth and lost two of their past three games, including an 81–65 defeat to Florida State. A win at Alexander Memorial Coliseum would put Carolina at 5–5 in the league and return it to .500 for the first time since January 14, with two winnable home games and a trip to bottom-feeder Virginia on the horizon.

It is, from all appearances, a critical game that should have the full attention of the Carolina players. But the Tar Heel coaches have learned over the past three months that predicting the intensity level of their players on any given evening is roughly akin to finding a parking spot in downtown Chapel Hill—sometimes you get lucky and sometimes you don't find what you expect. Privately, some coaches said their expectations for the Wake Forest game were very low, but the team played one of its more complete games of the season. Tonight, with expectations high, there is no guarantee of a commensurate performance.

The Yellow Jackets win the opening tip, and junior guard B. J. Elder hits a three-pointer. It is a sight the Tar Heels will become very familiar with over the next two hours.

Since working on the point zone defense in the days after the win over NC State, Roy Williams has increased the role that it plays in the Tar Heel attack. The benefits of the defense in general are numerous: unlike many zones, it keeps constant pressure on the ball handler; it keeps the best rebounders in the primary rebounding positions; and it tends to put the guards in good position to quickly make the transition from defense to offense and lead a fast break. For this depth-shy Carolina team, an added benefit is that it allows defensive players more rest than Williams's preferred man-to-man attack, and it was crucial in the win over Wake. There are also drawbacks. Like most zone defenses, it occasionally allows offensive rebounds because defenders have trouble finding their block-out assignments, and it can be susceptible to quick ball movement that leads to a three-pointer.

Fresh off the success in Winston-Salem, Roy Williams decides to employ the point zone late in the first half against Georgia Tech. The Jackets have gone on a 15–2 run midway through the opening 20 minutes, but the Heels break the streak with a Raymond Felton three-pointer. With 3 minutes left in the half, Williams gives the signal for the point zone—one raised index finger—to Felton, who has just scored. One of the point guard's basic responsibilities in the Williams system is to immediately get to midcourt after a made basket and signal the defense to his teammates. It has been a point of emphasis, but on this occasion Felton misses the signal entirely and the Heels spend the possession in man-to-man. Georgia Tech draws a foul, and during the free throws, Williams pointedly tells Felton that he wants the zone on the next possession.

The next time the Jackets bring the ball down the court, Felton inexplicably sets his team up in man-to-man.

It's not willful disobedience, it's not believing that he knows more about defense than the head coach. It's a subtle enough play that most spectators probably think Felton is simply tired and needs a rest when Williams yanks him in favor of Jackie Manuel. But it is exactly the kind of mental breakdown that has perplexed Williams this year, the kind that makes him think his players don't have enough trust in their coaches. Tech takes a 34–29 lead into the locker room.

After his game-opening three-pointer, Elder makes just one more shot in the first half, finishing with a meager 6 points. But after the break, he explodes. He makes 7 of his 10 second-half shots, including 5 of his 8 three-pointers. Some of those points come over the outstretched arms of McCants, who is not playing the same type of bulldog defense he showed against Duke. But as many points as he gives up on defense, he gets back even more on offense. He matches Elder almost shot for shot on his way to a career-high 31 points.

The difference in the game, however, is that Elder gets a minimal amount of offensive help from his teammates, while McCants gets none.

Melvin Scott scores 10 first-half points and zero in the second half. No other Tar Heel scores in double figures. With Tech holding a 70–63 lead with 5 minutes left, Felton misses a layup that would have cut the lead to a manageable 5 points. Tech turns the ball over on its next possession, leading to a Scott layup attempt, but he is hacked on the arm as he attempts the shot. No foul is called, and Williams explodes. He storms up the sideline after referee Ray Natili, who is part of a crew that has already drawn the ire of both head coaches. After Williams yells, "Call the foul!" Natili promptly turns around and zaps Williams with the ninth technical foul of his sixteen-year career. Will Bynum hits two free throws and Tech retains the ball. After a missed shot, McCants misses a box-out on Isma'il Muhammad, and the athletic Yellow Jacket sopho-more slams the rebound through with his left hand, igniting the Tech fans and essentially capping the Jacket victory. They hold on for an 88–77 win.

It is another poor performance for forward Jawad Williams, who hits 4 of 9 field goals and finishes with 9 points and 5 rebounds. Fellow junior Melvin Scott misses all four of his second-half shots; he will later say that he believes the Carolina offense was too focused on McCants in the second half, denying Scott the chance to get as many shots as he would have liked. But the two juniors, who play the most minutes of any upperclassman, don't seem broken up about the loss for long. As they shower after the game they are heard laughing and shouting with sophomore post reserves Damion Grant and Byron Sanders. The laugh-ter is so inappropriate and unexpected that it gets the attention of the rest of the players, most of whom have already showered and are getting ready for the plane trip back to Chapel Hill. Unfortunately for Scott and Williams, it also gets the attention of assistant coach Steve Robinson, who picked that exact moment to walk into the Tar Heel locker room. Still dressed in his suit and tie, he bolts into the shower area to inform the four players, in clearly understandable language, that laughter will not be tolerated just minutes after a disappointing ACC defeat.

"It hurts when you try to be a leader and you can't because nobody wants to follow," McCants says. "I'm doing what I have to do to put the team in position to win, but who else is doing the same thing? I can't just go out there and score 28 points in a half and nobody else really scores. . . . We try to put other people in a position to follow, but that's hard because everyone on this team has that confidence and swagger about them and doesn't understand why they need to follow instead of lead."

The loss puts the Heels right back on the NCAA Tournament bubble, where they have kept residence for most of the season. Their three remaining home games, against Maryland, Florida State, and Clemson, are now must-wins, and the road game at Virginia on February 24 also looks crucial. A Tar Heel victory in either of the two remaining road games—against second-place NC State or the regular season finale at Duke—would now be considered an upset.

The balance of the season, at this point, is no laughing matter.

The prototypical Roy Williams player does not laugh after a loss. The prototypical Roy Williams player does not even crack a smile after a loss. When introducing assistant coach Jerod Haase, who played under him for three years at Kansas, the Tar Heel head coach was quick to identify Haase's most endearing characteristic. "He's as competitive a kid as I've ever been around," Williams said. "He's the only player I've ever coached who I thought hurt as badly as I did when we lost, and that includes ten years as an assistant at Carolina."

That is the type of player Williams wants in his program. Since accepting the Carolina job, recruiting has been a top priority, with the emphasis as much on character as on talent. During the fall signing period, four players inked with the Heels: 6-foot-2 combo guard JamesOn Curry from Burlington, North Carolina; 6-foot-2 point guard Quentin Thomas of Oakland, California; 6-foot-5 wing J. R. Smith from Clarksburg, New Jersey; and 6-foot-8 forward Marvin Williams, a native of Bremerton, Washington. Williams and Smith are among the top ten players nationally in the high school senior class of 2004, and the Tar Heel coaching staff believe they are the best players at their positions in the entire class. Almost as important, both have the type of personality Williams wants. Smith originally tried to commit to Carolina while Doherty was head coach, but was told he needed to get his academics in order. When Roy Williams assumed the head coaching job, he told Smith he would follow his progress—academically, athletically, and socially. Roy

Williams's background with Marvin Williams was much deeper. The 6-foot-8 wing player had endeared himself to the Carolina staff when they watched him foul out of a summer AAU game and then serve as water boy for his teammates for the rest of the game, bringing them drinks at every timeout without being prompted. It was a small gesture, but the kind of team commitment that's frequently hard to find on the me-first AAU circuit.

Curry had committed to North Carolina during the Matt Doherty era, and although he wasn't a perfect fit for Williams's system, the new head coach decided to honor the previous scholarship offer. Despite Williams's generosity, Curry eventually cost himself the scholarship when he was arrested on drug charges on February 4.

It was the Thomas recruitment, however, that best illustrated Williams's recruiting philosophy. When Williams took over as coach, point guard was a key area of need due to the possibility that Raymond Felton might jump to the NBA after his sophomore season. During the July evaluation period, Carolina coaches watched Thomas intently, although as a native of California he seemed an unlikely fit for the Heels. The last player from that state to sign with Carolina was center Scott Williams in 1986, and over the past two decades the Heels had filled their roster primarily with East Coast players.

But Williams had experienced great success recruiting the West Coast for Kansas, which was able to recruit very few players locally. In addition, Jayhawk coaches learned early that they would have little success mining the East Coast.

"At Kansas, we didn't spend any time on the East Coast," assistant coach Joe Holladay said. "There was no need. We'd been successful on the West Coast, so we wanted to keep going back to where kids had had success at Kansas. On the East Coast, there is an image of Kansas that it's all flat, there are Indians everywhere, and there are cows in the streets. Why would you want to go there and leave the ACC, the Big East, and fly over the Big 10 and SEC? But out west, you've got to deal with the Pac-10, but there are no major conferences between there and the Big 12."

That meant that coaches like Holladay, who spent ten years at Kansas before moving to UNC with Williams, had virtually ignored high school programs east of the Mississippi River for the past decade. When Holladay arrived at UNC, he had to learn some new recruiting territories in his first months on the job. But his old ties still proved handy. Williams had been recruiting Thomas during his last year at Kansas, and the Jayhawks continued to recruit him under new head coach Bill Self. But despite the distance factor and despite Thomas's stated desire to play close to home, Carolina jumped into the recruiting fray.

"He has an eye for talent," says longtime friend Cody Plott of Williams. "He may not pick the top player in the eyes of recruiting gurus, but year in and year out he's always competitive. And when he decides who he likes and locks on, he goes for it. There's no coach who works like he does. If you want to go recruiting with Roy, you better take a box lunch because he's not going to stop for lunch. I sat with him in Las Vegas this year [at an AAU tournament] and he just went from game to game. We probably saw a dozen games."

Williams is able to see everything in his program through the eyes of high school recruits. When seats for a noon game in Chapel Hill weren't filled at tip-off, he pointedly told the fans that it wouldn't look good for potential recruits watching the game on television to see empty seats.

There is never a time that he is not recruiting, although he rarely lets outsiders into his plans. He coached in his first national championship game in 1991 at the Hoosier Dome in Indianapolis. Thirty minutes before the game, he called point guard prospect Jason Kidd from a near-courtside telephone to make sure he was watching the title game and picturing himself in a Jayhawk uniform. Several reporters walked up on Williams while he was making the call. "Hey, fellas," the head coach said. "Can't a guy talk to his dad?" The reporters left and, for one night at least, secrecy was preserved.

There were no questions about Kidd's talent, as he was the best point guard in his class. But reports from observers were mixed as to Thomas's potential to be a big-time Atlantic Coast Conference point guard. Typically, Williams didn't care about observers. He cared only that he had seen Thomas play, he thought Thomas was extremely talented, and he thought he had the mindset and competitiveness he demanded from a point guard. The lock was on.

In the meantime, as the summer ended the Tar Heels were among the front-runners in the recruitment of the top point guard in the country, Shaun Livingston, a singular talent with outstanding size (6-foot-6) and point guard skills. But Williams was aware that Livingston's father and grandfather, both of whom held considerable sway with the player, were enamored with Duke. So while most observers assumed that Thomas was only a fallback plan, Williams turned up the attention on the Oakland product. Thomas scheduled three in-home visits, which are essentially sales pitches from the schools involved. Arizona State, Kansas, and Carolina all received invitations, and all three sent coaches to the Thomas household during one busy week in September. Williams and assistant coach Steve Robinson handled the in-home duties for the Tar Heels, going through a three-and-a-half-hour visit to the Thomas home that featured talk about the Carolina point guard situation, the Heels' scholarship offer, and where Thomas might fit in Chapel Hill.

After the in-home visit, a prospect usually next visits the campuses of his suitors. Thomas visited Kansas on the weekend of September 26, just two weeks after Livingston had made the journey to Chapel Hill. On an official visit, the recruit will usually get acquainted with the campus and the team and then play some pickup games with the current players. Livingston's visit had been very positive, and at least two of the current Tar Heels felt certain he would commit to Carolina. So it came as a shock to the Tar Heel basketball world when word leaked out on the evening of September 29 that Thomas, just a day after returning from Lawrence, had phoned in his commitment to the basketball office at . . .

North Carolina.

Citing the fact that Roy Williams was the first major college coach to show interest in him—and without ever setting foot on the Chapel Hill campus—Thomas became the newest Tar Heel. It concluded a classic Roy Williams recruitment: he had identified a top target, paid little heed to the opinions of the Internet recruiting "gurus," allowed very little information about the recruitment to leak out, and wrapped it up with little fanfare.

Target identified, target locked, and target landed. All in approximately two months. The Tar Heels had their point guard, and would not have to spend the next six months worrying about Livingston entering the NBA Draft. Speculation began almost immediately upon his college commitment that he was likely to go straight to the pros, a prediction he fulfilled by signing with an agent and becoming the overall fourth pick in the Draft. The entire situation caused a major headache and a substantial hole in the recruiting class for his college of choice.

Which just happened to be Duke University.

12

TEAM	ACC	OVERALL
DUKE	10–0	21–1
NC STATE	8–2	15–5
GEORGIA TECH	5–4	18–5
WAKE FOREST	5–5	14–6
MARYLAND	4–5	13–7
FLORIDA STATE	4–6	16–8
UNC	4–6	14–7
VIRGINIA	2–8	12–9
CLEMSON	2–8	9–12

Roy Williams doesn't like the way his team looks. In the Smith Center locker room, just one hallway and a right turn from the arena where 21,750 Carolina fans are packed into the stands, he does not detect the fire in his players that he would expect with a 4–6 ACC record and a must-win game against Maryland just minutes away. It is part of the enigma of this team that it is almost impossible to say how the players will approach any single game of the season—with the exception of Duke. At Kansas, Williams usually had senior leaders like Nick Collison or Jacque Vaughn to set the tone for their teammates, not just in the locker room, but on the court.

At Carolina, the default setting for the players seems to be more laid-back than it was in Lawrence. It is perhaps the product of not winning as many games, and not understanding how enjoyable it can be to win. Basketball has occasionally been a chore for these players, three of whom grew to dread playing games during their 8–20 freshman seasons, and almost all of whom at least sometimes grew weary of the constant drama during the 2002–03 season.

There will be more drama if the Terps come into the Smith Center and get a key Atlantic Coast Conference win. The ACC continues to be the top-rated conference in the Ratings Percentage Index, a statistic given significant weight by the NCAA Tournament Selection Committee. The league is strong, which means it is likely to get at least six, and perhaps seven, bids into the field of sixty-four. Duke and NC State are locks. But the next five teams in the league have yet to write their postseason ticket. An 8–8 record in the conference would certainly be good enough to earn a bid. A record of 7–9 might require a win in the ACC Tournament quarterfinals, and 6–10 would be very perilous. That means the Tar Heels need to win their remaining home games against Maryland, Florida State, and Clemson and perhaps steal a road win at Virginia on February 24. Win those games, and the remaining road contests at State and Duke will be much less pressure-filled. Lose even one of the four easier games, and it's back on the fringe of the NCAA Tournament.

But Williams needn't have worried about the readiness of his team. The Tar Heels come out and play one of their best halves of the season in the first half against Maryland. The Heels dominate Maryland on the boards, gaining a 30–16 rebounding advantage, and hold the Terps to 30 percent in their field goal shooting. Jamar Smith, who so thoroughly dominated Sean May in their first meeting, makes just three of seven shots. Four Tar Heels finish the first half in double figures in scoring, including super-sub Jackie Manuel, who scores 12 points and grabs 4 rebounds in just 9 minutes of action, mostly in a stellar last 4 minutes of the first half. Carolina caps the 20 minutes with 2 minutes of surprise contributions from freshman backup guard Jesse Holley, who is better known as a receiver on the football team. Holley successfully leads a three-on-one fast break, which he finishes with a dish back to Manuel for a layup; then he converts a two-on-one break with a solid bounce pass to Melvin Scott for another easy basket. By the time Holley blocks D. J. Strawberry's shot at the halftime buzzer, Carolina bounds into the locker room with a sizable 55–35 advantage, their biggest halftime lead of the conference season. It is, as Williams will later say, a great half to be a coach.

Maybe it's the weeklong break that is only 20 minutes away. Maybe it's the false sense of security spawned by a 20-point lead. Whatever the reason, the Heels follow up one of their best halves of the season with one of their worst. Down 20, Maryland is forced to turn up the defensive pressure, a situation that seems to play right into Carolina's hands. Raymond Felton has spent the entire season carving up most of the half-court and full-court trapping defenses teams have tried, so the general expectation is that Maryland's increased pressure will lead to easier Tar Heel baskets in the second half. The Heels made 58 percent of their field goals in the first 20 minutes. A 60 percent mark in the second half doesn't seem out of reach.

That's exactly what happens on the first play of the second half, as Felton hits McCants for an easy layup. But on the very next possession, Felton turns the ball over attempting a bounce pass through three Terps to Sean May. So begins a second half that will later prompt Roy Williams to remark, "This is why they don't give guns to coaches."

The schizophrenic personality of his team is again apparent in 60 seconds of second-half action later in the stanza. During a defensive possession, Rashad McCants goes barreling out of bounds to try to recover a loose ball. That effort prompts a standing ovation from the fans in the lower level of the Smith Center. One minute later, nursing a 63–48 lead, Sean May hits McCants with a perfect outlet pass and the talented sophomore finds himself all alone in the frontcourt. Sensing a chance to make ESPN's *SportsCenter,* and perhaps with the previous night's NBA slam dunk contest fresh in his mind, he attempts a windmill dunk.

The dunk clangs off the front rim. Carolina recovers the ball, and McCants is eventually fouled in the act of shooting by Travis Garrison, sending him to the free-throw line for two shots. Roy Williams is incredulous. As McCants stands at the free-throw line in front of the UNC bench, Williams stares across the court at the fans in the midcourt seats. His arms are folded, his mouth a straight line. He is not yelling. Not stomping. Just standing and staring. He glances up into the rafters, where he has a perfect glimpse of the fact that the Tar Heels have not added any NCAA Tournament banners to the arena since 2001. And yet his players are trying windmill dunks with an ACC game still in doubt. Missing such an attempt would probably have resulted in an immediate benching from Dean Smith. Williams chooses to keep his leading scorer on the floor, but when McCants, pursuing a rebound, allows the ball to be swatted from his hands and then pleads with the official for a foul, Williams sends Reyshawn Terry into the game for McCants. "It's time we stopped begging people and wanting people to give us things," the coach will say later, echoing his comments from after the Kentucky game. "It's time we start doing things ourselves and making it happen. That's the reason I got mad and took him out." At the next practice, McCants overhears Williams saying he doesn't think the sophomore can make the dunk he attempted against the Terps. McCants, who is already holding a basketball, takes three steps, rips off a carbon copy of his failed dunk, and slams it through effortlessly. There is nothing the coach can do but laugh.

Carolina builds the advantage back to 68–50 but the Terps roll off a 16–4 run in the next 4 minutes. Felton gets in foul trouble and is removed with four fouls; he comes back in with less than 10 minutes to play, and then is yanked again after proving ineffective against Maryland's half-court trap. By this point, nearly every Carolina possession has turned into an adventure. A portion of Friday's practice was spent on press offense, but during most of the second half, the Tar Heels look like they are unfamiliar with the idea.

As Roy Williams could probably have predicted, Maryland eventually narrows the deficit to 3 points. The Carolina advantage is 5 with 2:10 remaining when Felton, who will end the game with 7 turnovers in 24 minutes, tries an ill-advised bounce pass to Jawad Williams in the post. Jamar Smith knocks the ball away and it trickles to McCants on the right wing. With the shot clock ticking down, McCants fires a 23-foot three-pointer that immediately appears to be much too hard.

The ball bounces off the backboard and straight through the rim.

Buoyed by this extremely fortuitous bounce, Carolina holds on for a 97–86 victory. It is not particularly artistic, and the second half leaves Roy Williams frustrated, but it is a victory. Felton's subpar performance is a concern, but Jawad Williams appears to have rediscovered his game, as he finishes with 23 points and 8 rebounds, and makes sixteen trips to the free-throw line. The Heels have six days off before their next game, a home date with Florida State, and their head coach gives them a light practice schedule during the first part of the week—Monday is an off day, and Tuesday and Wednesday are run-and-shoot days.

For the coaches, however, it will not be a weeklong holiday. There are no games, but the business of Carolina basketball demands that certain important tasks be accomplished over the next five days.

The first is recruiting. JamesOn Curry's legal situation remains unclear, as do the NBA prospects of several players already on the roster. Based on some of his comments, the coaches fear that recruit Marvin Williams may be considering a jump to the pros. With the break in the schedule, Roy Williams decides it's time to reconnect with the current commitments while also hedging his bets for 2004. He flies to the West Coast to watch point guard commitment Quentin Thomas. Assistant coach Steve Robinson is dispatched on a multiple-city trip that includes a stop in Detroit to watch uncommitted class of 2004 forward Malik Hairston. On the surface, Carolina doesn't appear to have a scholarship open for Hairston, but if Curry's situation keeps him from enrolling and a player jumps early, there would be room for the extremely talented Hairston. More important, Robinson also journeys to Bremerton, Washington to see Marvin Williams. His report on the status of Carolina's top recruit—at this point in February, no one even remotely considers J. R. Smith an NBA possibility—is cautiously optimistic.

"If people would leave him alone, I think the answer would be 'No,'" Roy Williams says when asked if Marvin Williams is considering the NBA. "I don't think he'd think about it one second. Every kid that has ever bounced a basketball thinks about going to the NBA. Every kid. But one of the problems we have now is that everybody says, 'What do you think? What do you think?' and then a kid who hadn't thought about it at all says, 'I wonder if I should be thinking about it.' If people would just leave high school kids alone, we wouldn't have half the problems. Agents and guys I call guys who crawl out from under rocks are going to be around all the time. Then the media and Internet and Web sites start talking about that stuff."

This week, though, Williams is only partially concerned with the future landscape of college basketball. He's also concerned with the history of hoops, specifically the history of Carolina hoops. The coming weekend will mark the first-ever Tar Heel Letterman's Reunion, a Roy Williams brainchild that was conceived almost as soon as he was hired. A total of 220 lettermen are returning to Chapel Hill for the event, which includes an invitation to Friday's practice, tickets to Saturday's game against Florida State, halftime recognition during the game, and a private Saturday evening banquet. It is the first reunion-type gathering since the Smith Center was dedicated in January of 1986.

That's not to say, however, that no one ever thought of having such a reunion. Matt Doherty mentioned the idea to the media during his first year at Carolina, and even made some initial inquiries into getting the process started. However, others inside the program realized that the new coach had already alienated enough alumni that the turnout could be dismal, which would be disastrous. Carolina trumpets its family, so to have a reunion with poor attendance would have been worse than having no reunion at all. Doherty brought up the idea again during his third year, but by then the chances of healthy attendance were even worse, and the event never got into the planning stage.

Roy Williams, however, has experience planning reunions. He'd instituted a policy of holding them every five years at Kansas, one of which was a massively popular event during the 1999 season that celebrated 100 years of Jayhawk basketball. The idea was simple: remind former lettermen of their impact on the program and remind current players of the deep ties that run through the institution.

Administrative assistant C. B. McGrath was put in charge of the planning for the reunion, a task he shared with basketball office staffers Emily Cozart, Armin Dastur, Jennifer Holbrook, and Kay Thomas. The response to the event was swift and positive. The entire starting lineup from Carolina's 1957 national championship team returned, and ninety-two-year-old Jim McCachren took a bus from Gainesville to Charlotte in order to attend. Everyone on the invitation list is invited to Friday afternoon's practice, which turns into one of the loosest sessions of the season. The group attending the practice is especially heavy on alums from the 1950s and '60s, older men who have no qualms about interjecting their opinions—sometimes loudly—during the practice. Any other afternoon of the season, the interruptions would have irritated

Roy Williams. This day, however, he takes it in good humor, even needling former NBA coach Doug Moe that he should come down to the floor and demonstrate how to run sprints.

A handful of players organize private parties that evening at a local Chapel Hill restaurant, sessions that former point guard Dick Grubar later describes as a lot of good friends, a lot of fun, and just a few lies. The current Tar Heels do their part to make the weekend memorable by holding off Florida State on Saturday afternoon with a 78–71 victory that returns them to .500 in the ACC for the first time in over a month. Carolina again struggles to maintain a big lead, as a 16-point halftime advantage dwindles to just 1 point with 5 minutes to play, but 17 points from Felton, yet another timely three-pointer from Rashad McCants, and a key McCants steal ice the win.

The real drama comes before the game. As the game clock counts down to 12 minutes before tip-off, longtime Tar Heel assistant coach and three-year head coach Bill Guthridge emerges from the tunnel and sits down next to Williams on the Tar Heel bench. One minute later, as the current team is leaving the floor after warm-ups, Dean Smith ambles quietly out of the tunnel, almost unnoticed. The stands are only about three-quarters full, but those in attendance quickly fall to a hush as Williams strides to midcourt and grabs a wireless microphone, followed by Smith and Guthridge.

It is one of Smith's few public appearances in the Smith Center since his retirement in 1997. He attends only the games that are not on television, choosing instead to watch them on television at home, where he can be nervous in private and, as he says, "think along with what Roy might call in different situations." Very few people have an idea of what is about to happen, as it has been a closely guarded secret throughout the week. At some schools, the honoring of two legendary coaches would have been an extravaganza complete with laser lights, fireworks, and teary-eyed tributes. Smith and Guthridge would never accept that type of adoration, however. As recently as the day before, Smith left five voice mails for Williams in an effort to get him to halt the proceedings. Finally, the current head coach had to play his only trump card against his former boss.

"Coach, didn't you tell me that if I took the job, I was going to be the head coach and it was going to be my program?" Williams asked.

"Yes," Smith answered.

"Didn't you say that I could do whatever I wanted to do?"

"Yes," Smith said again.

"Well, I want to do this."

Williams is well aware of the power wielded by the head basketball coach at the University of North Carolina, but he has a way of subtly using it that is endearing. The details are left to those more capable of handling them. But when, for example, a marketing staffer sells a large phone company the right to put 5,000 white T-shirts in the Smith Center stands before the FSU game, Williams—prompted by several other high-level administrators—intercedes. UNC is involved in a major effort to get fans to wear blue to the game, and the feeling is that white T-shirts send a contradictory message. So despite the fact that 5,000 shirts have already been placed on the seats, they are picked up hours before tip-off against the Seminoles. No hard feelings, no harsh words, but the white T-shirts are put back in the closet.

It's with similar grace that he coaxes Smith and Guthridge to midcourt. There are still a couple thousand empty seats when the banners are unfurled in the Smith Center rafters, and the crowd almost seems too surprised at the sight of the coaches to applaud. Instead of a sustained, rousing ovation, Smith and Guthridge receive a short burst of applause. They quickly leave the floor before anyone can appreciate them too much.

The duo seem much more comfortable later that evening at the private banquet. More than 200 lettermen, most of whom were introduced to the Smith Center crowd at halftime of the Florida State game, attend, and all receive an exclusive letterman-only T-shirt as they check in at the front desk of the UNC Alumni Center next to Kenan Stadium. There is a boisterous social hour before dinner is served, but the highlights of the evening are the speeches by six former players.

Roy Williams has given the current Tar Heels, who are seated at tables in the center of the ritzy, wood-paneled room, a simple set of instructions.

"Don't sit there and try to be cool," he tells them. "Don't sit there and think, 'When is that old guy going to shut up?' In fifteen or twenty years, you're going to be that old guy."

It is an important reminder for players who do, on occasion, seem overly interested in how they are perceived. Many know less about the Carolina basketball tradition than the regular fans who fill the Smith Center. The senior walk-ons, Jonathan Miller, Phillip McLamb, and Damien Price, all grew up cheering for the Tar Heels, but they—along with Raymond Felton and Rashad McCants—are a distinct minority. Jawad Williams readily admits that he rooted against Carolina and for Michigan in the 1993 championship game because the Wolverine players, known as the "Fab Five" and sporting black shoes and bald heads, were much cooler than Carolina. Every scholarship player on the roster was born after Michael Jordan hit the championship-winning shot against Georgetown in 1982. To them, anything before 1990 is ancient history.

They're also part of an era in Carolina basketball unlike any that came before it. In the past, former players made a habit of returning to Chapel Hill in the summers to work out with the current team. It was very much like a fraternity, with alums and current members mixing seamlessly. During Matt Doherty's tenure, however, that relationship began to crumble. In part, it was unavoidable. With the big dollars involved in today's NBA contracts, pro teams are eager to keep their investments nearby rather than allowing them to work out away from the watchful eye of their strength staff. Some players also were hesitant to return because of what they had heard about Doherty, both from other players and from former basketball staff members.

So the current Tar Heels are perhaps less used to mixing with other members of their elite group than any class that has come before. This evening is designed to make sure they understand their rich pedigree. The banquet is closed to the media and any non-lettermen or non-essential staff members. It is a closed society, and it is supposed to be. Lettermen are asked to sign the Letterman's Book, which will be placed in the Smith Center memorabilia room, using a pen with Carolina blue ink.

Roy Williams opens the evening with a few short remarks, and concludes by saying exactly what every letterman in attendance wants to hear: "I hope you'll always feel like this is your program." It's a sentiment that some in the room feel was lost over the past few years. Now, Williams is doing his best to restore it.

For once, the head coach of the Tar Heels is not the feature attraction. The former players who have been asked to speak are sent to the podium in chronological order. The first speaker is Nemo Nearman, class of 1950. He sets the tone for the hour of speeches that are to come, mixing the right amount of lightheartedness—at one point referring to Smith and Guthridge as "Dean and Bill," and then proclaiming that he doesn't have to call them Coach because he is seventy-eight years old—and family sentiment. "There's a thread in Carolina blue," he says as he looks directly at the current players. "It started back before me and it runs through you young gentlemen."

Criticized mercilessly last spring for their decidedly ungentleman-like appearance at Doherty's resignation press conference, the players are now being pulled back into the fold. Lennie Rosenbluth, the 1957 National Player of the Year and the player Sean May has said he most wants to meet—because Rosenbluth's name remains tattooed across Carolina's scoring records although he played only three seasons—is next at the podium. He delights the audience with his tales of adjusting from the Bronx, where he grew up, to Chapel Hill.

"One of the first things I realized was that everybody I met had three names," he says. "Billy Bob. Susie Joe. So I thought, 'Well, maybe I should have three names.' So the next guy I met, I told him, 'Hi, I'm Lennie Shootalot Rosenbluth.' "

Dick Grubar, class of 1969, speaks fondly of his time at Carolina and then exhorts the current players to remember that they're running, shooting, and defending on behalf of everyone in the room. He is followed by Phil Ford, who lights up the room with his story of the role Carolina basketball has played in his life. Although he is a favorite of many of the current players because of the way he can relate to today's teenager, Ford is also an emotional speaker.

"Think of all the little boys who grow up wanting to play basketball for North Carolina," he says from the podium. "I'm one of the lucky ones. When I went to the NBA, I met so many players who said they wouldn't go back to the same school. These were NBA players, so they were obviously very successful. I just took it for granted that everyone loved their school like I did."

He closes, as tears are starting to fill his eyes, with a pointed remark. It is nothing the current team hasn't heard before, but in this setting, it seems to hold new significance. Mindful of the occasional squabbles this team has had, and of the difficulties they've had in becoming a team instead of a collection of individuals, Ford looks straight at the current team.

"I'm proud of you," he says. "And I want you to remember, it's all about the University of North Carolina."

Al Wood, class of 1981, follows Ford to the front of the room. By this point the emotion is peaking, and it seems unlikely that anyone can capably follow Ford's speech. Wood does it. He speaks of the lessons he has learned from Smith and Guthridge, from the importance of completing every detail of every task, to being on time for appointments. They are humorous stories, and the lettermen in attendance laugh boisterously. It is when he turns to the more personal side of his experience that the room becomes dead silent.

"I battled alcoholism," he says. "And it got to the point that I didn't know what to do. The only person I could think of to call was Dean Smith. To me, that's what the Carolina family is all about. A family loves each other."

Wood leaves the stage to a standing ovation, one of many during the evening. The next speaker seems a somewhat odd fit. King Rice, class of 1991, was a much-maligned point guard who was once booed by the Tar Heel fans during a poor shooting performance in Chapel Hill. He was not a highly praised player, not like a Rosenbluth or Ford or Wood. In addition to his occasional on-court problems, he battled a series of off-the-court troubles, including a scuffle during a stint as a college assistant coach when he barreled into the stands to take on a heckler.

When he takes the podium, there are some raised eyebrows. By the time he leaves it, there are some tears.

He opens his speech with a touch of self-deprecating humor, pointing out that he realizes he is an odd fit among the All-Americans who have preceded him. Grabbing the sides of the podium, he admits his past mistakes and apologizes for any shame they might have brought to the

Carolina basketball program. He echoes a theme both Ford and Wood have mentioned: if I'd only known then what I know now, things might have been different.

The Doherty years have essentially been unspoken during the reunion. Most of the players from those teams have other commitments that keep them away from Chapel Hill, either in the NBA or in overseas professional leagues. It is almost as though those years didn't happen. But then Rice takes on the issue, and the decline in the number of returning players over the past few summers, with candor.

"Guys, everyone in this room loves you," he tells the current team. "When I was here, I had the former guys come back and get on me when I did the wrong thing. I'm sorry I haven't done that for you. I'm sorry we haven't been together like this. I'm ashamed of myself because everyone in this room has to come together to support you guys."

It is the capstone to an evening that could not have been better scripted. Rice chokes up, as do many of his listeners. With those five sentences, he seems to heal some of the wounds that have been lingering among the crowd. It appears to be the perfect message for a team that now has a better understanding of the status they hold as Carolina basketball players, of the family to which they belong. Current players—especially Jackie Manuel, who one year ago was miserable in Chapel Hill but who now seems determined to soak up every ounce of the UNC basketball experience—mingle with alumni well into the night. It seems no one wants to disturb the feeling of goodwill that hangs in the air.

The Tar Heels will travel to Charlottesville in three days to battle lowly Virginia. Bolstered by what they've seen and heard at the reunion, the Heels appear refreshed. New Carolina—the inconsistency, the individualism—seems to be dead.

Old Carolina is back.

13

Team	ACC	Overall
DUKE	11–2	22–3
NC STATE	9–3	17–6
WAKE FOREST	7–5	17–6
GEORGIA TECH	6–6	19–7
UNC	6–6	16–7
FLORIDA STATE	6–7	18–9
MARYLAND	4–8	13–10
VIRGINIA	4–9	14–10
CLEMSON	3–9	10–14

On paper, Virginia does not appear to present an especially tough challenge. The Cavaliers needed a last-second three-pointer from Todd Billet to defeat Clemson in their last outing, the second straight game in which Billet had hit a game-winning trifecta. Head Coach Pete Gillen is under considerable fire in Charlottesville, where construction is underway on a sparkling new arena that seats almost twice as many fans as the current venue, University Hall. The old arena has rarely been full this season as the Cavs stumble to a 14–10 overall record.

But logic rarely plays a role when Carolina goes on the road to Virginia. The Heels have lost four straight games in U-Hall, despite the fact that UVA rarely has an especially formidable team. It has been, traditionally, the definition of a "letdown" game. University Hall isn't a particularly glamorous place to play, and Virginia's players are usually just good enough to be dangerous if they muster a career game, which they frequently do. But Carolina is coming off the reunion festivities, a victory would give the players their first three-game winning streak since mid-December, and they thumped the Cavs by 19 just a month earlier.

Before the team boards the plane for the short flight to Charlottesville, Roy Williams puts his troops through a quick practice on the floor of the Smith Center. Virginia is Steve Robinson's scouting responsibility, and when the Heels take the floor for practice around 4:20 P.M., Robinson uses the Blue team—Damien Price, Phillip McLamb, Jonathan Miller, Wes Miller, and Damion Grant—to represent the Cavaliers. The Blue squad walks through two of Virginia's most frequently used plays, with Robinson explaining the options of each play as Roy Williams leans against the basket support next to the starters, who are lined up along the baseline. One particular play, called "Special," is designed to give Billet a pair of three-point options, one coming off a double screen and one coming off a single screen. Robinson shows the starters the best way to defend both the double and single screen to prevent Billet from getting an open look at the basket. Later in practice, the Blue team simulates the plays at full speed against the starters in order to accustom them to defending each set.

Just over twenty-four hours later, Robinson's dedication to his scouting report will become very important. The Tar Heels jump out to a 22–14 lead midway through the first half when Raymond Felton hits a three-pointer, but the lead quickly evaporates. Gillen, who is the most unconventional coach in the Atlantic Coast Conference—especially in the way he deploys his timeouts, eschewing the usual coach's inclination to save them until the end of a game—plays a box-and-one against Rashad McCants. The defense, which is a four-man zone with one player playing man-to-man against the other team's best scorer, is designed to make someone other than McCants take shots. J. R. Reynolds, a previously undistinguished 6-foot-3 freshman, draws the assignment on McCants.

The defense does exactly what it is supposed to do. Frustrated by the unusual attention, McCants spends most of the game standing idly on the wing. The best way to beat a box-and-one is for the offensive player being guarded man-to-man to keep moving and set plenty of screens, but Carolina's star sophomore does neither. By the time he is called for an offensive foul for swatting at Billet with 1:30 left in the first half, it's clear he is rattled by the trick defense. McCants picks up his fourth foul with 9:13 left in the game and walks to the bench, his face expressionless. He has taken just six shots, scored 6 points, and will finish the game with 8, his first single-digit scoring effort since the disaster at Kentucky. Although he has made dramatic strides in defense over the past few weeks, McCants's offensive frustrations carry over to the other end of the floor. At one point, the rest of the team lines up in man-to-man while he thinks the call is for a zone, forcing him to run out at Virginia's Devin Smith and foul the Cavalier sharpshooter as he attempts a three-pointer.

But Virginia is not an NCAA Tournament-quality team, and it appears the rest of the Tar Heels will be able to overcome McCants's struggles. Sean May converts a three-point play to boost the Heels' lead to 54–45 with 13:30 remaining. Even when McCants draws his fourth foul, the lead is still 62–54, and after May gets a generous no-call on what could have been goaltending of a Gary Forbes layup attempt, Carolina holds a 66–57 lead with 8 minutes left.

It is 68–59 at the 6:30 mark when Raymond Felton picks up a steal. The Virginia crowd, which has filled in throughout the contest, groans. This appears to be the dagger, as Felton leads a three-on-one fast break accompanied by David Noel and Sean May.

Then it all falls apart. As they cross the three-point line, Noel and May bump into each other just as Felton passes the ball. Neither sees the other, and they both reach for the ball as it arrives. Their collision sends the ball trickling away. After regaining possession, Devin Smith dunks for Virginia, and the 7,429 fans stir. A general sense of foreboding falls over the Carolina sideline.

"David and I were running," May says after the game. "He didn't see me and I didn't see him. I thought the pass was coming to me, and he thought it was going to him. We both pulled back. That's probably the difference in the game right there."

Blessed with an opponent apparently unable to get out of its own way, Virginia takes advantage of a handful of terrible decisions down the stretch—Felton attempts a pass while lying flat on his back instead of taking a jump ball that would have retained possession, Melvin Scott misses an unwise 21-footer, and May throws the ball away—to pull within 72–71 with 1:05 left. After a Gillen timeout, the Cavaliers inbound the ball near midcourt.

What the Carolina players see upon returning to the court looks very familiar: Virginia is lined up to run "Special," the very play Robinson drilled the Heels on a day earlier.

"We called out the play and we knew exactly what they were doing," May says. "At that point, I thought we were fine."

Felton shadows Billet around numerous screens, eventually forcing the Cavaliers to hunt for any available opening as the shot clocks melts away. Robinson's scouting works perfectly—the Tar Heels have eliminated Virginia's go-to play. Gary Forbes, who is making just 26 percent of his three-pointers, eventually has to heave a trifecta. As the ball bounces off the rim, it appears that Carolina has survived.

But the Tar Heels miss a box-out, allowing Smith to snatch the rebound as he is going out of bounds and throw the ball back into play. Jackie Manuel and Reynolds battle for it, the ball goes out of bounds, and the officials award possession to Virginia. It is Virginia's eighteenth offensive rebound of the game. Asked after the game whether offensive rebounding depends more on technical skill or effort, Raymond Felton will spit out just one word: "Effort."

There are 23.8 seconds left on the clock, but the rest of the game will take 15 minutes. Virginia runs a pick-and-roll for Billet at the top of the key. Elton Brown's pick eliminates Felton, and May steps out to put a hand in Billet's face. But as May leaves to go back to Brown, he steamrolls Felton, giving Billet an uncontested look at the basket and a potentially game-winning three-pointer. For the third straight game, he makes it, giving the Cavaliers a 74–72 lead.

As the ball falls through the net, the game clock keeps running—an error, since the clock is supposed to stop until the ball is inbounded. Roy Williams alerts the officials, who agree to review the courtside monitor to determine how much time should be on the clock, which currently shows 9.8 seconds. The Tar Heel coaches feel it should be somewhere around 11.5 seconds; the Virginia coaches, of course, would have happily let it run until it showed all zeroes.

Referees Ted Valentine and Karl Hess review the monitor for nearly 10 minutes. First, they set the clock to 13.6 seconds. But as Carolina is almost ready to inbound the ball, the officials reconvene at the scorer's table, and the clock is set back to 9.8 seconds. As the delay lengthens, McCants runs back and forth on the University Hall court to stay warm. Finally, the officials agree on 10.1 seconds.

As it turns out, it doesn't matter. Virginia has two fouls to give until the Heels enter the one-and-one, so Billet fouls Felton with 7.3 seconds left. The play is intended to disrupt whatever plan Carolina had drawn up during the lengthy delay, and it works perfectly. Felton and Roy Williams miscommunicate. Williams calls a new play, one that is designed to let Felton penetrate. But in the din, Felton doesn't hear him and runs the same play that was called during the break in play. His pass to McCants is knocked away by Jason Clark. Felton makes a last desperation heave off the loose ball, but it doesn't hit the rim.

Virginia students mob the court while Carolina players head for the locker room. The Cavaliers pile on Billet as soon as the buzzer sounds. When he emerges from the mass of humanity, he sees a strange sight: a solemn-faced man in a suit and tie, waiting patiently. It is Roy Williams, who has stayed on the court despite the increasing frenzy in order to shake Billet's hand and congratulate him on his game-winning shot.

Williams is not as pleased with his team. As he thinks about the game and the way the Heels lost the lead, it becomes very clear to him: things are about to change.

A storm is brewing. It is two days after Virginia, and the Tar Heels are practicing in the Smith Center practice gym because the main floor is being used by the traveling stage show performance of PBS's *Dragon Tales*. The practice gym, while a nice luxury on a day like this and just a few feet down the hall from the main arena, is set up in much closer quarters than the usual practice location. This is Carolina's first practice since the Virginia debacle, and their close proximity to the coach allows the players to see that he is not in a good mood. There is no joking. No smiling. His signature "Now then . . . ," with which he introduces each new segment of practice is clipped. He has had forty-two hours to recover from the loss in Charlottesville, but if anything the interval seems to have darkened his mood. He has instituted a new rule for this practice: every missed box-out results in every member of the offending team running a 33-second sprint—each player must run the length of the court six times in 33 seconds.

An hour passes without incident. But as the team works on half-court offense, Jawad Williams takes a running one-hander in the lane that is not a high-percentage shot.

Roy Williams, who is standing at midcourt, blows his whistle. There is complete silence in the practice gym. He rubs his forehead and walks over.

"Jawad, was that a great shot?" he asks quietly.

His junior forward correctly replies in the negative. The head coach begins a lecture on the importance of getting great shots—not just good shots, but great shots. His intensity rises with every word. Finally, his frustration boils over.

"You are six and seven in the league!" he yells, looking up and down the court at every member of the team. "You are in *seventh* place! You are embarrassing yourselves. I don't know if you have noticed or not, but every time the game is close, you get your butt kicked. Six and seven! And half of you think you are ready for the NBA Draft tomorrow. That's our problem. Everybody has got to get theirs."

It is an impressive explosion, and as he delivers it, each assistant coach edges to the other end of the court. As he finishes, he spits out, "On the line," and every player on the floor toes the baseline to prepare to run sprints. Before he blows the whistle to start the running, he looks around at the assistants and asks, "Do you understand what is going on out here?" They seem as perplexed as he is by the performance of the team. They all shake their heads.

The practice stretches to two and a half hours. At the end Williams leaves his players with just one simple thought. As they prepare for their customary end-of-practice stretching with strength coach Thomas McKinney, the head coach delivers a warning.

"Practice will be *harder* tomorrow," he says.

For several weeks, Williams has believed that he can't push this team as hard as he would have pushed some of his squads at Kansas. Weaker teams can't take as much practice pressure, he reckons. But the loss at Virginia has changed his mind. Practices go back to basics. He has never before had to use sprints as a punishment for errors so late in the season, but it seems to be the only way to get his team's attention. They go through a similarly intense workout the next day. The amount of running is reminiscent of some early-season practices in October, before games started.

But his players, who occasionally chafed in past years under extremely intense practices, respond well. Williams knows how to get his message across without making the criticism personal. The underlying message is clear even to those who bear the brunt of his intensity: he wants them to be a better basketball team, and his unhappiness does not extend past the court.

"It's been brutal," Sean May says. "But it's woken us up some. He knows what he's doing."

He'd better if the Heels are to win their next game, Sunday at 5:30 P.M. at NC State. The rivalry with Duke draws most of the national attention. But there is no more hostile place in the Atlantic Coast Conference for Carolina to play than Raleigh. At Cameron Indoor Stadium, there is always at least a hint of humor in the rivalry. At the RBC Center, it is pure hate that motivates the usually crass chants of the fans, and it seems to have increased markedly in recent years despite the Wolfpack's move from the cozy confines of Reynolds Coliseum. At Reynolds, coach Bill Guthridge was once nearly hit by a thrown battery. In 1987, Carolina freshman Scott Williams endured a terrible personal tragedy when his father shot and killed his mother and then turned the gun on himself. Later that season, Carolina played at State. As Williams made his first two free throws, the State student section repeatedly chanted, "Two for two!"

In those days, the chants were mostly invented on the spur of the moment. Now "cheer sheets" are passed out throughout the State student section. For the Carolina game, that sheet includes the instruction to chant "STD" at Rashad McCants, who is dating an NC State student, although the reason for the chant never becomes clear. Other references by the State students—for example to Sean May's weight, and to recruit JamesOn Curry's drug arrest—are clearer.

As the students bounce around in their center court seats just before tip-off, Julius Hodge and McCants cross paths at the scorer's table. Given the din—it's an intimidating atmosphere, which partly explains why the Pack is 14–0 at home this season—it's a challenge to be heard at courtside. But Hodge leans close to McCants and makes sure his Tar Heel counterpart can hear him as he utters one simple word:

"Pussy."

McCants does not respond, at least not directly to Hodge. But by halftime, when he has already piled up 13 points, it's clear that he's taking up the challenge issued by the State players and fans. Carolina holds a 40–27 advantage at halftime, and the gap was as large as 16 points during the first half. Roy Williams has deployed the Tar Heels in a point zone for much of the first half. State misses 10 of its first 11 shots against the defense, and makes just 3 of its 16 first-half three-pointers.

As has become their habit, the Heels eventually fritter the lead away in the second half. Marcus Melvin hits a three-pointer to give State their first lead of the half at 52–51 with 6 minutes left. This, it appears, will be another Tar Heel road collapse. But then the Carolina players appear to recall the Thought of the Day that was printed at the top of Thursday's practice plan: "Be mentally tough at the end of close games to execute and win."

Mental toughness has not always been a hallmark of this Carolina team. And the team is not perfect over the final 6 minutes; Felton makes some questionable decisions and May commits what could have been a crucial turnover. But Jawad Williams answers Melvin's three-pointer with a trifecta of his own, and after an Engin Atsur layup gives the Pack another 2-point lead with 4:20 remaining, Rashad McCants fires in a three-pointer to regain the lead for good. Williams switches his team back to the point zone for most of the last 4 minutes, and State continues their ice-cold outside shooting. After a Wolfpack miss, the Heels try to squeeze the shot clock. With the clock under 10 seconds, Felton tries to penetrate, but he loses the ball in front of the Carolina bench. McCants picks it up 22 feet from the basket, leans back, and fires it through the hoop over the outstretched arm of Hodge, all in one motion. It is a preposterous shot. But it goes in, and McCants finishes with 22 points and the two biggest baskets of the game. Hodge misses 7 of 11 shots, including 5 from three-point range, to finish with 13 points, and Carolina claims a 71–64 victory.

The victory is all the more impressive since it comes without defensive stopper Jackie Manuel, who sits out the game with an ankle injury suffered during Friday's practice. The Heels are back at .500 in the league, and defensively they have held opponents below 50 percent in field goal shooting for eight straight halves, the longest stretch of the season. Key to that improvement is Felton, who struggled to stop dribble penetration earlier in the season but who has become, in Williams's eyes, the team's best on-the-ball defender.

"I'm learning how to guard screens and keep my man in front of me," the Tar Heel point guard says. "I'm doing a better job helping out my teammates when somebody else has a lapse on defense. It took everybody a while to really understand what Coach Williams was trying to get across to us. But we're starting to get it now, trying to take charges every chance you get. Not being scared to use your body."

It has taken over four months of practice and twenty-five games. But Felton—and by extension, his teammates—may finally be getting it.

TEAM	ACC	OVERALL
DUKE	12–2	24–3
NC STATE	10–4	18–7
WAKE FOREST	9–5	19–6
GEORGIA TECH	7–7	20–8
UNC	7–7	17–8
FLORIDA STATE	6–9	18–11
VIRGINIA	5–9	15–10
MARYLAND	5–9	14–11
CLEMSON	3–12	10–16

Some occurrences in ACC basketball are rare. A Duke home loss, for example, or a Florida State win on the road, or a sportswriter passing up the pregame buffet. But only one game in the history of the league has thus far proven to be an absolute gimme: Carolina's home game against Clemson.

The Tigers have come to Chapel Hill forty-nine times in their basketball history and lost all forty-nine games. They've brought highly ranked teams, well-coached teams, and ACC Players of the Year to Carolina—and still lost every single game. It is a streak that defies logic. Duke, for example, does not come close to dominating the Tigers so completely. The streak was perhaps best illustrated by the January 28, 1998, game, when Rick Barnes brought a highly regarded Clemson team into the Smith Center. Under Barnes, the Tigers were known for extremely physical play, and the Tigers and Heels had already had several run-ins in recent years after what Carolina considered dirty play. The league office was well aware of the tension, and the officiating crew of Rick Hartzell, Steve Gordon, and Sam Croft whistled forty-one fouls on the Tigers, an ACC record. Six Clemson players fouled out of the game, forcing Barnes to end the game with only four players on the floor.

This year, under first-year head coach Oliver Purnell, the Tigers could expect at least to finish the game with the full set of players on the court. But they couldn't expect to win in Chapel Hill. Since their three-point explosion a month earlier at Littlejohn Coliseum, Clemson has returned to the doldrums. The Tigers made 85 percent of their three-pointers in that game; in the seven games since, they have made more than 39 percent just once.

They break the 39 percent barrier against the Heels, but not by much. The Tigers hit 7 of 17 attempts (41.2 percent) but can never generate any consistent offense against a Carolina team that also struggles offensively but seems to have rediscovered an interest in playing 40 minutes of defense behind Felton, who keys the defense while also handing out 9 assists against just 2 turnovers. The Heels force 23 Clemson turnovers and ride their best offensive weapon—Rashad McCants, who makes 8 of 13 three-pointers on his way to 30 points—to a 69–53 victory. McCants, who just two months earlier was seen by some as the poster child for what was wrong with Tar Heel basketball, has played himself into contention for the ACC Player of the Year award. His most telling play comes not on one of his successful three-pointers, but on one of the rare misses, when he hustles into the lane to retrieve the offensive rebound and dumps the ball inside for a chance at an easy basket. It is the kind of effort he might not have made earlier in the season. He is charming in the postgame media session and will delight reporters two days later when, for only the second time in his career, he agrees to do an interview with the collected media before a game. On Thursday he sits in the Smith Center press room and fields their questions for the better part of fifteen minutes, appearing to give genuine thought to every query and delivering what every reporter wants most—good, quotable insight—in nearly every response. Most tellingly, he makes eye contact with every questioner and never once rolls his eyes at a question. He is playing defense, he is scoring by the bucket-load, and he is interacting peacefully with the media. The fruits of Williams's sit-down with McCants two months earlier were not entirely immediate. But they are apparent now.

It's one of many subtle moves Williams has made this season to put his stamp on his first Carolina team. Another comes after the Clemson game, which is the last home contest for the squad's three walk-on seniors. After the final buzzer, which comes at 11 P.M., Williams hands the Smith Center microphone to each of the three seniors, in alphabetical order, to address the crowd. Thousands of fans linger, even at the late hour, to hear the short speeches. All three appear genuinely touched by being included in the day's festivities despite the fact that none played a full four years with the varsity team, instead beginning with the junior varsity and working up.

"It was a really special night," Jonathan Miller says. "It felt good that Coach Williams would go out of his way to make the night special for the three of us. Getting us to speak and then the little touches throughout the day, like the pins for our parents, made you feel really good."

The day isn't all about the seniors. Williams also takes time to speak to sophomore forward David Noel, who went scoreless in 20 minutes of action. Seeing Noel's long face after the game, the head coach approaches his stool. "You want to talk?" he asks Noel, who replies in the affirmative. The one-on-one conversation is their first extended talk about Noel's role, and he emerges from the chat looking more like the player who was one of Carolina's most consistent performers over the final month of the 2002–03 season. Despite his outstanding athletic ability, Noel is a player who needs consistent positive reinforcement to bolster his confidence. It was a call from Carolina alumnus Kenny Smith, who encouraged him to play more loosely—along with a highlight tape spliced together by Matt Doherty to show Noel the positive contributions he'd made during the season—that enabled him to break out of a slump during his freshman year. Now, with Jawad Williams still unpredictable, the Tar Heels need Noel to step forward again.

"Coach Williams wants me to play my game," Noel says. "He wants me to go out there and have fun and be a contributor to this team."

The practice on Thursday, two days later, could scarcely be more different from the previous Thursday's practice. With the children's show gone, practice is back in the Smith Center. And even though the game at Duke is just over forty-eight hours away, the mood is decidedly brighter than the previous week.

About an hour before practice is scheduled to begin, Rashad McCants walks out onto the Smith Center court. He finds a group of managers putting the team's newest training tool through its paces. The machine is the latest in a series of creations designed to allow a player to shoot without having to rebound his own shot. This particular model, known as Dr. Dish, is situated under the basket. A net swallows any rebound that falls near the hoop. From there, the ball is funneled into a lever-like mechanism that passes the ball back out to the shooter, allowing him to stand in the same spot and shoot jumper after jumper.

Walk-on point guard Wes Miller, McCants's longtime friend, is experimenting with the machine when McCants walks onto the court, where he is joined by freshman Reyshawn Terry. Miller and team manager Eric Hoots encourage McCants and Terry to try out the new device.

The two players don't know it, but they've just walked into a trap. Dr. Dish has one setting in which it delivers a pass only when the shooter makes a hand motion that catches an infrared eye. McCants and Terry don't know that, and Hoots and Miller "forget" to mention it. Instead, they tell the duo that the machine is voice-activated and passes the ball only when the shooter shouts, "Ball."

McCants lines up around the three-point line and calls, "Ball." Nothing happens. Terry tries it. "Ball!" he shouts. Nothing happens.

Unbeknownst to McCants and Terry, Hoots is holding a remote control device that signals the machine to pass the ball. When Miller pushes the pair aside and calls, "Ball!" Hoots presses the button, delivering the pass.

A look of disbelief crosses Terry's face.

"Man," he says, "that machine only passes it to white guys!"

Hoots and Miller dissolve in laughter before revealing the joke. It is one of the few places on the ultra-sensitive University of North Carolina campus where race can be joked about with such ease. A week earlier, Williams had set up the teams during one practice drill so that everyone on the team wearing white jerseys was, indeed, white. The head coach never noticed, but when Sean May pointed it out after the drill, the entire squad guffawed at the lily-white "White" team. "I never even noticed that," Williams told his players, and it's true—something that would doubtless please his mentor, Dean Smith, who played a significant role in integration in the state of North Carolina. Outside of the Smith Center, race matters. Inside, the only necessary credential is a good jump shot.

When Williams walks onto the floor shortly before the 4 P.M. practice, Hoots quickly tells him of the Dr. Dish experiment. Williams and Raymond Felton, who overhears the conversation, break into broad smiles. It is a loose but intense practice, nearly two hours long. Duke and NC State both lost the previous night, and Carolina, after concerns about missing the NCAA Tournament just two weeks earlier, now is a dead-certain lock for the field and could play itself as high as the third seed in next weekend's ACC Tournament.

Life, for the moment, is good. At the next afternoon's two-hour practice, Williams plays the role of the confident instructor, fielding questions from his players and watching quietly as Steve Robinson walks through a couple of Duke's key plays. The Tar Heels work on a new defensive wrinkle, the point-and-one—a variation on Carolina's usual point zone and a close relative of the box-and-one Virginia used so successfully on McCants—which they may deploy against Duke sharpshooter J. J. Redick. At the top of the practice plan is the regular season's final Thought for the Day: "What lies behind us and what lies before us are tiny matters compared to what lies within us."

The final activity of the practice is a competitive game. The White team wins handily, but as the clock ticks over the 4 minutes allotted for the drill, Williams keeps his team on the floor. "We've got to get one good stop with five guys boxing out, and then we're done," he says. "One good stop."

The White team forces a couple of turnovers but needs nearly 5 more minutes before they get the stop and defensive rebound Williams is waiting for. As his team prepares to do their end-of-practice stretching, he gives them a simple message: "We're going to have to have one big-time stop at some point in the game tomorrow night."

On Saturday night, the atmosphere inside Cameron Indoor Stadium is 50 percent basketball game, 50 percent carnival. ESPN has taken its *College Gamenight* highlights show on the road for the first time in history, and Rece Davis, Brad Daugherty, Jay Bilas, and Steve Lavin are broadcasting live just outside the doors of Cameron. However, by the time the network joins them at 8:00 P.M., one hour before tip-off, the raucous atmosphere that surrounded them earlier in the day has dwindled. By now, most of the famous Duke students have filed into their spots on Cameron's wooden bleachers, leaving outside only the unlucky few who didn't camp out in the week before the game. Duke ushers walk through the student section with dry-erase boards bearing the following message: "We have 1,000 people standing outside. Please turn sideways and move towards the middle."

In the front row of the student section, across from the benches, two different groups are dressed as characters from *The Wizard of Oz,* apparently in reference to Roy Williams's Kansas roots. The cheer sheet handed out to Duke students before the game—like at NC State, the Duke students plan their cheers in advance—includes no fewer than six references to Kansas. In the front row under one basket, three Duke graduate students (who are for some reason dressed as Vikings) are leading the undergrads through a choreographed rendition of KU's ominous-sounding "Rock Chalk" chant.

The Tar Heels are greeted with a typical razzing when they emerge from the locker room for their pregame warm-ups. Most of the players ignore the crowd. May has his ever-present iPod earphone in his ear. Rashad McCants, predictably, is the one player who engages the crowd. A year ago, he played to Duke's fans before the game, waving his arm to encourage them to get louder. This year, he punctuates his warm-up with a one-hand dunk, glances at the crowd, and then heads for the locker room.

With the last Tar Heel off the court and the Duke players still in their locker room, the carnival begins. A heavyset student at midcourt strips off a Carolina warm-up outfit to reveal a Tar Heel #42 jersey and shorts. Upon closer inspection, he even has a replica of Sean May's tattoo on his left bicep. The mini-May hops over the press table and onto the Cameron court. He is joined by one of the students dressed as the Wicked Witch of the West. The Witch waves her wand, apparently casting a spell over May, who is reduced to crawling on all fours. Then the Witch is handed a fishing pole with a Big Mac box dangling on the end. She casts it to one side of the court, sending mini-May scurrying after it. Just before he grabs it, she jerks it away, tossing it to the other side of the court.

Mini-May eventually pounces on the Big Mac. It is the second straight weekend that May's weight has been the subject of derision from an opposing student section. But at NC State, there was no hint of cleverness. In Durham, at least, the crowd has put some thought into their effort. May, as usual, takes it with good humor. Although he misses the Big Mac skit, he is later told about it. His reaction is a wide smile. "If they said something about my weight this year," he says, "I'd hate to see what they would have said last year."

Not all the Blue Devils are so unwelcoming to their visitors. When Mike Krzyzewski, a West Point graduate, emerges from the Duke locker room shortly before tip-off, he stops by the Carolina bench to shake hands with the Tar Heel coaches. As he shakes assistant coach Joe Holladay's hand, he leans in and asks, "Where's your son?" Holladay points to the seats behind the Carolina bench, where Army Ranger Mathew Holladay, also a West Point grad, is enjoying his first-ever Carolina-Duke game during a short break from his posting in Italy. Krzyzewski makes it a point to reach into the crowd and shake the younger Holladay's hand, as the West Point connection and the Duke coach's respect for a Ranger outrank even the Carolina-Duke rivalry.

As the game begins, there is one last sideshow: Donald Trump emerges just before tip-off to a chorus of "You're fired!" from the Crazies. It is Trump's first visit to Cameron, where he is the guest of a Blue Devil booster. His courtside seat gives him a prime view of Carolina racing out to an 11–5 lead with 12:30 left in the first half, propelled by a McCants dunk off the opening tip. Neither team is playing particularly well. It seems the Tar Heels' best offense is to miss shots, as they recover 12 offensive rebounds in the first 20 minutes to Duke's 3. That edge gives them a 33–30 halftime lead, seeming to prove the point that Roy Williams had included in bold type on the previous day's practice plan: "The game will be won or lost on the boards!"

McCants is 5 of 9 from the field, but no other player in light blue has made more than half his shots. Raymond Felton, who is 1 for 3, has to leave the game just before halftime after taking a hip check from Duke's Shavlik Randolph and suffering a hip pointer. After being examined during the break, Felton—who winced when he stood up from the bench to enter the locker room—determines that he will try to play in the second half. He does play, and is on the court for 17 of 20 minutes in the second half.

Duke blitzes the Heels with 6 straight points at the opening of the stanza, forcing a Roy Williams timeout. The main problem at the moment is Duke freshman Luol Deng, a versatile wing player who is too big for Jackie Manuel, too quick for Sean May, and too skilled for David Noel. Deng, whom Mike Krzyzewski called the best player on the team before the season, shot 1 of 14 in Duke's most recent game, but appears to have cured his shooting woes. He makes 7 of 10 shots in the second half and finishes with a game-high 25 points. Duke's vaunted perimeter game is relatively silent, as they shoot just 27.3 percent from beyond the three-point line. Jackie Manuel again locks down sharpshooter J. J. Redick, holding him to 3 of 9 from the field. But Deng makes up for the lack of offense from other players, scoring on a variety of mid-range moves and consistently providing Duke with a slim lead. Fresh off his talk with Williams, Noel struggles to guard Deng but is otherwise superb, finishing with 12 points and 8 rebounds, the first time in fourteen games he has finished in double figures.

McCants, meanwhile, is listless in the second half. Jawad Williams converts a four-on-zero fast break with a slam dunk, choosing not to pass ahead to McCants, and the talented sophomore spends too much time dribbling over the next several minutes. Instead of moving the ball and acting decisively, as he has done during his hot scoring stretch, McCants ponders his options, and the Tar Heel offense begins to slow down. But Carolina's defensive intensity—including McCants, who is effective guarding Daniel Ewing—keeps the game close. With the score tied at 54, May misses a wide-open 8-footer with 7:30 left, and after a

Chris Duhon miss, Felton misses a wide-open three-pointer. After Shelden Williams scores on an offensive rebound, Duke will not relinquish the lead.

The game's final seconds are hectic. Down 68–65, Carolina chooses not to foul. Ewing misses a three-pointer and the Heels secure the rebound, apparently getting the "one big-time stop" their head coach told them one day earlier they would need. David Noel fires an outlet pass to McCants, who is streaking down the right sideline in front of the Carolina bench. The clock ticks under 10 seconds. Facing defensive pressure from Redick and Duhon, McCants draws to a stop on the right wing, just in front of the three-point line, the spot where he has been most dangerous all season.

On Thursday afternoon, McCants met with the media in a press conference setting for just the second time all season. It is the type of environment he typically had shunned during his freshman season and the early part of his sophomore year, declining the requests of sports information staffers that he appear before the media. But on this day, he delivered perhaps the most insightful, engaging press conference of any Carolina player this season. He was thoughtful and humorous—he was the person his friends say he can be.

He is also unfailingly confident, which led to one of his last comments. Just before leaving the table set up in the press room of the Smith Center, McCants was asked about Redick. So far, the pregame buildup has been devoid of any trash talk or baiting by either team. McCants ends that trend.

"I don't find J. J. to be too much of a threat," he said, and then paused (nearly causing some eager reporters to fall out of their seats), "besides shooting three's. If he's not making shots, I don't think he's going to be too much of a factor."

It is fate, then, that it is Redick who reaches in and swipes at the ball as McCants gathers himself to attempt the game-tying three-pointer. The ball pops free, and Redick is instantly on the floor, scooping up the ball and signaling for a timeout. McCants never hits the hardwood, instead reaching for the ball with his hands while keeping his feet behind the three-point line, as if he wants to pick it up and still attempt the last-second shot. After the timeout, Redick makes a pair of free throws to ice the 70–65 Blue Devil victory, their fourteenth in the teams' past sixteen meetings.

McCants would later say he thought he'd been fouled on the game's final play. His head coach, however, thought a different decision might have been in order.

"It would have been nice if Rashad could have handled the ball a little better and passed to somebody else, since he had two people on him," Williams said. "But I like Duke's defensive intensity and their relentlessness."

That intensity seems to have a profound impact on Melvin Scott, who finishes the game 1 of 7 from the field. It is the fourth straight sub-par effort for the junior guard. His struggles lead him to make an unusually candid admission to Williams in the locker room. Ordinarily, Scott is the jokester, the player most likely to blow off a poor performance. This time, though, he is clearly shaken. "Coach, I'm really sorry," he tells Williams with emotion in his voice. "I really want to play well for you."

"I know you do," his coach tells him. "I know you do."

In some ways, the loss is not a complete disaster. Sean May continues to bounce back from his midseason slump, notching his twelfth double-double of the season and effectively taking Duke's touted Shelden Williams out of the game. May, who probably has the highest basketball IQ on the team, can sometimes be too analytical. During a January shooting slump, he spent hours in the film room, rewinding and pausing game tapes to try and discover the flaw in his game. But since the home loss to Duke, he has cut down on film work in an effort to rely more on his instincts—which are rarely incorrect.

Such a lackluster offensive performance would have resulted in a blowout earlier in the season. The Tar Heels continue to demonstrate a growing understanding of Roy Williams's defensive principles—for the eighth straight game, they hold an opponent under 50 percent shooting from the field. It's a small step, but a significant one.

Williams, however, knows there were problems hidden beneath the surface. Raymond Felton again struggles to control the end of the game in the way his head coach would like, and during a second-half huddle after a pair of late turnovers, the sophomore does not immediately accept responsibility for his mistakes. Jawad Williams plays just 24 minutes and is miffed about his declining playing time; he has played more than 30 minutes just twice in the past twelve games after averaging 34.5 minutes per game over the first month of the season. Part of the reason for that decrease is the return of David Noel, who lately has provided the energy and intensity the head coach wants; the other part is his inconsistent play following his rash of head injuries.

When the squad gathers for practice on Monday, Roy Williams has prepared a series of nine video clips that show the Tar Heels taking bad shots with 15 seconds or more left on the shot clock. It is well into March and the weather has turned spring-like. But Williams is still trying to bang through the same message he was preaching in October: we don't want good shots. We want great shots.

"The biggest thing that's caught me off guard is the idea that it's got to be us," he says. "The big picture was not as important as I thought it should be. The big picture is the name on the front of the jersey, not the back. It's human nature that if you haven't had as much team success as you would like, you have to look for some other way, and that's usually the individual. One thing I've always taken a great deal of pride in is that our team didn't give a darn about anything else besides our team. But if things haven't gone as smoothly as you'd like and you've been in college for a while and haven't been to the Tournament, you don't get your recognition that way, so you think you have to do it yourself.

"Earlier in the year I said I wanted our players to play together as a team more. That makes it sound like they are selfish or bad guys. But if things aren't going well, you're going to try and grab on to something to have good feelings about, and that might not always be the best thing for the whole team. It's been a much bigger sell than I ever thought it would be that it's 'we'—it's not 'I' or 'me.' "

15

THURSDAY

VIRGINIA

(8) versus Clemson (9) 7:00 P.M.

FRIDAY

DUKE

(1) versus 8/9 winner—noon

GEORGIA TECH

(4) versus Carolina (5)—2:00 P.M.

NC STATE

(2) versus Florida State (7)—7:00 P.M.

WAKE FOREST

(3) versus Maryland (6)—9:00 P.M.

In North Carolina, the Friday of the ACC Tournament is close to a state holiday. Games begin at noon and last until almost midnight, eight of the best teams in college basketball battling each other for almost twelve hours. In public schools, some teachers will allow their pupils to watch the afternoon games on television, occasionally sprinkling in math lessons based on three-pointers or free-throw percentages. Businesses across the state will notice a drop in productivity as workers surreptitiously listen to radios at their desks, the same way fans a generation ago might have listened to the World Series. On one Internet message board devoted to NC State sports, a thread entitled "Work Excuses to Stay Home on Friday" receives eighty-six responses, including, "The same aunt that has died for the past twenty-five years, has just passed away again. Funeral is Friday at 1 P.M."

Tickets to a Carolina home game are hard to obtain; tickets to the ACC Tournament are treasures. Raleigh actor Ira David Wood III scripted an irreverent stage retelling of Charles Dickens's *A Christmas Carol* twenty-five years ago that has become one of the best-loved holiday traditions in North Carolina's capital city. In one scene, the Ghost of Christmas Past asks Wood, playing Scrooge, why he left his longtime love, Laura, and never returned. It is an emotional moment.

"Well, I got these really great ACC Tournament tickets," Scrooge replies, prompting gales of laughter from an audience that understands exactly how prized those tickets can be. Getting tickets through Carolina for the Final Four is typically a breeze—the event is usually held at a 40,000-seat arena and the seats are only split among four schools. By contrast the ACC Tournament is held at a 23,000-seat arena and tickets must be split nine ways. Carolina receives about 2,400 tickets, nowhere near enough to fill the demand from the nearly 13,000 members of the Rams Club. Members receive one point for each hundred dollars donated to the organization and one point for each year of membership. To receive a pair of tickets for the 2004 Tournament through UNC, members were advised that a lifetime point total of 1,175 would probably be required; for four tickets, the point cutoff jumped to 1,750. When the Atlantic Coast Conference pursued expansion in the summer of 2003, one of the problems raised by UNC in its opposition to the plan was the impact on the ACC Tournament. Donors frequently increase their contributions in order to be eligible to buy tickets; with a depleted ticket supply, the concern was that donations would decrease. Although they will be full members in every other conceivable way, new league members Virginia Tech and Miami will receive only a one-third share of Tournament tickets in their first year in the league, and a two-thirds share in their second year. Even with that concession, Carolina's supply of tickets is expected to dwindle from 2,400 this season to below 2,000 in 2005. Already, fund-raising honchos are dreading the 2008 ACC Tournament, when the three new members will receive a full allotment of tickets, and so twelve schools will have to split 18,000 tickets for Charlotte's new arena.

In many ways, this is the last ACC Tournament as most fans remember it. Former NC State coach Everett Case was the first to come up with the idea for a postseason league tournament. He may have proposed it in part because he knew he had the best team in the conference—and also the only gym, Reynolds Coliseum, that would be suitable for the event—but for whatever reason, it worked. The ACC played its first postseason event in 1954.

It's not the oldest postseason tournament in the country (according to the NCAA, the ACC was the fourth league to organize one), but it is the best. State's Reynolds Coliseum hosted the first thirteen tournaments before it began to travel. Case's idea didn't take long to catch on—the last public sale of tickets was in 1965. In the early years, when the NCAA Tournament field was much smaller, only the ACC Tournament champion earned a chance to play for the national title. That created epic battles, like the 1974 clash between NC State and Maryland. Both teams were clearly among the top five in the nation, but only State—after dispatching the Terps 103–100 in overtime in the league final—advanced to the NCAA Tournament.

The expansion of the NCAA field means that six schools—Duke, State, Wake, Georgia Tech, Carolina, and Maryland—journey to Greensboro fairly confident that they'll be selected for the NCAA Tournament. The Tar Heels are generally expected to receive a fourth or fifth seed when pairings are announced Sunday evening. A string of victories in Greensboro might elevate them to a third seed; an early exit at the hands of the Yellow Jackets could drop them to sixth.

While countless column inches are devoted to the passing of the ACC Tournament as fans have come to know it, Roy Williams is not as sentimental. Journalists and fans enjoy the Tournament; for Williams and the other eight head coaches in the league, it's a source of considerable stress. The ACC is, by consensus, the best basketball conference in the country this season. The teams have spent three months beating up on each other. Now they'll go to Greensboro and do it all over again over a seventy-two-hour period. Williams's team has already sealed a bid to the NCAA Tournament, so in essence, he's just exposing it one more time to the threat of injury. He is the only coach who doesn't take his team to practice at the Greensboro Coliseum on Thursday, noting that his Tar

Heels have already played a game there earlier in the season. The move draws some complaints from the media, but his is a coach's perspective, not a fan's.

"When you're concerned about your team winning, you could care less who is playing Thursday night. I am not going to watch that game. It's a fact that it's part of the ACC Tournament, but I could give a flip. I'm concerned about 2:30. So all that pageantry and all that, if I were a fan, I might be sad. But I'm not into all that stuff . . . I'm coaching North Carolina. And if we lose, I'm not going up there and watch the game Sunday afternoon. I'm going to be here practicing. It's much more for the fans. I don't think it's for coaches at all.

"Do I love the Tournament? No, I don't love the Tournament at all. In some ways, it's just a huge cocktail party for four or five days. People put so much weight on the NCAA Tournament, so the ACC Tournament is just something we do between the regular season and the NCAA Tournament."

His comments cause a stir. One reporter asks a follow-up question that begins, "Coach, you said you don't like the Tournament all that much . . . ," a sign of how the comment will be perceived in the days to come. Williams never says the words, "I don't like the Tournament." Instead, he says he doesn't love it. To him, the distinction is important. He is a man who chooses his words precisely, so the difference between "like" and "love" to him is crucial. But by the time he explains the difference to the reporters, the comment has already begun to take on a life of its own. Even some Carolina fans, like the Rams Club donors who pony up the hundreds of thousands of dollars it takes to secure tickets, are slightly miffed that their coach doesn't seem as enthralled with the event as they are.

Williams consistently downplays his interest in the event to the media. But with the players, he takes a different tone.

"Guys, we've got to play this weekend," he tells them in the Smith Center locker room on Wednesday. "So we might as well win it." When the travel itinerary is issued later that day, his players can't help but notice that it's a four-day schedule. The listing for Sunday at 1:00 P.M., the time of the championship game, is a simple line of text: "UNC vs. NCSU/FSU/WFU/MU winner."

As they take the court for Friday's second quarterfinal, the Carolina players are greeted by the usual split reaction. The game is being played in Greensboro, a Tar Heel stronghold that is traditionally packed with UNC supporters. When the Heels played in the same arena earlier in the season, Roy Williams marveled at the passionate support provided by the Greensboro crowd and used it as an example of what he wanted the Smith Center crowd to become. According to the way the tickets are split, only about 2,400 should be in the hands of fans wearing light blue. But at other less basketball-crazy schools, like Florida State and Clemson, fans are less fanatical than those along Tobacco Road. They sell their tickets to brokers or give them to friends, creating a thriving secondary market for tickets. Close to half the building, it seems during warm-ups, is rooting for the Heels.

But the other half is decidedly anti-Carolina. Upon the arrival of Dean Smith in 1961, the Tar Heels became the ACC's flagship basketball program. That inspired envy and jealousy from fans of their league brethren, and in the late 1970s, a curious phenomenon began to develop: the "ABC" fan. The letters stood for three words: "Anybody But Carolina," and it became a mindset throughout the league. If you were a Maryland fan, and your team was eliminated early in the Tournament, you stayed to root for your new favorite team: Anybody But Carolina. The same was true at the other conference schools, especially at Duke, Wake, and NC State.

That hatred has dimmed somewhat due to Carolina's struggles over the past two years and Duke's dominance. The Blue Devils came to Greensboro having won an amazing five straight Tournament titles, prompting senior guard Chris Duhon to remark that "everybody else is playing for second place." ABC, a backhanded way of showing significant respect, was in danger of giving way to ABD. Or as Roy Williams says, "The mystique is not the same as it was when I left."

At most road venues, his statement is true. But at the ACC Tournament, where most of the fans are old-money donors who have been around the league for decades, the hatred of Carolina still burns. North Carolina Senator and John Kerry running mate John Edwards is in the minority when he leaves his courtside seat for a television interview and proclaims, "I'm a Tar Heel fan."

Roy Williams isn't overly concerned about the makeup of the crowd. He's more interested in his team building on the points he emphasized to them after the Duke game—playing an up-tempo yet still controlled style of offense that results in great shots. His team does get good shots early, but not in the way he might have planned. Rashad McCants appears to have reverted to his early-season offensive form: on at least three first-half possessions, he catches the ball and then ponders his next move, seemingly oblivious that his deliberation is breaking down the Carolina offense. On one play, he and Jawad Williams execute a smooth pick-and-roll, but as Williams breaks free under the basket, McCants instead chooses to loft a three-pointer.

It would be easy for Roy Williams to be frustrated with his talented sophomore, who received the most votes in the conference for All-ACC honors, which were announced earlier in the week. But McCants compensates for his errors by continuously putting the ball in the hoop, and by the time he converts an old-fashioned three-point play with 10 minutes left, the Heels hold a 24–13 advantage. Even without Jackie Manuel, who picks up his third foul with 12:11 left, Carolina still boasts an 11-point advantage with 7:30 remaining in the first half. The fifth-seeded Heels are the trendy pick to win the Tournament, and they give a dozen minutes of championship-caliber effort.

Then the momentum changes. An athletic, high-flying Tech squad scores 7 points in the next minute. They tie the score at 33 with 4:10 left in the half as Carolina's defense turns into a sieve, prompting Roy Williams to run his fingers through his salt-and-pepper hair. The postseason is supposed to be the time of year when upperclassmen provide leadership to their younger teammates. That is not what is unfolding on the Greensboro Coliseum court for Carolina. Instead, when Jawad Williams allows Anthony McHenry to breeze by him on a give-and-go for a layup, the head coach has to remove his junior for the remainder of the half in favor of walk-on freshman Justin Bohlander. Two minutes later, B. J. Elder slashes through three flat-footed Heels for a layup, giving Tech a 41–35 lead at the 2-minute mark. Foul trouble and defensive lapses leave Williams juggling some unusual lineups—Carolina ends the half with no players on the court who have scored a single point (Bohlander, Byron Sanders, Jesse Holley, Melvin Scott, and David Noel). Not surprisingly, Carolina ends the half with a 42–39 deficit, having allowed the Jackets to make 51.9 percent of their first-half field goals.

"The first half was a nightmare for me," Roy Williams will say. "I had no idea what offense we were running. It wasn't the offense we try to coach. When the ball goes to one guy and it stops there for a long period of time, I think that offense is easier to guard."

The halftime break provides little relief. On one of Carolina's first possessions, the stagnant offense continues as Rashad McCants holds the ball for a full 9 seconds before attempting a contested jump shot. Manuel picks up his fourth foul 7 minutes into the half. The loss of one of his best man-to-man defenders forces Roy Williams to try some zone defense. Isma'il Muhammad promptly gets an alley-oop dunk, and Marvin Lewis hits a three-pointer to give Tech a 61–52 lead. Some of the conflicting personalities within the Carolina team are starting to have an impact on the floor. With 8 minutes left and facing an 11-point deficit, Sean May loses the ball in the paint. It bounds to Jawad Williams, who for a split second appears to have a clear passing lane to Rashad McCants wide open under the basket. Instead of delivering the high-risk pass, however, Williams backs the ball out and restarts the offense. McCants cocks his head at his teammate, throws his hands out, and rolls his eyes, muttering, "Come on, man!" The possession ends with Raymond Felton kicking the ball out of bounds.

Most of the Carolina players and coaches believe any off-court disagreements are left behind when the Tar Heels step onto the hardwood. Still, some members of the program believe there have been instances this season when off-court personality conflicts have carried over onto the court. Moments like this one lend credence to the charge. At least one Tar Heel will openly say that the personalities rather than the plays have sometimes determined passes or shots for this year's team.

"It's sad to say, but I do think some of that stuff carried over to the court," David Noel says. "You look at a couple of the games, and you could see the frustration coming out. You don't expect that at the University of North Carolina, but it's true."

Williams misses five straight opportunities from within 5 feet with 6:45 left. Suddenly, though, something clicks. Even the players and coaches can't quite diagnose it, but the Tar Heels abruptly revert to their more fluid first-half ways. A Sean May steal sparks a fast break, May hits a layup, and Felton hits a three-pointer. Frustrated Carolina fans are out of their seats and roaring as the Heels close to within 1 point with 3:45 on the clock. Tech looks rattled, and Carolina has become the more assertive team. Elder scores to provide a 3-point cushion, but Felton promptly answers with another trifecta. After a defensive rebound, Felton—who is on his way to a sparkling 20-point, 6-assist, 3-steal performance—hits David Noel with a laser-guided 40-foot bounce pass for a layup, and Carolina holds an improbable 79–77 advantage with 2 minutes left. Tech battles back to tie the game with one minute remaining.

The second half has been a microcosm of Carolina's season. The Heels started strong, using stellar individual performances to overwhelm a less talented team. But then they went to sleep on defense, allowing Tech to creep back into the game. Now, with a minute left and the game tied, they need only the "one big-time stop" Williams has so often stressed to them in order to get a chance to win the game.

They get it. Manuel closes out perfectly on Elder, forcing him to pass to Jarrett Jack for a desperation three-pointer that clangs off the backboard with 45 seconds left. After the rebound, Carolina's first offensive option is a backdoor pass from Felton to McCants, a play that has already worked twice in the game. But although McCants appears to have a sliver of daylight, Muhammad makes a diving, twisting play and swats the pass away with his left hand. The ball trickles to Sean May, who is fouled while attempting a potentially game-winning shot. May has already nailed 10 of his 12 free throws, but on this occasion he makes just one of two. After a timeout, Tech controls the ball near midcourt with under 10 seconds left. As the Tar Heels break the huddle, Roy Williams tells his team, "Let's play the best twenty-two defense [one of Carolina's man-to-man defensive calls] we've ever played. Let's make them shoot over our hands."

But Carolina's defense over the next few seconds is a textbook example of how not to defend a last-second play. Jack inbounds the ball to Marvin Lewis, and Felton incorrectly leaves his man—Jack—to track Lewis. That leaves McCants on Jack at the top of the key, and the Yellow Jacket point guard smoothly cruises right past McCants, who chooses to swat at the ball from behind rather than moving his feet and staying in front of Jack. The misplay gives the Jackets a variety of options—Jack can shoot or he can dish to Elder or Lewis, both of whom have a clear look at the basket thanks to the confused Carolina defense. Jack decides to take it himself. As the Tech point guard moves inside the three-point line, Carolina radio analyst and former standout point guard Phil Ford lets out an audible, "Oh no" as Jack elevates for the final shot. Just as Ford feared, the shot finds the bottom of the net, giving Paul Hewitt's team an 83–82 lead with 1.4 seconds left.

Roy Williams wants his team to call timeout in this situation any time the clock is under 7 seconds, and as soon as the ball falls through the net the head coach is screaming for a timeout. In the last huddle, he had reminded his squad that two timeouts were left—something Sean May remembers. He grabs the ball and makes a T with his hands around the ball while stepping behind the endline. But no one in the officiating crew of Duke Edsall, Les Jones, and Jamie Luckie sees him. When the timeout is not immediately granted, May fires the ball inbounds in the direction of McCants. Marvin Lewis easily steps in front of the pass, intercepts it, and dribbles out the remaining time.

The frenetic ending stuns the crowd of 23,745. There is an intermission after the second quarterfinal game on Friday, and usually by the end of the second quarterfinal, the crowd is sparse. Most fans duck out to the parking lot in the second half to try and grab something to eat during the three-hour break.

This year, however, it appears that virtually no one has left. There is no mad rush up the Coliseum steps to make the short drive to Stamey's, a local barbecue institution. There is very little movement at all except for Jack's victory dash around the court, which he punctuates by stopping in front of the Carolina cheering section and yelling, "Go home!" The fans, however, can't seem to do it. Many sit, motionless, as their team walks off the court. It will likely be the last time that many of these fans see the team in person this year. With the loss, Carolina has assured itself of being shipped out west by the NCAA Tournament Selection

Committee, which will not grant a favorable location or seed to a team that has an 18–10 record and two straight losses on its résumé.

The Tar Heel players themselves provide perhaps the best glimpse of the year into the psyche of the team. While addressing the media, Rashad McCants—who will soon pull his hooded sweatshirt over his head and decline any further questions—says, "This team has too many leaders and not enough followers." About ten feet away, Jawad Williams provides another explanation for the loss, a pointed reference to a team-mate's last-second lapse: "If we don't get beat on defense at the end, we win the game."

The game is a perfect illustration of the season. The three ultra-talented sophomores have solid games, as Felton scores 20, McCants 25, and May 27. But the rest of the team combined contribute only 10 points—Melvin Scott is 0 for 4 from the field, and Jawad Williams is 3 of 11. Individuals, as Roy Williams has been telling them all season, do not win meaningful games. It takes a team effort, and today the Tar Heels did not resemble a team.

The quarterfinal loss means that only the NCAA Tournament remains. True to his word, Roy Williams tells his players to pack their belongings for the one-hour bus trip back to Chapel Hill rather than staying in Greensboro for the rest of the Tournament. They do not gather to watch the conference championship game. Instead, they are practicing on the floor of the Smith Center while Maryland and Duke tip off in the league final. Williams stops practice at 1:00 P.M. to remind his players that the championship game—where they had hoped to be—is beginning. He stops practice again once the Terps get the over-time victory to let his team know that another group has claimed the league title.

Later that evening, the entire squad gathers at Williams's home to watch the NCAA Tournament selection show. It is the second straight year the Tar Heels have watched the show as a team. One year ago, Matt Doherty, who harbored fleeting hopes of an at-large bid, gathered his troops at his home, located on the same leafy Chapel Hill street where they meet with Williams, to watch the pairings. The mood is less somber this year, but not as excited as Williams might have guessed. On some campuses, when a school's name appears on the screen, the players jump out of their seats and exchange high fives. But when CBS unveils the words "North Carolina" about halfway through the show, matched up against Air Force, the reaction in the Williams living room is muted. The indifference surprises their head coach, who expected more celebration after a two-year absence from the Tournament. His mood does not improve when, as he addresses his team in what is intended to be a quiet, team-only moment, his speech is interrupted by a phone call from a local radio show seeking an interview later in the evening.

The fact that the Tar Heels are coming off a lethargic effort against Georgia Tech does not lessen expectations. By the time ESPN concludes their three-hour breakdown of the NCAA Tournament brackets Sunday evening, alleged experts Steve Lavin and Andy Katz—perhaps blinded by the raw talent on the Tar Heel roster and the big win over Connecticut —have already picked Carolina to beat Duke in the regional final and advance to the Final Four. Beginning in November and all the way through mid-March, Roy Williams has told anyone who would listen that his team and the words "Final Four" do not belong in the same sentence. Over the next three weeks, his team gets the chance to prove him wrong.

Roy Williams has the sixth-best winning percentage in NCAA Tournament games of any active coach. He has won 70.8 percent of his games in the field of sixty-four, and his thirty-four Tournament victories leave him fifth among active coaches, behind only Mike Krzyzewski, Bob Knight, Lute Olson, and Jim Boeheim. With the Tar Heels' selection this year, his active streak of fifteen consecutive NCAA appearances is second only to Olson's twenty. His teams have made it to four Final Fours.

And yet the NCAA Tournament continues to be, in the minds of some, his albatross. He has never won a national title despite, on at least one occasion, believing that he had the best team in the country. His teams have occasionally experienced surprising upsets in the postseason, including a 1992 upset to Texas-El Paso, a disappointing defeat to Virginia in the regional semifinals in 1995 in a game played in Kansas City, and a 1998 loss to Rhode Island. But the key moment, the game that he will have to apologize for until he wins a national championship, came in 1997. The Kansas Jayhawks had the best team in the country that season. Led by Raef LaFrentz, Paul Pierce, Jerod Haase, and Jacque Vaughn, they blitzed through the Big 12 regular season with a 15–1 record and entered NCAA Tournament play with a 32–1 mark. This was, it appeared, ol' Roy's year. The Jayhawks crushed the competition in the Big 12 tournament, whipping Oklahoma State by 15, Iowa State by 24, and Missouri by 27 to win the league title. They came to the NCAA Tournament having had only one game closer than 12 points in the past month.

Kansas defeated Jackson State and Purdue to move into the round of sixteen against a youthful Arizona team. But it was the beginning of a guard-heavy era in the NCAA Tournament, and the Wildcats had plenty of guards. On the way to winning Lute Olson's first national championship, the Wildcats got 21 points from Mike Bibby, 20 points from Michael Dickerson, and 17 points from Miles Simon to claim an 85–82 victory. Arizona got the victory only after a furious Kansas rally closed the deficit from 13 with 3:30 remaining to 3 points on the last possession of the game, when Kansas had three chances to tie the score. All rimmed out.

"We had three straight chances to tie the game," Williams recalls, the game still fresh in his mind. "After that season was the biggest study of myself and my philosophy that I've ever done."

Oddly, one of his most painful defeats turned out to be a critical building block in his self-confident approach to coaching. In the wake of the loss, he spent endless nights analyzing and reanalyzing the way he had coached the team. Friends believed he had reached a point of being overly self-critical. He was near the top of his profession; he had pushed his career winning percentage over the unheard-of figure of 80 percent. But he wondered if he was a good coach.

He still retained, however, his above-average intelligence. And so he eventually recognized that what his friends—both inside and outside the coaching business—were telling him was true: college basketball was not the same as the NBA. Instead of a seven-game series, college teams played a one-game-and-out format that occasionally allowed for a hot streak or a lucky bounce to impact the outcome. Sometimes the best team simply didn't win.

And after critiquing every move he made during the 1996–97 season, Roy Williams came to an important realization: he would have changed very little. There was no clear error in his coaching, no obvious flaw that allowed his team to lose.

"Every year, I take time after the season to get away and go through the thought processes of what I'd change and what I wouldn't change," he says. "I talk to other coaches. And over the last fifteen or sixteen years, what it's taught me is that I do enough thinking about it beforehand that very seldom would I change any of it except the results."

The seeds of that more mature outlook were planted in 1997.

"As he's gotten older, he's started to realize that sometimes you just have to rely on eighteen-year-old kids," close friend Cody Plott says. "You prepare them and get them ready. Sometimes they just may not make the shot."

Sometimes they may not make the shot. It's a lesson that, if Williams hadn't learned it already, would have been driven home by the 2003–04 Tar Heels during the regular season and the ACC Tournament. Carolina entered NCAA play having lost seven games by six points or less, all of which were winnable games in the final minute of play. Carolina had lost by technical foul (Maryland), by buzzer-beaters (Duke), and by desperation three-pointers (Kentucky). It had lost nail-biting conference games in triple overtime (Wake Forest), single overtime (Florida State), and in regulation (at Virginia). Only twice all season were they truly out of a game in the final 60 seconds. Usually, the Tar Heels had a shot to win or tie. Sometimes, however, the shot didn't go in.

National observers seemed to believe the Tar Heels were simply snakebitten, rather than having some fundamental flaw that caused them to lose close games. On the Monday after the NCAA Tournament brackets were announced, the Heels became the trendy pick to advance at least to the final eight, which would present an Armageddon-type clash with Duke for the right to advance to the Final Four. The two teams had never met in the NCAA Tournament. Now, the NCAA Selection Committee had cast that bait into the water.

Roy Williams isn't biting. He is one of the few human beings in America who has never filled out an NCAA Tournament bracket. Instead of looking at Carolina's region as a whole, he prefers to view it as a series of 4-team tournaments. By Monday, he has looked no further than the Heels' potential second-round matchup, which would be against the winner of the Texas-Princeton contest. He and his team have significantly more media-related responsibilities in the 72 hours before their meeting with Air Force. NCAA rules require teams to be on-site more than 24 hours before their first game, which means Carolina's charter leaves the Raleigh-Durham airport Tuesday evening. When it arrives in Denver, the players tell their head coach they are thinking of shaving their heads en masse as a sign of team unity. "You going to do it, Coach?" they ask. "If we make the Final Four, I'll shave my head," he promises. His only request is that the media not find out, because he doesn't want it to become a big story—as a chrome-domed Roy Williams certainly would.

Wednesday, the squad is required to practice at the Pepsi Center in a 50-minute session open to the public. For most teams, it's a chance to show off for the fans. Texas has the workout time before the Tar Heels, and the Longhorns spend the majority of their time determining which player can throw down the most crowd-pleasing dunk. Head coach Rick Barnes observes from afar, sitting casually atop a press table while chatting with CBS sideline reporter Bonnie Bernstein. Bernstein, of course, is best known as the reporter who badgered Roy Williams into saying, "Right now, I don't give a shit about North Carolina," on national television after the 2003 NCAA championship game. That fact is not lost on Barnes, who has a sly sense of humor and loves to deliver straight-faced jokes. When Williams and the Tar Heels emerge for their practice, Barnes is still talking to Bernstein. As Williams comes within earshot, Barnes pointedly says, "Bonnie, I just want you to know something. I do give a shit about Texas." It's a good line, but unfortunately for the head Longhorn, Williams doesn't hear it. He is too focused on what his team needs to accomplish during their practice. Earlier in the day, he put his team through a 90-minute session at Cherry Creek High School, just 5 minutes from the team hotel, and the practice did not go flawlessly. The Blue team is struggling to pick up some of the nuances of the Air Force offense, which consists of various principles borrowed from the Princeton offense, where Falcons head coach Joe Scott played and served as an assistant coach. Air Force lacks top-tier athletes, but its patient offense makes use of frequent cuts and screens. It is the perfect strategy for a squad that will usually have less talent, but at least as much intelligence, as its opponents.

"We play the way we play for games like this one," Scott says before the game. "If we just wanted to have fun, we could go out there and run up and down and throw up shots. But we want to win. And the way we play gives us the best chance to win."

The way Air Force plays also can't be learned overnight, which is why the Blue team spends more than a few minutes bouncing off each other at Cherry Creek. Their struggles ensure that the Heels will devote at least part of their public practice time to refining their defensive and offensive approach. It's not especially crowd-pleasing—although the fans, one of whom is sporting one of the "Jackie Manuel has a Posse" T-shirts that are sold in Chapel Hill, don't seem to mind—but Roy Williams makes sure his starters get plenty of exposure to Air Force's strategies during the Pepsi Center practice session.

"Air Force is a very dangerous team," Rashad McCants says on Wednesday. "They make hard cuts and use thirty-five seconds to get a shot off. It's frustrating to sit on defense for thirty-five seconds and let them do what they want."

That patience on offense is what concerns the Carolina coaches, since they know they have a team that has occasionally struggled to play 40 minutes of defense. One lapse against the Falcons will lead to a backdoor layup. At least partly for that reason, Melvin Scott is replaced in the starting lineup by Jackie Manuel. The Heels have tried to stay with Scott through his late-season struggles—he hasn't made more than 50 percent of his field goals in a game since the February 15 win over Maryland—but in a one-and-out situation, they have to go with the player who gives them the best chance to win. At the moment, that's Manuel, and by beginning the game with Scott out of the lineup they also get more flexibility and ballhandling in case Felton gets winded early in Denver's thin air.

There is some concern about how the Carolina junior will take the move, which Williams is careful to note is "not a demotion." Scott, perhaps more than any other player on the team, is sensitive about his role; he chafed as a sophomore when Matt Doherty required him to come off the bench. But he is in good spirits as his first-ever NCAA Tournament game approaches. When the team gathers on Wednesday night, Scott gets his teammates to follow through on what they talked about the previous day. Razors are fetched, and the Tar Heels shave their heads. Even managers consider going bald, but eventually decide against it.

There is precedent for the clean-shaven look in Tar Heel history. In 1993, Donald Williams began shaving his head during the NCAA Tournament and went on to win Most Outstanding Player honors as the Tar Heels captured the national championship. In 1995, the entire team went bald—except for the long-locked Dante Calabria, who decided to keep his much-talked-about hair. This time, everyone on the roster gets trimmed down to the scalp, and there is much good-natured kidding about the results. Jawad Williams has sported a shaved head for years, so his role is primarily to provide commentary on his teammates. Walk-on senior Jonathan Miller, it is decided, bears a striking resemblance to Charles Manson. Raymond Felton is the last player to get shaved; more than anyone on the team, he seems to think seriously about the consequences of what he is about to do. Eventually, however, he emerges hairless, and so an entire team of newly-bald Tar Heels greet the coaches at their 11 P.M. meeting. The session begins on a lighthearted note as the coaches evaluate the new haircuts. Upon reflection and after viewing his shiny-headed team, Williams will say that the jocular mood that evening is one of the first times all season that his players have truly acted like college students rather than world-weary basketball lifers.

That feeling lingers into the next day. For Williams and his staff, a first-round NCAA Tournament game is routine. For everyone else on the roster, it is a completely new experience. For the first time since 1975, when Williams was just a fledgling high school coach, North Carolina puts a team on the floor in an NCAA game that has no experience in the Tournament.

It shows in the first half against the Falcons. Playing just 75 miles from their campus in Colorado Springs, the Falcons have the benefit of a boisterous partisan crowd that leaps to its feet every time the Air Force band breaks into a zesty rendition of "Off We Go Into the Wild Blue Yonder," the school's unofficial fight song. The first Falcon field goal is—no surprise—a backdoor layup, as A. J. Kuhle takes advantage of a defensive lapse to sneak under the basket for an easy hoop. The culprit on the play? Melvin Scott, who is burned almost immediately after coming off the bench. But the Baltimore native doesn't sulk, and when he hits his first shot of the game, a three-pointer from the left corner with 13 minutes to play, he gives the Heels a 10–9 lead and appears to be capable of providing the offensive boost from the bench Carolina desperately needs.

The Falcons play a textbook opening stanza. Their matchup zone stymies the Tar Heel offense, and Rashad McCants doesn't score a point until just 2 minutes remain in the first half. Versatile center Nick Welch proves to be a thorny problem for Sean May, who isn't quick enough to stop Welch's dribble penetration from the top of the key. When May sags off Welch to prevent the drive, Welch simply steps back and tosses in a three-pointer. Reserve Jacob Burtschi tosses in a three-pointer at the halftime buzzer, and Air Force goes to the locker room with a 28–23 lead.

For the Tar Heels, it is a predictable opening half. They appear impatient, trying to blow out the eleventh-seeded Falcons on every possession rather than slowly building a lead. Out of nine first-half field goals for the Academy, three were backdoor layups and five were three-pointers. Carolina commits ten turnovers in the first half, a dismal number made worse by the fact that, because of the tempo of the game, possessions are even more valuable.

Before he sends his team onto the floor for the start of the second half, Roy Williams tries to emphasize the importance of patience. "Let's do this one possession at a time," he says, looking his starting five in the eye.

"Yeah," Jawad Williams echoes. "One possession at a time."

Apparently, it's just that easy. McCants explodes from his lethargic first half with 5 quick points in the first 2 minutes of the second half. By the time Raymond Felton hits Jackie Manuel for a basket with 17:10 remaining, the Tar Heels have seized a 32–30 lead.

There is one last hiccup: David Noel picks up his third foul 1 minute later and is outwardly frustrated with his performance. He is on his way to a 3-point, 1-rebound effort—of which there have been too many in a season he expected to be a breakout campaign. Three and a half minutes later, the situation gets worse when he fouls Joel Gerlach as the Air Force captain is sinking a three-pointer. It is Noel's fourth foul, it is a 4-point play for Gerlach, it gives the Falcons a 44–38 lead, and it prompts at least two-thirds of the Pepsi Center to explode in cheers for the underdog military academy.

It also, unexpectedly, refocuses the Tar Heels.

"Guys finally realized it was do or die," Sean May says later. "We don't want to go back to Chapel Hill with shaved heads talking about how we came together and then lost."

May proceeds to ignite his team with a 3-point play; then he sprawls headfirst to pick up a loose ball, which he corrals and passes to Felton, who gets it to Manuel for a dunk. On the very next defensive play, Felton hits the floor in pursuit of a loose ball. Suddenly the lackadaisical Tar Heels of the first half have turned into a scrappy bunch that isn't yet ready to exit the NCAA Tournament. Felton's play leads to perhaps the nicest possession of the season for Carolina. Melvin Scott passes up a three-pointer and passes to Rashad McCants, who pump-fakes and then passes up a good shot to get the ball back to Scott. The Carolina guard is open, but instead of shooting, he dishes to Felton, who is wide open. The Tar Heels have made three crisp passes around the perimeter and stretched the Air Force defense to the point of ineffectiveness. They have—as Roy Williams surely notices—passed up good shots in an effort to find a great shot. That Felton nails the three-pointer is almost immaterial. This is how Williams wants his teams to play basketball.

"That possession right there was pretty basketball," he says. "We had three different guys who could have taken the shot. That's how I like my teams to play. Move the ball and be unselfish."

Carolina zips off on an extended 21–3 run over the next 10 minutes, making the final score of 63–52 deceptive. Away from the crowd, back in the safety of the locker room, there is a strange combination of exhilaration and relief. The players have rarely let down their guard enough to be giddy after a victory. Instead, they usually try to maintain their facade of coolness.

This time, there is no coolness. Jawad Williams, who has endured an 8–20 season and an NIT bid, cries. Even Roy Williams, who has frequently been frustrated with his team, will remark that this is the proudest he has been of them all season. In the past, first-round NCAA Tournament wins were formalities for North Carolina. This one almost has the feel of an upset. Virtually every player on the roster had a part in the ending of some impressive Tar Heel basketball streak. Now, they've started one of their own.

"It was one of the biggest games of my career," the usually impassive Jawad Williams says. "Finally getting to play in the NCAA Tournament was a dream come true."

The players and coaches realize the gravity of the moment. They are jovial as the team bus rolls back to the hotel where they are sequestered, about twenty minutes from downtown. Roy Williams's mood is darkened, however, when he looks out the window of the bus and sees . . . nothing. At Kansas, any NCAA Tournament win was cause for Jayhawk fans to gather at the team hotel and greet the squad. That's never been the tradition at Carolina, where the location of the team hotel was frequently a well-guarded secret during the Dean Smith era. Many Denver-area Tar Heels will later complain that they would have been happy to greet the team but were never informed of their whereabouts. It's a situation that will be remedied in future years, but for now, it hits Williams the wrong way.

"It's part of that fan culture we've been talking about," he says. "We've got to change the culture."

The moment passes quickly. Before the sun comes up, the Carolina head coach wants to review some tape of his team's next opponent, the third-seeded Texas Longhorns. It's not a completely unknown foe, as Texas was a frequent opponent during Williams's tenure at Kansas. He is well acquainted with Rick Barnes's team and is immediately aware that the Longhorns pose two serious problems: they are deep and they are tall. Barnes uses four players who stand 6-foot-8 or better, and during the course of their 24–7 season to date, eleven players have averaged at least 11 minutes per game. Any of the four Longhorn post threats would probably start for Carolina.

The team goes through a closed practice on Friday, but it's unlikely the Tar Heels can simulate the mass of tall, talented athletes they'll see Saturday evening.

Because of the tidal wave of post players Texas can unleash on the Tar Heels, it's especially important to get Sean May and Jawad Williams off to good starts. Both players are prone to overthinking their actions on the court, and May was visibly frustrated against Air Force. It is not a good sign for the Tar Heels, then, when he misses the first shot of the game, a turnaround jumper that rims out. But 3 minutes later, Felton gets a steal, leads the fast break, and drops the ball to a trailing Williams for a one-handed slam dunk over onetime Tar Heel recruiting target Brad Buckman. Buckman also fouls Williams, giving the Tar Heels a momentum-boosting 3-point play early in the game.

Carolina's first-half highlights begin and end with that play. Over the next 17 minutes, the Tar Heels will play some of their worst defense of the season. Texas, which came into the game shooting just under 44 percent from the field, takes advantage of the porous play and makes 60 percent of its first-half field goals. Even without quality contributions from shooting guard Brandon Mouton, who makes just 2 of 7 attempts, Texas gets virtually any shot it wants, and ten Longhorns score in the first 20 minutes. Rick Barnes gets 20 points from his bench, while the sum total of bench production for Carolina is a field goal from David Noel and two free throws by Reyshawn Terry.

Despite the seemingly overwhelming stats, Texas holds just a 44–39 advantage at halftime. Roy Williams spends halftime once again begging his team for effort, something that seems strange in the NCAA Tournament environment. After the Air Force game, he'd told his squad, "There are only thirty-two teams in the country that have a chance to win the national championship, and we're one of them." Now, though, with a chance at the Sweet Sixteen just 20 minutes away, he doesn't feel the urgency from his players that he knows is required to win a championship.

The kind of urgency he wants is demonstrated by Texas guard Royal Ivey just minutes before the first media timeout of the second half in a play that illustrates, all at once, everything that is good and everything that is bad about the NCAA Tournament. Before the game, Carolina team manager Eric Hoots had set up the Tar Heel bench area exactly as he'd been doing all year. Cups in a certain location, water cooler in a certain location, towels in a certain location. Because of NCAA limitations on the number of people who can be on the bench during the Tournament, Carolina was using fewer managers than usual, and Hoots knew he'd be in action for every minute of the game to pick up duties usually covered by others. When he first walked up to the bench, one of his first moves was to push the water cooler and cart holding the cups a few feet down the bench. Almost immediately, an NCAA site official informed him that the cooler could not be moved; it bore the logo of a corporate sponsor and was placed where it was to get maximum television exposure in the prime spot behind the bench.

So Hoots had to move the cooler back to its previous spot, and there it sits when Ivey comes barreling toward the Carolina bench early in the second half. The Longhorn guard hurdles the bench, crashes into the cooler, and sends gallons of sticky sports drink rushing onto the walkway behind the bench. Had the cooler been where Hoots originally placed it, out of harm's way, Ivey would have missed it. But then the NCAA wouldn't have reaped the advertising bonanza from its corporate sponsor—money that is never passed on to the athletes.

As soon as Ivey returns to the court, a horde of Pepsi Center officials descend on the mess behind the Carolina bench. In a matter of seconds, four men, all carrying walkie-talkies and wearing suits and ties, are down on their knees cleaning up the liquid with Disney World–type efficiency. Minutes later they have dried every inch of the floor, laid down a strip of carpet to prevent slippage, and handed out towels to nearby fans and media to ensure no one has suffered due to the incident. The yin and yang of the NCAA Tournament, all in one moment.

Roy Williams, meanwhile, is unable to appreciate the efficiency taking place just behind his bench. He is too busy watching Raymond Felton and Rashad McCants run some type of foreign offense with which he is not familiar. The Tar Heel head coach yanks his two star sophomore guards just 2 minutes into the second half and blasts them on the bench for their selfish play. Texas, still chugging along without any spectacular plays but with steady contributions from everyone on the roster, stretches their lead to 57–44 with 13 minutes left. On the next Carolina possession, Felton holds the ball at the top of the key, prompting Williams to slap his hands together and yell, "Move!" The point guard swings the ball to McCants, who drops in a three-pointer.

The next 2 minutes are not pleasant for Carolina's players. As soon as McCants's shot falls through the net, Williams signals for a timeout. Even before his players can reach the bench, he is on them, a whirlwind of intensity.

"The game is *not* over!" he yells. "If you want to lay down and take a twenty-point butt-kicking, fine. Do it! But we can come back from this."

Then he says something sharp to Noel, who at 6-foot-6 has spent most of the night looking up at taller Longhorn players. Noel can't help but notice that although he is not the tallest Tar Heel on the floor, Carolina's bigger players, Jawad Williams and Sean May, are continually taking the defensive assignments on relatively smaller players. Noel is fuming by the time he reaches the bench.

"David, you have to *do* something," Roy Williams yells.

"I think the whole frustration of my season came out at that moment," Noel says. "I'm only six-six and I was guarding six-nine, two-hundred-eighty-pound guys. They were all coming at me and there were four of them. I was on their biggest guy but I wasn't the biggest guy on the court for our team. I'm getting pummeled and people are getting offensive rebounds on me. When Coach said something to me, it sparked me. I was staring a hole through him. From that point on my facial expression changed, everything changed. I was already mad when I came out of the game and I got madder."

It is easy to read the sophomore's frustration in the huddle, and he remains on the bench after the timeout. While his team takes the floor, Williams turns his back to the court and lays a hand on Noel's knee.

"Coach, I'm so pissed right now," Noel says, weary from waging an undersized war against Texas's talented post players.

"Son, do you think I'm stupid?" Williams says. "I know I am asking you to guard guys who are bigger than you. But you have to step up for us."

While the teaching session is going on, the team is responding to Williams's admonishments during the timeout. By the time Sean May makes a putback with 9:20 left, Carolina is riding an 11–0 spurt and has closed the deficit to 57–55.

But depth is about to become an issue for the Tar Heels. May, Felton, and Jackie Manuel all have 4 fouls with 5:33 remaining. There are no capable substitutes on the bench for that trio. Williams keeps rotating in Scott and Noel, but both players are well on their way to very ineffective performances—Scott with just 3 points and Noel with only a pair. After edging back out to a 69–58 advantage, Rick Barnes switches his team to a zone, and the Longhorns pay very little attention to Scott, whose profile would seem to suggest a capable zone-buster. Instead, his confidence almost completely shattered, he poses little threat to the zone.

Even without his help, the Tar Heels have one more run. May hits a pair of free throws to trim the Longhorn lead to 73–66 at the 2:00 mark. But McCants misses a three-pointer and then commits a questionable foul with 20 seconds remaining on the shot clock, leading to one Ivey free throw. Felton responds with a three-pointer to cut the deficit to 5 points, but then the Heels commit another silly foul when Manuel picks up his fifth with 4 seconds left on the shot clock. Mouton hits one of his two charity tosses, and then Scott—who this time doesn't hesitate— immediately pulls the trigger and nails a three-pointer, his only basket of the game.

Carolina is clawing back. Mouton hits a pair of free throws for a 77–72 lead, but Felton hits another three-pointer, Carolina's third in the last minute, with 11.1 seconds on the clock. Then the Tar Heels foul Texas's P. J. Tucker.

The irony is thick. Tucker is a native of Raleigh who desperately wanted to play in the ACC. Carolina gave him scant attention, due at least partly to his questionable academic record, and he committed to Texas. Now, with 8.9 seconds left in a second-round NCAA Tournament game, the freshman has the chance to end the Tar Heels' season.

He makes the first free throw with a calm smile, but misses the second. The rebound falls to Jawad Williams. Roy Williams calls a play that requires Noel to set a screen for McCants, who would then—in theory—have an open look at a game-tying three-pointer. It is the kind of shot McCants has made all season. But in the final 9 seconds, the play unravels. Noel never gets in position to adequately set the screen. After receiving the ball in front of the Carolina bench, McCants has to pump-fake to free himself from 6-foot-8 Brian Boddicker. In doing so, he takes one step forward, putting his lead foot squarely on the three-point line. He fires a last-gasp shot that is irrelevant—with his foot on the line, the shot would only be a two-pointer. The shot sails over the basket, the final seconds elapse, and the season is over.

Jawad Williams puts his hands over his face. Raymond Felton punches the air. Sean May, who fouled out seconds earlier, stands by the bench and leaps as McCants releases the shot, then drops his head as the shot misses. Team manager Hoots pounds the stack of towels behind the Carolina bench. Roy Williams shakes hands with Barnes and then heads for the locker room.

It is a solemn place. The head coach has warned the players that in NCAA Tournament play, the last game of the season comes with sudden finality. No one, except perhaps for the sacrificial sixteen-seeds, enters a game expecting it to be the last game of the season. "That's the most difficult thing about the NCAA Tournament," he tells them. "The swiftness and the suddenness and the finality with which it is over."

There are tears from virtually everyone, especially from the three walk-on seniors who have played their last game and from Hoots, who has been such an integral part of the program—and a close friend to most of the players—during his tenure at Carolina. McCants turns the final play over and over in his mind, wondering what he might have done differently.

NCAA rules require that the locker room of the losing team be opened to the media 15 minutes after the final buzzer. At the 10-minute mark, a crowd is beginning to gather outside Carolina's locker room. At the 15-minute mark, it's a veritable throng, including UNC Chancellor James Moeser and Athletic Director Dick Baddour. A miscommunication at the 19-minute mark prompts one reporter to throw open the door, but as a sliver of daylight shines through, the door is slammed closed before he can enter. Inside, the team gathers in a circle for one of their final official acts as the 2003–04 Tar Heels. Eyes red, they offer a prayer.

Once the media enter the room, they find a sober group. Melvin Scott sits in the middle of the room with his jersey pulled over his head for the first five minutes of the interview time, unable to compose himself enough to offer any coherent thoughts. After the media leave, McCants and May huddle in one corner of the room.

"I can't believe it's over," May says. "There's nothing tomorrow. No practice, no meetings. Nothing."

In the moments after the Texas game, Jawad Williams describes the just-completed season as "stressful." Raymond Felton calls it "bumpy." Rashad McCants calls it "interesting" and says he has never experienced a season so full of ups and downs.

The players and coaches have pushed, cajoled, and snapped at each other for five months. It was not a particularly well-assembled team; it was a group of individuals who sometimes struggled to subvert their individual desires for the good of the team. But in the wake of their final loss of the year, as the realization begins to set in that they will never be together quite like this again, something unexpected happens—they exhibit a certain closeness.

As his players describe their reactions to the season, Roy Williams suddenly interjects. "You have to understand," he says hoarsely, "that a big part of the frustration and the bumps is that I'm not an easy guy to play for."

The admission is somewhat out of character for the head coach. His players have known it, the coach has known it, but it's been mostly an unspoken truth throughout the past few months. Now it has been said out loud, and his players seem to appreciate the candor. Felton, Williams, and McCants accompany their coach to the postgame interview room, where they sit at a podium in front of a blue curtain and field questions from the assembled media. The NCAA requires that questions be asked of the players first, who are then free to leave, and then the head coach. When they finish their interviews, the trio has to walk by their coach on the way out of the room. Each one, even the usually stoic McCants, pauses and pats Roy Williams on the back. It is a telling gesture, one not unlike the tacit thanks of a teenager who has chafed under a parent's discipline but who silently appreciates the boundaries.

At the beginning of the season, four Tar Heels—Felton, Jawad Williams, May, and McCants—were giving at least a passing thought to the NBA. But even before his sophomore season ends, May has proclaimed he will return to college for his junior season. Felton makes a similar decision within a month after the Texas game. Because of his injuries and his uneven season, Williams's draft position is not optimal, and he too will be a Tar Heel for the 2004–05 season. Most of the players watch at least some of the remaining games of the NCAA Tournament, and they notice something about the teams that advance as the field dwindles from thirty-two teams to sixteen to, eventually, the Final Four of Duke, Connecticut, Georgia Tech, and Oklahoma State.

"It's a matter of everybody putting aside their egos and coolness to enjoy being teammates with this guy or that guy," Melvin Scott says. "That's what it's about. I looked at some of those other teams and envied how together they were. That's one thing I would never think we'd lack at the University of North Carolina, but it was a big thing we lacked."

David Noel takes the same notion further, even bordering on sacrilege.

"I respect Duke so much," he says. "It's hard for me to say that. They play together. Those five guys are buying into it and playing with reckless abandon. I will say right now, and you can mark this day, that we will play that way next year."

The Heels have a solid recruiting class, although it shrinks from four players to two. JamesOn Curry pleads guilty to six felony drug charges in April, eliminating any chance of playing for Carolina—although Oklahoma State snaps him up. Shooting guard J. R. Smith, who openly lobbied for a scholarship offer from North Carolina, suddenly decides that coming to Chapel Hill isn't his dream after all when he has a high-flying performance at the McDonald's All-American game. Roy Williams meets with the Smith family and tells them his NBA sources say J. R. will be picked in the twenties in the upcoming draft. He gives them the salary figures for the twenty-fourth pick—approximately $2.4 million over three years. Left unsaid is the salary slot for Syracuse's Carmelo Anthony, who went to college for one year, won a national championship, and vaulted to the third pick, earning a contract worth $8.67 million over three years. Smith's father Earl believes his son won't fall past the ninth pick, and Smith announces for the draft on May 3 and signs with an agent less than three weeks later. Even without those players, the Heels will be national contenders in Roy Williams's second year on the job. Before the last piece of net is snipped in San Antonio by the 2004 national champion Connecticut Huskies, Dick Vitale installs Carolina as his preseason number-one team for next season. Even in the moments following the loss to Texas, when bitter comments might be expected, players are optimistic about their future. "I love playing for Carolina," Felton says. "This is the only school I wanted to play for."

Next season will be Roy Williams's seventeenth as a head coach. The sixteenth was, in many ways, harder and more frustrating than any of the previous campaigns. His team barely finished in the top half of the conference, lost in the ACC quarterfinals, and was dispatched in the second round of the NCAA Tournament. None is a result with which he is happy. But assistant coaches Steve Robinson and Joe Holladay tell him he may have done the best coaching job of his career. And another, less likely person agrees.

"I think he probably did the best job of his career," Rashad McCants says. "There were a lot of egos on this team. It's difficult to deal with. Anybody else would have broken. The winning and the losing, the up and the down, it's really frustrating."

McCants is named Most Valuable Player at the team's annual banquet, an honor voted on by his coaches and teammates. If there were an award for Most Matured Player, he would likely win that one too. At the podium after accepting his MVP honor, he looks into the crowd of hundreds of Carolina basketball supporters and Rams Club members.

"I know I can be hard to be around sometimes," he says. "But I want you all to know that I'm a good person. I'm a good kid."

Seven months earlier, McCants had stood in the same building and declared that he didn't care what anyone thought of him, that it wasn't his job to try and please people. Now he is making an extra effort to appeal to the crowd. In the pickup games that have taken place since the end of the season, his teammates say he has been unstoppable. For the first time, he has developed an off-court personality that complements his basketball talents rather than detracts from them.

It is also a different Roy Williams who attends the banquet on April 13, exactly 364 days after he accepted the job in Chapel Hill. The red tie he wore at his introductory press conference has given way to a Carolina blue one, and a few more silver hairs are visible. Last season, he skipped the Tar Heel banquet, feeling it wasn't appropriate for him to attend, since the event celebrated a team he hadn't coached. This year, he not only attends, he is already making plans to tweak the banquet to make it more entertaining and less predictable next season. He uses the occasion to point out the poor quality of the video boards in the Smith Center. He is the picture of a coach in control of his program.

One other thing is different about him. The Kansas University Final Four ring he proudly displayed on April 14, 2003, no longer resides on his right ring finger. He removed it near the end of the regular season, convinced that it wasn't serving its intended purpose—to motivate this year's Tar Heels to earn similar jewelry. Most of his players don't notice when he removes it. Sean May does.

"He said the teams in the past didn't play the way we have played," Sean May says. "They always listened. He said he thought maybe him talking about Kansas too much was bringing us down. I looked at it as motivation. I want to be the first to get him a national championship ring. This is the first time anyone on this team has tasted success. We've learned how fun it is to win. And we've learned how hard it is to win."

It is early June 2004, and this year's first camp game is just a week away. Former Tar Heels are already beginning to trickle back to Chapel Hill to work camp and play in the annual summer pickup games. After lifting weights each day, the current Heels gather with any alums who want to play for approximately two hours of pickup action. The faces are much the same as the summer of 2003, including the ever-present Shammond Williams. From a distance, the games are virtually indistinguishable from last summer's.

Up close, however, something is different. Instead of being glorified one-on-one contests, players repeatedly set picks off the ball to free teammates for a shot. There is less bickering, more focus on the game.

Late one afternoon, after several games have been played, Raymond Felton gets control of the ball, his team just one basket from victory. Sean May posts up, Jackie Manuel slides to the wing, Jawad Williams bodies up on defense. From the top of the key, Felton surveys the opposing defense and his four teammates. As he is dribbling the ball, he says something just loud enough for them to hear, almost as if he is trying to remind himself of something, trying to reinforce a point in rhythm with the bouncing basketball.

"Let's go," he says. "Let's get a great shot. A great shot."

Epilogue

In late April and early May, the curious are easy to spot.

They roam the halls of the Dean Smith Center, peeking their heads into each doorway. If what they are seeking isn't present, they move on, cameras clutched in one hand. Sometimes, they speak.

"Excuse me," a woman from Robbinsville, North Carolina, says one Tuesday afternoon. "Do you know where I could find the trophy?"

She doesn't specify exactly which trophy she's hoping to find. She doesn't have to. There is only one trophy that makes the curious drive from across the state—she has come from the far western edge of the Tar Heel state, almost in Tennessee—just in the hopes of catching a glimpse of a wooden trophy that's no more than knee-high to Sean May.

It's the 2005 national championship trophy. And it's taken up permanent residence in the Smith Center. Its whereabouts remain a popular topic throughout the summer. Most fans just want to take a picture. Some want to touch it, which occasionally proves difficult since it usually resides in a glass case in the lobby of the Carolina basketball office.

It didn't make a shot during the 2004–05 basketball season, didn't win a game. But it is the proof. It really happened: Roy Williams really took a 19–11 bunch of squabblers and shaped them into a 33–4 national championship team.

Fans aren't the only ones who still marvel at the achievement. David Noel sits in the Smith Center memorabilia room—for the record, that's not where the trophy is kept, at least not at the moment—in early May considering the events of the last month of his life.

"It's been crazy," he says. "You dream of coming here and playing ball and winning a national championship. Then when it happens it happens so fast. It doesn't even seem real. I think I'm going to have to see the ring for it to seem real."

The ring will come later. Right now it is time to reflect.

• • •

The change is immediately noticeable upon watching any Carolina basketball practice.

During the 2003–04 season, the prepractice mood in the Smith Center usually seemed to be tense. Not angry, but nervous—the way the air feels when two strangers meet on a blind date. There was little of the personal banter that usually accompanies the best teams. The individuals were there—the elder statesman trio of Jackie Manuel, Jawad Williams, and Melvin Scott, plus the talented sophomores Raymond Felton, Sean May, Rashad McCants, and David Noel—but they simply didn't mesh. They came into the season as individuals and, for the most part, left it as individuals.

2004–05 seems different almost immediately. In one corner of the Smith Center, Jackie Manuel and Wes Miller are firing one-liners at each other. Walking down the hallway toward the locker room, suddenly boisterous shouts come from the players' lounge. It turns out Marvin Williams has just upset David Noel in a game of Sony PlayStation2 basketball.

The noises are testament to something many people realized only after the Final Four appearance: the individuals have become a team. That's why Rashad McCants takes almost 100 fewer shots as a junior than he did as a sophomore. That's why the minutes per game of every player in the rotation other than Jackie Manuel decrease. In the past, those two stats were kept religiously by almost every player on the team.

This year, they pay attention to just one number: wins.

The change manifests itself in a much happier atmosphere surrounding the team. Players joke with their teammates, coaches joke with coaches, and coaches joke with players.

Roy Williams spent most of his first season begging his new team to "buy in" to his system. Only Jackie Manuel ever did so with significant commitment. But as if they had flipped a switch, his entire team did it almost as soon as the final buzzer sounded against Texas in the second round of the 2004 NCAA Tournament.

A players-only meeting was held shortly after that game. The theme was simple: we can continue to hunt shots, to get jealous of each other, to try to post the gaudiest individual stats that we can. Or we can win.

They chose the latter.

It was easy to be skeptical in the preseason. In September, Jawad Williams was asked his personal goals for the 2004–05 campaign.

His response: "If we win, we'll get the awards and rewards. That's what happens when you win as a team."

The quote is one Roy Williams first mentioned at his introductory press conference at North Carolina. He repeated it throughout his first season in Chapel Hill. That his players are now quoting it verbatim qualifies as progress. But quoting is easy. Acting on it is hard.

Sean May acted on it by transforming his body. After the magical tournament run, it will erroneously be described as simply "losing weight." The junior did need to lose a few pounds, but he also needed to redistribute some weight, to move some of the extra pounds around his middle to his biceps, so he could deal out some of the punishment he'd sometimes taken during his first two years in the ACC.

He has given up the pizza and fried foods that had been staples of his diet. He now eats only lean meats. At 7:00 in the morning, he wakes up to go running with former Carolina strength coach Thomas McKinney. They run sixteen 100-yard sprints per day. He lifts weights, he plays rigorous games of pickup.

The workout plan pays off when he goes to tryouts for the USA Basketball Under-20 team. May is dominating a drill. An assistant coach blows his whistle and pauses the action.

"Do you want to know why he is kicking everyone's tail?" the coach asks the assembled players.

He does not wait for an answer. "Because he came in here in shape and no one else did!"

For other players, the transformation is less tangible. Jawad Williams and Rashad McCants have always been wary of each other. Both have tracked not only their own stats but those of the other player. Each believes—as most top athletes do—that he deserves to be the go-to player in the clutch.

Those beliefs, which have checkered their two years together at Carolina, are set aside as the players enter the 2004-05 season. McCants is the go-to player, at least as preseason practice opens. He is the player who has made the big shot in the past. He is the player who can be counted on to make that shot again.

Williams, meanwhile, will be one of the many beneficiaries of the arrival of Marvin Williams. The Bremerton, Washington, native shows up for the second session of summer school and promptly begins throwing down jaw-dropping dunks in pickup games. First-time observers arrive skeptical, firmly believing that tales of his talents have been exaggerated. They depart as converts. He is 6-foot-9, but he has the shooting range of a guard and the inside skills of a post player. He is, quite simply, the type of player who rarely attends college in the twenty-first-century LeBron era.

His basketball talents make him unusual. His personality makes him unique.

Even before he arrived at last year's McDonald's All-American game in Oklahoma City, Marvin Williams knew he was different. Most of the other twenty-three players in attendance at that game weren't new to him. He'd played against them during AAU tournaments, had hung out with them during the inevitable down time that surrounds those events. And it hadn't taken him long to realize exactly what people in Chapel Hill began to realize last fall: this Williams kid isn't like other prep basketball superstars.

"I noticed I was different right off the bat," Marvin says. "You meet some real characters at those games. Those guys are so basketball serious. And it shows, because some of them are in the NBA right now. Basketball is something I love and I'm thankful I can do it, but they have a different passion for it. They can play or talk about it all day long, seven days a week. Sometimes I just need a break."

One of the most basic things—and most flattering things—you can say about Marvin Williams is that he's, well, pretty normal. Close friend Ian Mateikat, who has known Marvin Williams since high school, says being a *SportsCenter* fixture didn't change his buddy.

"We don't really talk about basketball stuff that much, but when I ask him about a game, usually he says, 'I did alright. I got a dunk,'" Mateikat says. "I'll say, 'Was it on somebody?' and he says, 'No, not really.'

Then later I'll see the highlights or read about it and find out he dunked all over some guy."

Moving to the other side of the country from Mateikat, Josh Johnson, and Phil Houston—the close circle of friends Marvin had grown up with in Bremerton, Washington—wasn't easy. The night before he left to enroll at Carolina, the quartet went to a Bremerton tattoo parlor and got matching tattoos that included their initials and the words "B-Town's Finest." It was an emotional night.

But that's not the tattoo Marvin touches before he shoots each one of his free throws. Before he releases the ball, he taps his left bicep with his right hand, rubbing his fingers over the word "Andrea." It was his first tattoo, inked when he was just fifteen years old. It's on his left arm, but it's the one closest to his heart.

Andrea Gittens is a single mother who has somehow managed to raise three respectful sons while simultaneously holding down a full-time job that pays the bills for everyone in the house. And not just any full-time job. The daily routine until Marvin left for college was for him to drop off Andrea at the Washington State Ferry at 6:45 a.m. While Marvin drove the boys to school, their mother took a one-hour ferry ride from Bremerton to Seattle. The ferry would depart at 7:20 a.m.; miss it by even one minute, and the next one didn't come until 9:00 a.m., which meant staying at work two hours later to make up the lost time. Andrea would arrive in Seattle at 8:20. Take the 25-minute walk uphill to her bookkeeping job. Leave work at 6 p.m. Take the ferry back to Bremerton. Arrive home—hopefully—by 8 p.m.

Every day.

So it's no wonder that Marvin and brothers Dimitrius (sixteen years old) and J'Tonn (thirteen) are more than capable around the house.

"She taught us how to cook and clean and I still do that to this day," Marvin says. "I can get on the stove a little bit." Andrea could be tough—any sentences directed at her that didn't include "please," "thank you," or "ma'am," were usually met with, "Did I hear you say something? I don't know who you're talking to"—but her boys saw her sacrifices.

Roy Williams gives his team the weekend off just before the season opener against Santa Clara and there is very little doubt where Marvin Williams will spend it. He's mentioned the open weekend to his mother, but told her there was a good chance a recruit would be in town and he'd need to stay in Chapel Hill for the festivities. But he's simultaneously making plans with his uncle to fly back to Seattle and catch a ride to Bremerton.

Around 11 p.m. West Coast time one November evening, Andrea Gittens gets a telephone call from Marvin. "What are you doing?" she asks, well aware that it is 2 a.m. in Chapel Hill.

"Just chilling," he says. He happens to be standing in his mother's kitchen, pawing through the refrigerator, but she is in her bedroom and hasn't heard him yet. He pulls a snack out of the cupboard, hangs up the phone, and switches on his mother's bedroom light. Standing there in the suddenly bright room, he looks like Dimitrius, who stands 6-foot-3.

And then she realizes it is Marvin.

"I had cried literally for a week when he left," Gittens says. "And when he was standing there, I just screamed. It was the happiest day."

Marvin's departure for Carolina was the fulfillment of a lifelong dream to play for the Tar Heels. Although he grew up on the West Coast, he was captivated by Dean Smith, by the way teams from Chapel Hill carried themselves with a dignified air. While talking with Mateikat recently, he had a moment of wonder, asking his friend, "Ian, it's so weird. Can you believe I'm actually playing for Carolina?"

He knows the tradition he represents and fits in flawlessly.

"Class is the way you carry yourself," he says. "I like people to act professionally. You have to be classy with Coach Smith here. You don't want to do anything crazy."

When Marvin was younger, his father, Marvin Williams, Sr., had made sure he noticed not just the way Michael Jordan played basketball, but the way he handled himself in post-game interviews. Level-headed. Cool. Classy.

That philosophy extends even to the way Marvin dresses. The team frequently wears suits on the road. But even when suits aren't part of the dress code, Marvin checks with Jawad Williams to find out what the senior is wearing. If the elder Williams, who makes a habit of almost always being dressed impeccably, is planning to wear a suit, odds are Marvin Williams will come out of the locker room dressed like he's about to go to a bank meeting.

Coaching the prodigy seems to invigorate Roy Williams. He greets the rookie every day on the practice floor with the same refrain:

"It's a Marv-elous day in the neighborhood."

His player's response is usually the same: "OK, Coach."

The addition of Marvin Williams to the team means more than just one more talented player on the roster. It means David Noel, who became frustrated with his role in the paint battling bruisers during 2003–04, can move to the perimeter. The athletic junior pays huge dividends on the wing, as he teams with Jackie Manuel to give the Tar Heels a powerful two-headed defensive monster. Manuel's defensive prowess is well known. He is all arms and legs, a spidery combination that makes it difficult for opposing guards to release shots over the top of him.

Noel is the perfect complement. Manuel starts the game harassing his man with quickness, using his exceptional first step to always stay within swatting distance. When he gives the tired signal, Roy Williams turns to Noel, whose 6-foot-6, 232-pound frame is conducive to playing a more physical game. The Durham native was undersized in the post but is the perfect foil for ACC wings used to trying to post up—or go around—their defender.

Duke's J. J. Redick, the best sharpshooter in the league, shoots a combined 9-for-25 against the duo in two games. NC State's Julius Hodge shoots 7-for-16 against Manuel and Noel in a crucial February 22 game in Raleigh and is outwardly frustrated by the middle of the second half. Neither Tar Heel is a big scorer, but both are critical pieces of the burgeoning team chemistry.

Marvin Williams also lessens the burden on Jawad Williams. Since Jawad's arrival at Carolina, he's been squeezed into a post role. But while his 6-foot-9 height suggests that's where he belongs, his game is more suited to the wing. With Marvin Williams on the roster, suddenly it's not automatically Jawad Williams's responsibility to be the secondary rebounder behind Sean May.

The various pieces illustrate the complicated nature of building a basketball team. It's not just a simple matter of adding a talented player. It's adding the talented player while factoring in the effect he will have on the existing roster.

• • •

The existing roster, as it turns out, is good enough to have one of the most dominating seasons in Carolina basketball history. A season-opening loss to Santa Clara is largely disregarded because of the absence of Raymond Felton, who had to sit out a one-game NCAA suspension due to playing in an unsanctioned summer league. A gritty road win over Indiana early in the season gets little national attention—the Hoosiers are down from their Bob Knight–era peak—but is a key turning point. Road games have been troublesome for the program in recent years. But after the Tar Heels swagger out of Bloomington in front of the most raucous environment they will face all year—Sean May is a Bloomington native and his father was a Hoosiers superstar, a combination that unleashes IU fans' blood lust on May—there is a noticeable change in attitude. It is no longer a question of beating opponents. It is a question of how badly they will beat opponents.

The Tar Heels survive a mysterious virus that sidelines Rashad McCants for the final four games of the regular season. They defeat Florida State in the penultimate home game, clinching a tie for the regular season.

And then they play one of the greatest games in the history of the rich Duke–Carolina series.

Trailing 73–64 with three minutes to play, the Tar Heels head to the sideline for a timeout. It is a season-changing moment.

Their head coach gathers his team around.

"If you'll do exactly what we say, and you'll give me a total commitment on every possession—not to do well, but to do the best—we're going to win the game," he says.

Jawad Williams, who is facing the prospect of ending his senior year with a season sweep at the hands of the arch-rival, drops his head. Roy Williams turns to him.

"Jawad, get your head up!" he says. "We're going to win this game. It's going to be you, and you, and you, and you, and it's going to be a total commitment. You have to do it right now better than you have ever done it before. If you do that, we're going to win this game. And I'll tell you something else: I promise you we'll win this game."

Even three months later, the head coach still gets cold chills recounting the moment. His team proves him to be a prophet, as they mount a furious comeback that is capped by a Marvin Williams three-point play. The Smith Center is as loud as it has ever been. The Tar Heels are the outright regular season champions.

They perform dismally in the ACC Tournament, due partly to the emphasis they had placed on the regular season championship. Players admit they don't feel they have anything to prove in the tournament, which is held in Washington, D.C. It shows, and Georgia Tech eliminates Carolina in the semifinals.

After an intense practice on the Monday before the start of the NCAA Tournament—Roy Williams takes the rims off the goals in the Tar Heel practice gym and sends his squad through thirty minutes of drills devoted entirely to defense—the dominant version of Carolina returns. They breeze through Oakland and Iowa State, survive a game effort from Villanova, and overpower Wisconsin. One of their best performances of the NCAA Tournament comes in the second half against Michigan State, as they shut down the burly Spartans and simply speed into the national championship game.

From there, it becomes a series of unforgettable moments. Carolina wins the game, and the national title, with a 75–70 victory over Illinois. Sean May is crowned the tournament's Most Outstanding Player after a dominant finish to the season. In the minutes after the victory, streamers explode from the Edward Jones Dome ceiling. Roy Williams looks into the crowd and locks eyes with his wife, Wanda. He walks away from his team and toward Section 101F. She's offered the opportunity to come join him on the floor, soak in the celebration first-hand, but she declines. She has to descend about eight rows to meet Roy A. Williams. And then he hugs her the way you see in the movies, one of those hugs that makes your eyes a little moist just watching. All those previous Final Four nights that ended in disappointment, with a shoulder to cry on, deep in a concrete dome somewhere. All of those nights pour out in that embrace.

Williams has never been one to shy away from showing emotion with his children, so their time comes next. First Kimberly, then Scott.

Hundreds of Carolina fans are standing right there, shouting, "We love you, Roy!" and "Congratulations, Roy!" and "You're the man, Roy!" at their basketball coach. But it is clear that none of it matters, that at that moment there is just Roy Williams and his family and the rest of the world has stopped turning for just a second.

Eventually he leaves them and returns to his team for the traditional post-championship celebration. The 2005 Tar Heels—the national champions—are herded onto a platform to watch the CBS staple "One Shining Moment" highlight video on the dome's video board. It is a striking moment. The team is gathered together for one of the last times as a group, with championship hats turned frontward, backward, sideways, and wide smiles on their faces as they watch what they have accomplished.

The board shows highlights from the three weeks of the NCAA Tournament. One of the clips is a slick pass from Raymond Felton to David Noel for a slam dunk against Michigan State. Noel throws his arms out wide, soaking in the moment. So does the man next to him—his coach, Roy Williams.

Sitting on that couch in the Smith Center memorabilia room a few months later, the memory of the moment still makes Noel crack a megawatt smile.

"One Shining Moment," he says. "We did it, all of us together. Can you believe it?"

Just then, a fan wanders into the memorabilia room. He is clearly awed by the presence of Noel but he is also clearly on a mission.

"Hey, guys," he says. "Do you know where they keep the trophy?"

Index